T0387640

THE BOOK OF

CHANGES, TROUBLES, PROBLEMS, LIGHTNESS, AND CALM

The I Ching as Oracle & Teacher

PETER MULLER

Translated by RALPH BERKIN

Destiny Books
Rochester, Vermont

Destiny Books
One Park Street
Rochester, Vermont 05767
www.DestinyBooks.com

Destiny Books is a division of Inner Traditions International

Originally published in Hungarian in 2001 and again in 2015 under the title *Jóskönyv: Ji King a ma emberének* by Rivaldafény Kiadó
First English edition published in 2025 by Destiny Books

Cataloging-in-Publication Data for this title is available from the Library of Congress

ISBN 979-8-88850-273-0 (print)
ISBN 979-8-88850-274-7 (ebook)

Printed and bound in India at Replika Press Pvt. Ltd.

10 9 8 7 6 5 4 3 2 1

Text design and layout by Debbie Glogover
This book was typeset in Garamond Premier Pro with Gill Sans MT Pro, Gotham, ITC Legacy Sans, Minion Pro, and Palatino LT Std used as display typefaces

To send correspondence to the author of this book, mail a first-class letter to the author c/o Inner Traditions, One Park Street, Rochester, VT 05767, and we will forward the communication.

Scan the QR code and save 25% at InnerTraditions.com. Browse over 2,000 titles on spirituality, the occult, ancient mysteries, new science, holistic health, and natural medicine.

✳

I would like to thank Gábor Kosa for his work and inspiration, László Deseő and Mária D. Nyikos for their high inspiration, Mihály Beöthy and Lajos Pressing for their thoughts, and Hua Ching Ni and Master Huang for helping me to understand the message of the ancient characters.

Thank you to Rudolf Ritsema, Stephen Karcher, and the Eramos Fountain for their help.

I am grateful to Daniela Alder, who discovered that my book has a special value in the abundant world literature of the I Ching, because it was written not by a scientist, but by a playwright who, in the 64 signs, wrote the dramas of our lives, which we are currently playing out on the stage of our destiny. Thus, the text, on which she worked extensively, is written in beautiful, literary language.

As ever, thank you to my son, Péter Sziámi Müller, who, as in life, has also been my partner in the creation of this work.

I also have to thank my spiritual Master for not only raising me in the spirit of the I Ching for so many years but for making me ready for the cooperation from which the Oracle was born.

In response to these words, he would say:

"Thank yourself!"

Contents

Recommended Reading

Reflections on the Oracle

I wrote this Oracle for myself. This is my research diary.
The best thing would be if you continued writing it yourself.

I have been studying the I Ching, perhaps the world's most ancient oracle, for more than twenty years now. It is said to originate from a supernatural source to help humankind to live and to shape our fate.

In ancient China—in much the same way as in our ancient Christian world—emphasis was given to a relationship with *holy spirits* (in Chinese: *shen*) who healed, taught, and prophesied. Of course, prophesying did not mean the same as predicting the future but, in every situation, the seer told the individual how to live, what is "blessed" and what is "cursed," or in other words, what will lead to a "bad" future and what will lead to a "good" future.

So, I have for the longest time been searching for the answer to what "will be good," and not in the general sense, but in the smallest of questions in my everyday life. For more than twenty years I have been working with the I Ching, seeking advice from it for myself, for my friends, and for all those who turn to me with problems related to their fate.

It was not too long before I came to realize that the Book of Changes sees much deeper and further than I. So many times, people would turn to me with their problems and I would say, "I have advice that I would give, but let's first consult the Chinese holy book." In every case, it turned out that the answer provided by the Book of Changes was the correct one.

The I Ching itself—the Holy Book of Changes—is no more than a couple of thousand Chinese characters. Each character is a dense symbol. These were interpreted by wise priest-mediums who were able to communicate with the higher spirit world. I am convinced that this connection is still in place to this very day.

This book is the result of my meditations, my studies, and above anything else, the work that I have done together with my Master. That is why, if you find an instruction in it with an exclamation mark, such as *Stop! The fulfillment is ripening but don't hurry! Patience! The moment of action has arrived!* you should know that this is what the Voice said to me when I asked a question related to my fate or that of others.

This Voice is not simply the voice of my Master but also the voice of my "better self," who in moments of inspiration has a clear view of my life and is able to judge what constitutes a beneficial step for me and what I should definitely avoid. I had to say this right at the beginning of the book. As Carl Gustav Jung says in the beautifully written forward to the *I Ching*, "The person who uses this book will receive a helping spirit and the book itself behaves like a wise master to whom a person can turn for advice."

We must become used to the idea that in ancient tradition *knowledge* and *listening* were very closely linked. A sage was not just the one whose head was full of knowledge, but also the one who was in contact with the supernatural, heavenly world. The "Wisdom" (*sheng*) character depicts a large ear and a little mouth: wise is the man who "has an ear to hear," as Jesus said.

It is this "ear" that the I Ching develops in us.

Knowledge is, of course, necessary. I had to read a great many books to access the secrets of the I Ching. Over thousands of years, every period in history has left its mark on these ancient symbols—just as each geological and astronomical event has left its mark in the layers of the Earth's crust. Each age sought not only to decipher the symbols, but also itself; that is why library shelves have become crammed with collections of commentaries and explanations of the I Ching.

So, as time passed, I moved deeper and deeper—in the end, I simply had to attempt to *experience* the message of these ancient Chinese Oracle Signs, asking myself, *what would a shaman really have thought upon seeing this or that character?* This was a glorious journey through time, during which I did not forget for a single instant that the ancient treasures that I unearthed have to be used by us in the here and now.

You will also come across the odd Chinese word or expression in the book. I thought it important to introduce you to these since Chinese words have multiple meanings and they cannot be translated by simply one English word.

I have gained a great deal from the work that I have done on my own and together with others. I have collected my experiences and my meditations; virtually every Oracle Sign has my own personal story or that of a friend or colleague behind it. Eventually, a time came when I no longer referred to books but rather consulted my own notes. This is how the Oracle was born that I now place in your hands.

It is not a completed work—it cannot be completed—but a writer should not keep anything to himself over the age of sixty. The best way for you to use this work is to add your own notes based on your own experiences. In time, this will mean that the Oracle is not only mine but also, truly, yours.

PART ONE

HELPFUL SPIRITS

1

The Book of Fate

The I Ching is the only book that you can converse with.
You can ask it a question and it will answer you like a
living master.
The question can take hundreds of thousands of forms and
yet it is always the same.
"This is my problem here and now. What should I do?"
The I Ching is the book of fate shaping.

To use more modern parlance, it is an interactive book—according to ancient Chinese concepts, it is a "helping spirit" that directs, advises, cautions, and shows the way. This way is, in all cases, the way of Tao—in modern terms, following the will of God.

The role of the book is to make wiser a person who regularly turns to it. It is not by general teaching that the reader is made wiser, but by advice given for the smallest problems in life—demonstrating the hidden forces of fate that operate everyday events and how to sensibly resolve them.

A person who spends a lot of time with it doesn't feel as if they are reading a book but rather that they are talking to a wise master. It is no coincidence that it was once written, "Even though you have no teacher, turn to it as you would to your parents." That comment was written relatively late on, 2,500 years ago, when the world was in turmoil—as the 36th Oracle Sign says, "The Light has gone dark." It was in this era that books took over the teaching role.

As the I Ching is primarily an oracle, you can ponder this sentence: it does not say "if you have no teacher," but "even though you have no teacher." Sages who peered into the magical crystal ball of times to come, *knew exactly that we would no longer have living, flesh-and-blood teachers, that we would learn from books how to live and seek answers to the deeper meaning of life in general.*

Who is it that you can go to today and ask what you should do for the best outcome? Who is it that can see so deeply into your heart that you accept the advice that they give? No one. And the sages of the I Ching *knew this.*

It was not always like this. The truth, the holy knowledge was carried by people of the Earth, mortal humans, and they passed this living word onto living people of whom anything could be asked. But a catastrophic event changed something in us; our spiritual eye became blind, our heavenly being dropped to the depths of the subconscious and was replaced on Earth by a too clever, too selfish, too unhappy, too deceitful, too rational, too godless, too lonely, too egotistical human race—to which we also belong.

There is not a single person among us—including the saints themselves—who would be free of these qualities. In fact, the "purer" a person is the more precisely they are aware that they "see through a glass darkly." And even though they know what is good, they still do bad, and they do not play the role of the authentic teacher or faultless guru because they know themselves.

Jesus never promised living teachers. He no longer believed in the living chain of knowledge between masters and pupils—he promised us the help of the Holy Spirit: "I still have a great deal to tell you but you are not yet ready to accept it: when He comes, the Spirit of Truth, and leads you to the whole truth; because he does not speak from himself but tells the things that he hears and *announces things of the future to you*" (John 16:12–15).

That part of Christian tradition that works and is still genuine is based on the exact same relationship with the spirit world as the I Ching, in which divination and knowledge of things of the future are just as important as the recognition of the truth.

The I Ching comes from a supernatural source. It comes from a relationship with the "spirit of Truth" or as the Chinese knew it, the "light gods" and "holy spirits" (*shen*). It was an initiated shaman, a priest-medium, or a holy king himself with abilities as a medium who maintained the relationship with the heavenly order of the supernatural world. It worked in exactly the same way as a Christian priest has to work today—or at least how they should work.

While this contact lived, there was no need for books because the knowledge was passed from master to pupil, and this was kept alive by the relationship with the higher spirit world. The light, however, went out. Something went wrong about which all traditions know.

Humankind plummeted along with its sight. It also lost its purity, its humility, and spiritual ability that made it capable of such a relationship and it was now that the sages thought: the time has come to write these words of wisdom down. Like the captains of a sinking ship, the order was issued: "Here's the lifeboat—row on your own from now on!" The I Ching—the Holy Book of Changes—was written "*to help light the gods.*"

It is not only humans who find themselves in need of help, but also the holy spirits whose job it is to help us—they are not able to do this as we have grown deaf. We cannot hear, we have lost our direction, and we are being tossed around on ever more treacherous seas. This book was written for us, the shipwreck victims.

All of a sudden, a very familiar face looks out at us from behind the wise words. And like one who is no longer able to contain itself, it says, "*The writers of the book had a lot of problems and troubles.*" Yes, they did too.

Our fellow in fate speaks to humankind from one of its oldest books. Neither is he afraid—like the guardians of ancient traditions—that he is placing sacred secrets into profane hands. He says, "If you are not true, no sense will appear to you." There are two types of people: those who understand the message of the book and those who don't. Those who have an ear to hear—and others who do not.*

Both "people" are within us: sometimes we hear and sometimes we do not. There is no one, even in the lowest of states, who does not know, if even just for a split second, that there is a difference between the selfish self and what God wants. There is no one who is completely "deaf," who does not know inspiration or even the glimpsing moments of a spiritual state, and who at such times does not suspect that life has a higher meaning and that it is more than meaningless piracy and stealing everything in sight before disappearing into the grave of eternal passing.

This does not require us to forget about God, but ourselves: to forget that we are People. Many have managed this in recent times, but I am not convinced that the process was complete.

J. F. Yan, an American-Chinese biochemist, warned that it was not possible to translate the book without knowledge of the Chinese soul. When, for example, I quoted, "Turn to me as you would to your parents"—this does not just mean with great respect, but a great deal more. It means with the reverence with which you would approach the gods! In ancient China, the family was a spiritual family, a sacred community where the father was the Creative and the mother the Receptive, while the siblings embodied some dignitary or other within the hierarchy. When one of Professor Yan's students who suffered from a feeling of inferiority was advised by a Californian psychologist to "speak bravely back to your father," the boy burst out of the clinic and ran all the way home convinced that he had been the victim of a terrible practical joke.

---

*I will write about this in greater detail later on; this does not describe two types of people but rather two qualities of spirit.

My father, however much I respect him, can make mistakes—but the "father" of those for whom the above words were written could not make mistakes as they were gods! In other words, this phrase means that the book is *infallible*. However, *you* can make mistakes because your "childish" knowledge means that you cannot always correctly interpret advice—but the I Ching never makes a mistake.

Wherever possible I have done my best to experience not only the words but also the meaning of the characters. Each and every ancient character communicates a great deal. It was Confucius who said, "Everything depends on the correct use of words." Sometimes understanding of the whole Oracle Sign depends on understanding one single word. *Any misunderstood word can lead to misunderstanding everything.*

THE ORIGINS OF THE I CHING

The origin of the I Ching is veiled in legend. The ancient—"before the Sky"—version is considered to be the work of the mythical, holy king, *Fu-hsi*. Fu-hsi originally represented a god, much like the Greek Zeus or perhaps more appropriately Prometheus, who brought fire down from the sky. If it is at all possible to speak about time, he lived more than five thousand years ago. Where? On Earth? In the spirit world? Or in the soul of humans? It is difficult to say—in the same place as Zeus and Prometheus and Jupiter and Seth and Wotan, and perhaps even Abraham.

There is something very edifying in the history of Fu-hsi and characteristics of the Chinese approach to life.

We know that civilization began to deteriorate, first becoming materialistic and then rationalistic, and finally the last phase is when it begins to decay. This is the stage we are at now, where we are no longer idealistic, no longer religious, and no longer materialistic. If someone falls, they no longer have principles. "You are galleries of all of that you once believed!" is how Nietzsche described us. In recent times, materialism and rationalism have also failed and we know that nowadays people's lives are poisoned by scientificism and all manner of "isms," but there is nothing that can be done: the world is falling and, beyond money, there is no longer any form of working ideal and no God.

Decline always begins with hate: they want to destroy the spiritual world and the world of ancient beliefs. This also happened with Fu-hsi, as well as the I Ching itself, which people attempted to burn on a number of occasions. The cunning Chinese sages then said that Fu-hsi was not a god but just a simple, earthly king. They even invented a time and a place where he ruled, they drew his official "portrait," and they quite possibly recorded what sort of robe he wore and the size of his shoes. They lied that the I Ching was a technical work that could be used as a reference for healing. They managed to hide the sacred secrets behind the word *scientific* much in the same way as holistic wisdom hides behind the expression "natural medicine" today.

This is how Fu-hsi and the I Ching managed to avoid complete destruction. Prominent figures in both Greek and Roman culture were destroyed because they were not willing to betray their gods.

The Chinese sages—who were always extremely *flexible* in their approach—said, "If the blind do not see, we will tell them the truth even if this has to be done through touch." And they brought Fu-hsi and his ancient mythology down to earth and they made use of the I Ching for social, political, and agricultural purposes. As you can see, there are two permanent and constant things in the world: one is divine truth—the other is human stupidity.

C. G. Jung used the I Ching over a period of thirty years. He initially used Legge's translation and later a translation by Richard Wilhelm, to which he also wrote the preface. Jung carefully concealed his mystical and spiritual experiences his whole life because he thought that, if uncovered, it would lead to him being rejected by the scientific world. That is why, before he sat down to write the preface, he turned to the Oracle itself for advice. It responded by telling him to be very careful as it would result in him being ostracized by his colleagues.

The reason that I mention all of this is because I want to give a sense of the approach that most of the signs in the Oracle use and that later became the fundamental strategy of virtually all martial arts from the Far East. This is preserved change, the wise art of adaptation that is symbolized by a tall reed: the reason that it does not break under a heavy load is because it bends and, if need be, it can bend completely to the ground. Despite this, it still remains a reed, and when the burden is no longer present, it starts to make its way up again.

So, what is today known as the I Ching and what the Chinese refer to as the *Chou I*, was written in its final form by King Wen and later his son, Prince Chou—to give some indication of the date, this was around 1000 BCE. This was in the Dark Ages.

King Wen lived as the prisoner of the tyrant Chou Hsin whose drunkenness, thirst for power, and merciless nature was comparable to that of Stalin. The I Ching was therefore born in prison, in dire circumstances. Wen pretended that he was insane in order to avoid torture and execution.

Legend has it that he scribbled on the wall the Yin and Yang oracle lines that later not only meant the fall of Chou Hsin, but also the blossoming of his people, and the creation of Chinese culture itself that would last for a thousand years. It is from these mysterious signs that Taoism, Confucianism, Chinese art, social order, politics, morals, religion, ceremony, wisdom, medicine, science, feng shui, all martial arts, and especially the order of everyday life were all born.

King Wen went beyond Fu-hsi's "Order before the Sky" and created a new "Order after the Sky" as it was his aim *to make the sacred knowledge usable by ordinary people.* It teaches how to live wisely.

I have described the story of how the book came to be written because this is integral to the essence of the book. They say that King Wen himself lived according to this spirit. He used the Oracle for himself. He asked it for advice in all situations. This is how, with miraculous tactics, he managed to free himself from prison; he then convinced his son—who had been born to fight—to organize an army that toppled the rule of the much-feared tyrant and that laid the foundation for a new empire that for so long lived and blossomed in the spirit of the I Ching.

The reason that I write all of this in the past tense is because currently not only China, but the whole world travels the path that the Oracle refers to as "trouble" and "shame." The worst is when a person knows that their actions will lead to trouble and yet still goes ahead. This is where we stand today.

King Wen teaches that only a person who is aware of the danger can create peace within themselves. You should not turn your back on danger but face it. One who does not do this will "be shamed."

Preserve the joy of the heart in all circumstances at the same time as maintaining a cautious vigilance of thought: this is the only way to differentiate beneficence from trouble and to fulfill all things on Earth that are difficult.

The I Ching does not believe in positive thinking based on turning a blind eye. *A person who is cautious rarely makes a mistake.*

2

Change, Trouble, Problem, Lightness, Calm

If we are to use the Oracle, we need to get right inside of its soul. This is a very enjoyable task: you have to experience the meaning of several ancient words and you have to think a little with the head of a wise, Chinese master. *Ching* means "legal code," "canon." The meaning of *I* is "Change, Trouble, Problem, Lightness, and Calm." All five at once! All over the world, it is translated as the Book of Changes, as Western languages lack this degree of complexity. It has the same place in Chinese tradition as the Bible does in our world.

The precise title is the Book of Changes, Trouble, Problem, Lightness, and Calm. How does this all come together? Let's take things one step at a time. The Chinese do not say that "everything changes," but that there is nothing other than change! There is not 100 millionth of a second of life in which something exists without change. It is this continuous flow that we call "Life"—but we cannot talk about "what" or "who" because "what" and "who" undergo constant change and transformation.

What we refer to as "material" is nothing other than a continuous Dance: it is so dazzlingly swift that it cannot be seen by our eyes and appears to be solid and dense. But this is not the case. In Hinduism it is said that in the same way that you see a quickly spinning cyclone as a solid ring, this is how you see the density of the material world; your eye doesn't see the movement but only the constructed illusion that makes you think that it stands, it exists, and that you can touch it. Our consciousness is only able to see *static images*, but life is a moving image, a continuous flow. It is a path on which there is no stopping.

Path and Life and Reality are One. There appear to be two directions on this path: your past pushes you toward your future via your present. And your future pulls you, along with your past, toward it via your present. You are also trapped here because you only know the first direction, but your life is not only directed by your experiences in the past but also by the fact that, deep down in your soul, you know who and what you should become, and this is the direction toward what you aim to achieve.

A seed not only contains the past but also potentially contains the future: everyone has written inside them not only what they once were but also what they have to—or should—become. Your fate is not only written in your body but in your whole being—whether or not you realize this depends on you. The I Ching sees into this wonderful process and that is why it is known as "Change," and that is why it can be used for divination. The problem is that we are afraid of change.

We are condemned to death the moment that we are born. Our cells multiply and continuously die, we struggle to achieve something that, no sooner have we done it, turns to dust in our hands; we suffer so that something can become ours and when it is ours, we suffer so as not to lose it. We are afraid if we have it and afraid if we don't; a person feels under constant threat from change and not without cause because this is nothing other than fear of transience and the certainty that "sooner or later, everything and everyone I know will be gone."

This is why *I* also means "trouble" and "problem." It means trouble if chaos constantly threatens order . . . if dark threatens light . . . if death threatens life. This is the drama of Creation and we are all in it up to our necks—it is our drama too.

Trouble and problem.

As our Spirit (shen) is timeless and eternal—it does not feel good in this world of transience and change and death. And it is afraid. It worries. It feels uncomfortable.

The Chinese language uses *I* when something suddenly falls apart, when the floods come or fire or when a person, a family, or a society crumbles—in other words, when chaos breaks into something that we thought of as Order and as being permanent. This is *trouble*. This is the *problem*.

As change is eternal, trouble and problems are also eternal. It is constantly present, even now, as I write this book. Will I really manage to get it written? Will I succeed in completing it? (I could die at any minute.) Will I manage to get it published? Will you understand it? What will happen to me, my family, and my health? How many people will look down on me, reject me, hate me because of this Oracle?

I look at one I love and in my mind's eye I can already see them at their funeral.

Problem. Trouble. Big problem. And unfortunately, this is because of change. This is why *I* is change, trouble, and problem all at the same time. The three together, indivisible.

And there is still the fourth to come. This is the wonder of the book. The fourth meaning of *I* is "lightness." That's the most staggering thing: how can you take this whole thing *lightly*?

This is now dealing with you. It is about your soul, about your consciousness, about your spiritual vision or blindness, and about how to live wisely with change so full of worries, problems, and troubles— lightly, relaxed.

What does this mean? In brief: selflessly, unselfishly, with no ego. A person who knows that they are immortal and the world that they are born into is changing but they are not, has nothing to fear. Jesus said, "Be wanderers." Those who live with this knowledge know that life is not solid but liquid and is continuously flowing. And that is why they are extremely careful not to stiffen, freeze, or lose their lightness or freedom for a single minute—*they keep their consciousness in a constantly fluid state.*

They are afraid of nothing; they insist on nothing—only freedom. They do not fight against passing and they do not fear it; they take things and events *lightly* because they do not get bogged down in them and they do not identify with them.

A phrase that we use today would be that they are at peace with the will of God. In other words, they live their fate and do not swim with all their might against the tide, they don't push, they don't want, they don't connive, they don't flail around but they *live in the current with the current*, and that is why everything is easy for them because everything helps them. They see the constant battle between chaos and order but as they look with eyes of the soul, they also see that order is invincible.

The Chinese say Order is the sum total of disorder. This also means that every upset, problem, and failure has its own deep cause and meaning . . . and in the end, Order is restored. Those who live with this knowledge are *calm* and their lives are *Light*. Not only their lives, but also their every tiny action is Light. And that is the point.

The action about which the I Ching speaks we would refer to as "inspired" action. We can only experience it for a split second because it is completely spiritual and selfless action, and our ego has obstinate, evil, and tyrannical strength. It will not allow itself to be pushed from power.

All it takes is one instant for us to know what this is all about. We sometimes refer to this with the term "spiritual presence." When, in an emergency, you calmly swerve your car, you suddenly throw your coat over a flaming gas canister, or you grab the arm of a child who is about to step out into traffic without consciously realizing what it is that you are doing because perhaps you don't *see* but you *sense* the approaching danger: this is all *I*—Light and inspired action.

It is only afterward that the problem appears difficult, complicated, and problematic—but while you were acting, it was so *easy* that you did not even sense that you had done anything at all. The ancient view says that it is not you but your most inner self that acted and what it did it did with help from the Holy Spirit.

The Oracle says of such deeds that they are *fu*, which means that your inner and outer self *harmonized* for a moment in time and the most important thing of all is that the Holy Spirit worked together with you. It is at times like this that we say, "God is with us." However, this only lasts for a couple of minutes. Then the inner and the outer part company once more. The spirits leave us and we are left with trouble, problems, and uncertainty.

Preserving Inspiration or Spiritual Presence takes a massive amount of work. We refer to this work as *Ta Ye*, which means "Great Undertaking." Those who build the I Ching into their everyday lives receive a "Helping Spirit" as they set out on the difficult but wondrous path of spiritual development where they become wiser. They get to experience that free spiritual consciousness for longer and longer periods that lifts them above problems and troubles, and they see through the amazing meaning of their own lives and the whole world drama.

In fact, the martial arts also practice Ta Ye based on the I Ching. I will speak more about this when I discuss interpretation of Oracle Signs because they very sensitively express the way in which people battle in the world drama. A body-to-body struggle much more sensitively expresses spiritual strategy than a complex political battle does or one that takes place in a person's private life.

I would like to say this: the aim of the masters is *to keep the consciousness of a warrior in a constant state of flow.* In this floating, free, and inspired state everything runs and flows and continuously changes; if someone stops, that is the end of them.

If a warrior's thinking stops . . . let's say that the sight of sword speeding toward his head stops him thinking with "Good God, that sword is going to cut my head off!" then the sword will cut his head off. Practically speaking, this is because he becomes paralyzed where his spirit froze, and he misses out on those opportunities that would avoid the problem.

Everything changes and passes—even thought. The three seconds that appear to stand still for you is an endless sequence of changes for an initiated warrior; that is why he can fight with seven or eight adversaries "at once," like a Karate Kid, because for him this is not *at once* but many versions of the available options. He doesn't think in a fixed image but in continuous changes.

This is what can only be achieved with endless meditation and practice. But the essence is floating, soaring, and sailing with the current. This is freedom.

I Ching means The Holy Book of Changes, Problems, Troubles, and Liberated Lightness. And because it deals with the manifestation of fate, it has been used for making divinations since ancient times.

3

Divination
and Fortune-Telling

The I Ching does not tell fortunes, it divines. There is a decisive difference between the two. A fortune-teller says what will happen to you, while a divination tells you what to do to ensure that what happens is good. Divination has been used by traditional cultures and religions for millennia. Fortune-telling is a superstitious and foolish offshoot of divination. The future is not "finished." It is very rare for things to have collected in the invisible so that future events can be clearly seen. The future is in a state of continual birth, it is shaping and forming and you cannot be left out of this as you give birth to, shape, and direct the process.

We are the children of the Creator, who breathed divine spirit into humankind and bestowed the greatest gift: the power of creation. We all take part in the creation of ourselves and the world around us. We are all magicians; we dream ourselves and our lives into being. We form ourselves with our desire, our will, our faith, our false beliefs, and mainly our "life imagination" that lays hidden deep in our consciousness. We then give birth to ourselves and our own future with our magical creative powers.

If we achieve something, it is not because a foreign hand placed it in front of us but because this is the path that we chose—we create all that our future lays before us. We are fate-creators, divine beings. We don't like to admit this because it means we have to take responsibility for all that happens to us. This is the essence of all divination and prophecy.

The present, the Now, is where the soothsayer (or prophet) is able to reach into your life. This is a threat to Jews, a warning to Greeks, and a mild recommendation to the Chinese not to use "black" magic but your "white" magic—in other words, live your fate and not your tiny life that ripens a selfish, greedy, and dark future.

Forget the unproductive debate of free will versus predestination. No power controls you. Neither God nor the world has cast a spell on you so that you live your life in a trance and only do what they want and only play the part that you are given by a tyrannical director.

At the same time, you should not deceive yourself that you can do whatever you want because your will is "free." The only thing that is free is choice. You can choose a path. Everything else is determined. Movement on the path is strictly controlled, but the path you choose depends on who you listen to inside yourself.

The essence of the I Ching is reflected in the gospels when Jesus says, "Let your will be done, Father, and not mine." He stood with two paths before him. One was suffering and death on the cross. This was his fate task and the path of his undertaking that he had often divined to his disciples—the path to Golgotha. We can only guess at the other path because he did not follow it, but it is a very familiar one: the ego takes fright, fleeing, hiding—the path to survival.

One was Fate and the other the path of a minor life. Or as the Chinese say, one is the path of a Great Life and the other is the path of minor existence. Jesus decided, he chose the path of his fate. Could he have chosen any other way? Of course he could. That is what makes this story true. If the Father had not given his son the choice, this mythical story would have become godless and inhuman—it would have simply been the story of a hopeless slave and a merciless tyrant. Such a Father could not be loved and such a son could not be followed.

Jesus also said, "I and the Lord are one," which was to say that the drama was not between "I" and "Him" but that it mainly took place in Christ's soul where a choice had to be made between the divine Self and the will of the human ego. Before Jesus decided, he still had two futures before him. Two paths. We only know the one that he chose and the one that he took.

The Jewish prophets also placed a decision before their people. They never predicted the future, but they made divinations. The most beautiful example of this was the glorious prophecy that Moses made before his death. "Look," he said, "I hold before your eyes, life and salvation or death and damnation." He called upon his people to choose. He poetically described the blessed and cursed versions of the future. Two scripts were still available before the decision was made: a blessed and a cursed version. The blessed version showed a happy nation while the cursed version showed a Jewry living in exile all around the world. This divination was read again and again over thousands of years with great sadness because it literally came true.

The shaman, the *wu*, and the Eye of Delphi all work in the same way as Moses: they tell a person who is facing a decision what a good future contains and what a bad future contains. They reveal which inner voice should be listened to. In other words, they describe what will happen if a divine path and the way of Tao is followed and what will happen if one's own, stupid head is followed.

The future is not finished. A person asks for a divination if they have "trouble in their heart," which means that their life and fate have come into conflict with each other; they have doubts and must make a decision. Our future is not finished—our life is not a one-way track that we trundle along toward an unavoidable destination, instead it is constantly forming and we have many possible futures that we ourselves can choose from. Man is not only a player but also the author of the drama of life.

I will not talk about the process of the formation of our fate beginning long before our birth as I have dealt with this in my other books.

Everyone arrives on Earth with their own life plan that we do not prepare alone, but with many others, because life is a team game. The formation of the drama of our life begins in the spirit world based on many experiences of the past, but we also make this for ourselves from ourselves; we create a character from the infinite richness of our soul. It was not the idea of a "director from beyond" that I should be Peter Muller, but my idea because that was the result of many incarnations and experiences both good and bad. This "role" covers me and only I can play it because he is the creation of my own divine spirit together with the life plan with which he arrived.

With this life plan, we really have created an unbreakable framework for ourselves; there are certain karmas that we are not able to modify—but the process of free choice is not completely closed to us either because fate creation and self-creation are constantly in operation. What we dream as a spirit, we realize as a person—but the reality will never be anything like the dream because life is a live process of creation and new dreams, new desires, and new fears weave new threads into the tapestry of our lives.

There is music buried deep down in our consciousness, but a musician likes to improvise. At times like this, the tension becomes increasingly painful between the basic melody and the improvisation—this is referred to in psychology as a "problem"—and this is the point at which it is a good idea to consult The Book of Fate and ask it what you should do.

FRAMING THE QUESTION

The future is open in many ways. This "open future" is not only part of the I Ching but also found in the Chinese language itself. This is because the I Ching and the language stem from the same spiritual root. It is impossible to ask a question in Chinese like "Should I go to town?" In Chinese it sounds more like "I to go, not to go (the) town?" So, the question takes the form "Should I go to town or shouldn't I go to town?" So, this contains both possibilities, despite the fact that I only asked one.

There is a song that begins, "Should I go for your dark eyes, or shouldn't I?" If I go for your dark eyes, it will mean a different future than if I don't go for your dark eyes. One means that I fall in love with you and this will lead to marriage and children, while the other one means no love, no marriage, no children, and I go off to Canada to become a lumberjack.

I choose my fate. The fact that I choose one means that I give up another. Modern science refers to this as the many-worlds theory. This means that I realize one of many virtual futures while the others lie dormant on the nonmaterial plane. For example, I leave for Canada because that is the path that I have chosen and all I do is dream about you all the time and your dark eyes that I "should have gone for" but, unfortunately, I didn't and now I can't and I'm lonely. The other option is that I live in a bad marriage and I stare into your dark eyes and I torture myself for not having gone to Canada. Everything is there all the time on different levels of reality.

The reason that I am talking about this is because when we reach the practical part of the book, you will see that you can't simply ask the I Ching "What should I do?"—you have to carefully describe your problem. The book will never decide for you. You are the one who has to choose. But it is important that you do this with a vigilant spirit and you do not listen to the ignorant encouragement of short-sighted ego and take a step that leads to trouble and shame.

WHAT THE ORACLE WILL REVEAL

Our forefathers invented the game of chess to deal with the question of "what step should I take?" This is much more than a game; it is an initiation and it symbolically represents our whole life. The board is the field of life. It is made up of black and white—Yin and Yang—pieces and squares and there are exactly sixty-four fields of fate, just like the number of Oracle Signs in the I Ching. The pieces represent different strengths of your being.

No one tells you where you should move with them—but as with all individual and life dramas, a chess game is controlled by strict rules. One is the law of *dharma*, which means that there is an unavoidable order controlling the field of life. This is a world law that cannot be broken. You cannot move pieces around the board in any way you like.

The second is the law of *karma*, which says that you can freely move your pieces, but all moves carry consequences. This is true of all the pieces on the "battlefield" of life. You make one move with a pawn and you alter the whole dynamic and, with it, the fate of all the other pieces on the board. Here—just as in life—everything is linked to everything else. My fate is linked to his fate is linked to our fate is linked to your fate.

Each move that you make changes everybody's life. Furthermore, a game of chess symbolizes the drama that is played out in your everyday life with such intensity that there is a "stance," an external dynamic, a "world situation" and although you have participated in its creation, you experience it in the form of the outside world that either helps or threatens you. You are in a situation that is outside of you.

Here is the point. The better a person can play chess, the further they can see. And the more they are aware of what move will lead to what, the better they are able to divine. This is because when one is able to see into the invisible dynamic, one is able to see what changes will take place and the culmination of a given dramatic situation.

Everyone can choose freely. You can step wherever you like but if you cannot play chess, you will lose one of your pieces. Sometimes this will happen straight away and sometimes it will happen eight moves on—but the eye of the master sees this eighth step. This is the karmic consequence of a bad move.

The I Ching has the eye of a master and is able to recognize the inner and outer dynamic that you happen to be in, and if you listen to the advice that it provides, it will be as if you are playing chess with a grandmaster whispering into your ear.

Our life is art. The wiser we are, the better we play. The better we play, the better the result will be. We can avoid checkmate and the "death of the ruler" (our ignorance leading to the death of the divine within us).

4

Thoughts of God

Since I wrote this Oracle for everyday use, I would like to speak about its soul rather than its theory. We are able to use a compass without having to understand the theory of how it works. (I have provided a detailed bibliography at the end of the book for those of you who are spurred on to carry out further research on your own.) When I attempt to speak *lightly* of heavy matters and *simply* about complex matters, I examine myself; I can always speak simply about that which is my own. I usually need complicated explanations when I myself don't really understand what it is that I am talking about.

Albert Einstein once said, "I would like to know what God is thinking." The I Ching allows us to see more clearly, perhaps not what God is thinking, but the fundamental thinking behind creation. This is true in the sense that if you were to look for the philosophical background of the results of the most modern research, you would find it in this most sacred of books. If a physicist really becomes absorbed in the science, they will involuntarily become a Taoist. This is the only valid philosophy today. Today, physics is metaphysics.

It is another matter entirely that knowing this doesn't get us anywhere at all; if someone plunges helplessly down a steep slope, *they aren't concerned with abstract philosophical questions*. It's far too late in the day.

Once upon a time, people sought the truth in order to make their life better, more sensible, and more human. Today, in an age of madly dashing around and mental collapse, knowledge of the truth is the passion of but a few individuals; truth, principles, and morals no longer have anything to do with life. The majority of mankind is only interested in one working "truth"—how to make as much money as possible as quickly as possible!

The person who knows the real truth possesses the "Sages' stone," but people don't even listen to these individuals because they know better than anybody that this whole world order based around money, banks, and the economy is dancing on the rim of a volcano and its days are numbered.

The reason that I say all of this is because I am now going to discuss something about which one of man's ancient traditions and the most modern scientific theories largely agree.

THE GREAT ANCIENT BEGINNING

Chinese people think in pictorial terms and they describe God's thought in picture form.

There is a circle.

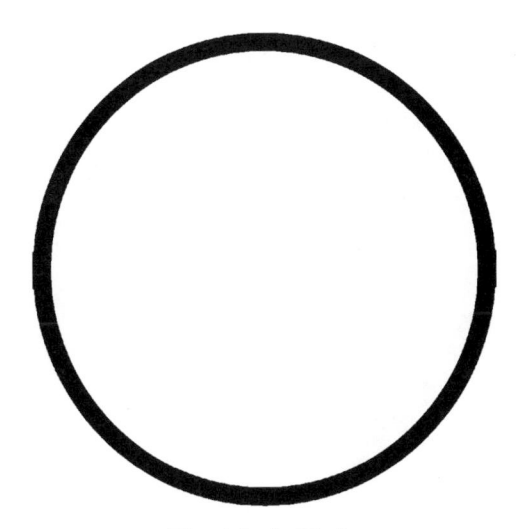

Fig. 4.1. A Circle.

This is Ancient Reality. We say that it is "empty" because we see nothing inside of it. However, this emptiness holds the whole universe. Ancient Reality is just like a magician's top hat; it is empty and yet everything and everyone pops out of it. The number of the circle is One.

The divine magic begins when some kind of split creates Two out of One—and the two halves begin to attract and repel each other, love and hate each other. The dance between the two sets everything in motion, they begin to multiply, make war, make peace, spin out, and pull in, repel and yet still attract; the two of them begin to spin, the dance begins, the spiral twists—and this creates polarity and with it eternal and continual change.

One half of the circle is white—that is Yang. The other half is black—that is Yin. And, as you can see, the white Yang is not completely white; it carries a little spot of Yin. And black Yin also has a little spot of white Yang within it. These tiny little spots will have enormous significance later on. The two together—held together by the Great and All-Embracing Ancient Circle—form the symbol of Tai Chi, the Great Ancient Beginning.

As you can see, the ancient forces of black and white do not split the picture completely in two because the Great Divine Circle embraces

Fig. 4.2. The Yin / Yang.

everything: they struggle, turn, and change inside it like fighting twins in their mother's womb.

We say, "*We are all in God.*" Frigyes Karinthy, the Hungarian author and poet, describes the secret of creation when he said, "I dreamt that I was two cats and I played with each other." Exactly the same thing is happening here as well. In the dream of the Great Ancient Beginning, Yin and Yang are the two cats that are playing with each other for as long as the Ancient Beginning sleeps within us and until it finally awakes. We experience the drama of polarity in everything. Dark and light, attraction and repulsion, male and female, positive and negative, sun and planets, nucleus and electrons, electrical and magnetic; life constantly vibrates and undulates, embraces and repels; all that was, is, and will be is born from the drama of these two ancient powers before it passes and is born once more.

We have polarity within ourselves and it is a question of approach whether we operate via digital or analog means: our heart beats, we breathe in and out, our brain pulsates, and we have two kinds of blood circulation; this is why we change, are born, grow old, and die. We are driven by a desire for satisfaction toward the other pole; that is what makes us fall in love, make love, be faithful, be unfaithful, be good, be bad, weak and strong, cowardly and brave, and that is why we have light and dark periods in our lives—the one doesn't exist without the other, all joy contains sadness, and even in the unhappiest of moments, something sparkles in the deep like a coin tossed into a wishing well.

It is really quite unbelievable that the whole universe all comes about from the drama of Yin and Yang. Everything. Even me! Not to mention my computer on which I type these lines and on the screen of which a message just arrived from the far side of the globe; this wonderful operation came about from the interplay between two pieces of information, between 0 and 1. It is amazing that this endlessly rich, cosmic conjuring trick has such a *simple key.*

But this is the truth and this also forms the basis of the I Ching. If you ask the Oracle, all it tells you is the current state of the drama of Yin and

Yang. It shows a dramatic dynamic that is the kind of thing that a chess grandmaster sees behind the pattern of black and white pieces in a game of chess. You can see a long way from this position. You can determine what steps to take in order to take the match to a favorable conclusion. You should know that a chess master—as Géza Maróczy said—doesn't see chess pieces but *senses the invisible, dramatic drama*. That is why a master can play simultaneously on up to thirty-two chessboards.

The I Ching shows the very same dynamic—Yin and Yang, positive and negative, the momentary juxtapositions of 1 and 0—and everything is in that. From this you have to read what future burdens the present moment and how to beneficially open this up. In order to understand a divination, you need to have analog sensitivity. What does that mean? The wonder of the "conjuring trick" is that just two invisible forces above can result in hundreds of millions of things and events down here. There are just two pieces of information behind the whole of the great Nintendo game that plays itself out on Earth, and just one dynamic can lead to any number of games.

You are the one who has to sense what the Oracle's answer pertains to. It might be an inner problem and it might be an external problem. It might be about you or those around you; it might be about how you relate to others or, the opposite, how others relate to you.

Friendship, love, family, vocation, health, battle—the drama can be acted out on one of many stages of your fate, and the stage in question might be your inner spiritual world and it might simply be the outside world—nine times out of ten, my experience has been that it was both at the same time. There is a connection, an analogy between the many different versions.

I will write about this in more detail in the section that talks about how you should use the book. All I want to say here is, it is always your problem that selects the answer from the endless list of analogies. The question hiding in your heart attracts the answer to itself. A force-cyclone forms at the point in your fate where you sense a problem and a difficulty to be solved, and it pulls the answer to it.

This is where the Holy Spirit and the word of the master once provided help: they translated the general answer given by the book into your language and told you what it is that you should do here and now. I am convinced that we did not lose this help in the age of solitude and if we have sufficient self-knowledge, and if we make our spirits more sensitive, conversations with the I Ching will lead to the *aha* sensation of sudden inspiration appearing more and more regularly in our lives. We are not alone today either. If you use the I Ching with a giving heart and open mind, you will receive a helping spirit.

The essence of analogical thinking is that a supernatural world exists beyond the natural world and if what exists there as an invisible ancient force, pattern, or idea becomes visible down here, it can turn into myriad forms, beings, or events. The Pattern is up there and it's invisible. What it creates is here is visible, and has hundreds of millions of variations. Analogy does not mean that certain earthly things are similar to one another but that they come from the same spiritual root.

What we see in the world and what happens to us is the reflection of invisible ancient patterns. The reason that we feel similarities between them and that they appear to rhyme with one another is because they have the same *Mother* and *Father* and they all resemble them in the spirit world.

This is the essence of the I Ching. It links us to the invisible world. It links you to the morphogenetic fields of your own inner and outer world and allows you to take a look at the Forces that direct your fate.

THE SIGNIFICANCE OF 64

There are 64 signs; there are 64 divine patterns; the whole of creation is within these 64 divine "thoughts." The number of squares on a chessboard is 64. The number 64 was of great significance in the creation of the computer.

The double helix, known as "the secret of life," is based on the ancient principle of the Yin Yang. European and Chinese biochemists recently discovered that the amino acids that make up our genetic code are combined in a total of 64 basic patterns. Biochemical formulae are analogous to the Oracle Signs of the I Ching to such an extent that if we synthetically create a chemical, it has a similar effect on the human body as its equivalent Oracle Sign. For example, the structure of the antidepressant called tryptophan, is the same as the 35th Oracle Sign* that is known as Advancement (Emergence). The message of the Oracle Sign is exactly equivalent to the biological effect of tryptophan: it makes an excellent antidepressant.

These 64 Oracle Signs are the 64 scenes of the world drama. The 1st Oracle Sign, or "act," is where everything is created; this is the overture of the Creative. In the 63rd Oracle Sign and penultimate act, everything is Fulfilled. It is in the last act that we discover that as everything comes to an end, a new cycle begins because change is eternal and nothing ever really comes to an end—when a person thinks that the end has arrived, everything starts all over again from the beginning.

If you flip through the Oracle, you can see that each Oracle Sign is made out of six Yin or Yang lines—these can be seen as scenes or mini dramas within an act—and also that a whole Oracle Sign is made up of two types of ancient symbols that are formed with three Yin and three Yang forces. The technical literature refers to Oracle Signs as *hexagrams* as they are made up of six Yin Yang forces. The two ancient symbols that form the hexagram are known as trigrams because they are made up of three Yin Yang forces. I don't use these expressions. It is much more important that you get to know the approach to being that the ancient book offers.

You first need to know the spirit of something and then follow this with the practice. A lot of people have asked me how to call up a spirit. Or to be more precise, what needs to be done in order to establish contact with the Holy Spirit? I answered by saying, "In order to make

---

*Wang, B. "The Eight Trigrams of the I Ching Provide a New Avenue for Characterizing the Association between mRNA Codons and the Hydrophobicity of the Encoded Amino Acids." *Open Journal of Philosophy* 10, 1–8.

contact with the Genius of Music, the best violinist in the world can do nothing better than to put bow to string, hair to gut, and rub away. Perhaps, at most, they should carefully apply resin to the bow beforehand. This is practically all that has to be done and no more."

The "more" is in the spirit: the Tuning, the Knowledge, the purity of Giving, and the humble attention of the Inner Ear with which to hear and experience the message of Genius. It also requires unbelievable amounts of concentration, meditation, and practice. This is first and foremost with the I Ching. It is important to become acquainted with the fundamental spiritual and life secrets that the individual Oracle Signs—thoughts of God—offer.

The reason I give the following chapter the title "The Art of Life" is because, for me, *art* means to do something as beautifully, as well, and as wisely as possible. In the East, war is also referred to as being an art. The martial art Pa Kua Chuan is nothing other than the drama of the 64th Oracle Sign, the 64th "divine drama."

The world drama has 64 acts. It has 64 dramatic situations. And each has its own optimal combat strategy. The reason that I prefer to talk about the tactics of open struggle is because it creates a much clearer and spectacular image of the choreography that cunningly hides inside a love affair or, even more so, in a problematic spiritual situation.

The important thing to know is that there are only 64 dramas of being, 64 archetypes. There are no more. And if one alters, it turns into another. If you step out of one situation, you step into another—there is no in-between state, there is no transition, there is no "mutation."

The patterns transform into one another. Each pattern (Oracle Sign) boils, tenses, enriches, and forms within and when it reaches a certain limit, it instantly changes into another pattern. Either butterfly or caterpillar or chrysalis—there is nothing in between: only struggle.

The whole of your life is made up of nothing other than an endless sequence of Oracle Signs (patterns), one turning into the next.

5

The Art of Life

In order to live in harmony, we need wisdom. This is what the I Ching teaches—and now I will describe a few essential basics that you will come across when using the I Ching on a regular basis.

FUNDAMENTAL PRINCIPLES OF PRACTICE

1. Either You Lead in the Dance or You Are Led

It is always timeliness that dictates whether leading or being led is beneficial, and when. There is no greater problem than when someone is not willing to lead when they should lead—or not allowing themselves to be led, deliberately treading on the toes of the other and ruining the dance.

There are two ancient forces: Yang and Yin. Yang initiates, directs, leads, wants, creates, determines, is active, is positive, moves forward, and spreads out centrifugally. Yang leads in the dance. Yang is the first in a fight, the attack, and the validation of self will. It has the male role in this world. If Yang overflows it will become aggressive, obstinate, pigheaded, willful, rough, uninhibited, or self-important. My mother always spoke of people with overly powerful Yang as "really being." This is not just a trait but a force: time also has Yang periods.

If the helping spirit of the Oracle sees that you happen to be standing at the beginning of a Yang period, it encourages you to become active, to step into the field of action and act, or as the Chinese say, "Cross over the Great Water."

The sign of Yang is a single, solid line.

Yin accepts, welcomes, is passive, embraces, and allows itself to be directed or led in the dance. It is giving, ripening, patient, waiting—it creates what Yang wants. Yin is the second in a fight, it only retreats and responds; it survives by the errors of its rival and when its rival "oversteps," it attacks. Yin is the genius of defense. It is the feminine role in the world. If Yin overflows, it will become lazy, weak, cowardly, helpless, materialistic, shy, nervous, and defenseless. My mother described overly weak Yin people "as if there was no one there at all."

If the helping spirit of the Oracle sees that you are standing at the beginning of a Yin period, it warns you against initiating, wanting, or directing. It advises you to wait, stay quiet, retreat, or follow a will that is worth following.

The sign of Yin is a soft, broken line.

All this appears to be natural, but if you come into contact with the wise spirit of the Oracle, you will be surprised to experience that you muddle the two forces, and that will be the main reason for your unease. You complain when you should wait, you speak when you should remain silent, and you wait when you should really be doing something. You interfere in quietly ripening processes and you put off taking a step in a decisive moment.

We are not "life artists" but "life wreckers." We lack wisdom and move frantically around the chessboard. To make matters worse, we make the mistake of not feeling the unity of the two ancient forces, that however emphasized the one is, it is never separate from the other—the two are halves of the same One and one cannot be lived without the other.

The Kung Fu master Bruce Lee said, "If you set off on a bicycle, you don't press down on both pedals at once because you'll tip over. If you want to get anywhere, you *press* one pedal and *release* the other. Pressure and release together: that is the secret of moving forward."

Strength and softness work at the same time in a harmonious person with one on the outside and one on the inside—or the reverse—and the secret is always doing the right thing at the right time. For us—however natural this may sound—it is the most difficult thing to achieve.

In our consciousness, the world is broken into pieces and if there is anything we are incapable of experiencing, it is this: the wonderful unity of opposites.

2. Always Seek Harmony

Some who are led by the I Ching never look for conflict. They strive to maintain harmony in all situations and if this is lost, they do all that they can to see it restored.

They don't willingly attack—only if it is unavoidable. "The meek shall inherit the earth." The basis for such peaceful conduct is to trust in the fact that life is not against you but for you. That you are in the Tao like an embryo in its mother's womb. What happens to you is *ming* (fate).

In essence, Christ's advice is much the same: "Love your enemy as yourself." The trouble is that nothing came of this. The divided churches have been living in unresolved hatred for more than a thousand years and this obstinate hostility characterizes every aspect of our culture.

It is important for us to know this as the Taoist approach has not been built into our spiritual makeup. We are not the only ones, our ancestors didn't understand the language of harmony either—the glorious experience of oneness only exists in our books or in hypocritical lies; our history is dominated by disharmony, hate, and the conviction that others have to be conquered with aggression or, better still, they have to be destroyed altogether.

We do not have any real experiences of love or unity with the world. At least, if we do, they are very few and far between. Our real experience of being is that we live as strangers in a hostile world that can only lie above love. It is impossible to live with a consciousness like this. The I Ching wants to create harmony and this happens with the balancing of opposites, with the balancing of Yin and Yang. This is why it gives that timeless and yet true advice to "life artists" not to see the world as their enemy even if that is how the world sees them!

Try to live like a good sailor: however stormy and treacherous the sea may become with towering waves tossing the boat and wanting to swallow everything up—the sailor still doesn't see it as an enemy. The sea is the element of the good sailor. It is their spouse, their love, their life with which they may battle from time to time, never in the same way as with an enemy but as with their own body, their own soul, their own entirety. They couldn't live without it because it is theirs, it is one with them. That is why they never curse the storm—they know that it will happen and they also know that it is in their fate—and they always try to keep on their feet even in the most deadly storms. A good sailor knows that even in the most enormous storms, the key to the solution is in their hands. If it isn't there, then it is with God. But they never, ever hate the sea.

A "life artist" never sees anyone as their enemy, even when others see them as theirs. This is also the fundamental rule of martial arts. They encourage everyone to empathize and they discourage those pupils who are aggressive and who only see another person as a stranger to be defeated. This type of approach is not merely moral but it also has a practical aspect: you cannot conquer with hate. The good fighter lives as one with the opponent—that is how they know their thoughts. That is why they can defeat them and that is why they show mercy to the last minute. But not afterward! The samurai is peaceful but it would be ill-advised to question their honor or threaten their life.

3. Avoid Exaggeration

The secret of the two ancient powers is not only that they wrestle with each other but also that they individually change within themselves. Yang wants to spread out—and if its inner tension steps over a limit, it breaks up and becomes Yin.

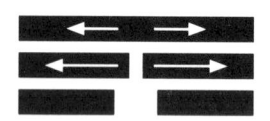

Yang spreads outward to become Yin.

And the same is true in reverse. Yin wants to pull in together—and if its inner strength oversteps a limit, it implodes and becomes Yang.

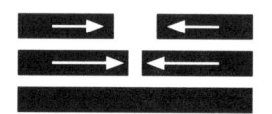

Yin pulls inward to become Yang.

The law of change dictates that when phenomena go beyond a certain level, they become the opposite of themselves. So, the drama is not just between the Yin and Yang but it is going on all the time, separately in each. (If you remember the Tai Chi picture: the little black spot begins to swell in the white until it dominates virtually completely—and the same is true in reverse: the little white spot begins to swell in the black womb. It spreads and swamps the black.)

A cowardly person, when cornered, suddenly breaks out and becomes a demon of daring; an unshakeable hero suddenly bursts out in floods of tears and breaks down in what appears to be a completely insignificant situation. This is how Iago ruins Othello, a tough solider who does not fear death, with nothing more than a handkerchief—he draws the envious and nervous lovesick child out of him. Someone who has won everything until this point, loses the battle, crumbles at the peak of success, becomes an alcoholic, and falls into ruin.

The *switchover* not only results in failure but can often mean illness or even death. A life that runs over the speed limit leads straight to a hospital bed, a wheelchair, or crutches; from this point on, an individual has to be patient and experience what it means to be vulnerable. At the same time, an overly lazy, passive life can culminate in divorce, independence, and revolution.

This is, in essence, the law of karma; it often operates in more than one life and plays out on the shady and sunlit shores of newer and newer incarnations. An overly Yang life is often followed by a Yin life, and if this becomes too much, then it can only be balanced out by another Yang life. (For example, a life of arrogance and power may be followed by a life of servility and if this overflows, it may lead back to a life of arrogance once more.) It is hard to avoid going from the sublime to the ridiculous. However, the aim of the life artist is exactly that—to remain in the middle. This is the essence of the strategy of both Buddha and Lao Tse.

The nearly full moon is the symbol of the *fulfillment* of a desire, a want, a love, or a large piece of work. In other words, this is a state that comes to a stop *a tiny little bit before the peak*. It doesn't switch over. It doesn't make it all the way to the summit because, in that exact minute, it will begin to fall. The full moon is already beginning to darken. The same is true of the noonday sun.

The 55th Oracle Sign, Abundance, cautions against over happiness, and it warns the questioner not to be sad that their path can only lead downward from here. It tells you to begin something new and not to become bitter at exactly the point at which it appears that everything has been achieved.

The life artist never aims for extremes but always the middle way; seeks consensus rather than makes war; stops rather than steps over; pushes the plate away before they have eaten their fill. It is better to be satisfied with less than to ruin yourself with too much.

And in relationships with others—even in the most passionate of love affairs—they stop halfway at the "boundary" of their own being and wait for the other party to arrive at the same point. The life artist doesn't drive right over them and doesn't want to "over own" the other being—this is the basis of all long-term relationships. Because, whoever we "over own" for whatever reason will revolt sooner or later. On the other hand, anyone who doesn't come to that boundary will stay lonely.

Everything is good in moderation.

4. Preserve Your Center Point

The symbol that appears again and again in the I Ching is *chung*.

You often see it in on the front of Chinese shops or Chinese restaurants along with another sign, *kuo*, as this means "China" or "Chinese."

Separately, it means "center." China refers to itself as the "Empire of the Center." This word is extremely important; it signifies the secret of a whole people: it is called "chung" and everything has a "center." This is the heart of a hurricane where there is quiet, calm, and silence while the storm rages all around. Everything comes from here: from emptiness. There is no Yin or Yang here, only calm. Symbolically speaking, this is where God lives. Your soul has a center as does your body and all of your problems.

Whatever battle you find yourself in, however wildly the storm rages within you or around you, whichever way the whirlwind spins and threatens to swallow you up, you always have the opportunity to retreat to the center, to the calm of chung from where you can take a clear view of the whole swirling confusion.

I've written a great deal about this and I've described the meditation practice that, whatever the problem, can lead you to the calm of your center point. This is the "Peace of the Heart" in Christian tradition—and Jesus is shown pointing to it in popular prints. Everyone misunderstands the symbolism of the heart. We think that this is where pure emotions live in the same way that we think of love as being some kind of warm, well-intentioned, and sentimental emotion. This is not the case.

A person who "sees with the heart" sees clearly, seeing the Whole, together, with no emotional bias of any kind. They see what is really there *because they aren't tangled up in the drama.* There is no Yin and no Yang here—it is exactly between the two—and that is why here there is no turmoil, dizziness, time, and clambering around; everything can be seen clearly from here and a decision can be made as to the best solution to an unfathomably complex life situation.

Let's take a simple example: there can be many different kinds of tension between a man and a woman that can be solved not only according to the truth of the man but also that of the woman. The two "truths" are not the same because they see the world with different eyes and they can both be "right" in their own, individual way. But it is not as simple as this, because it is possible for them to look at this question not as a man and not as a woman but through the eyes of a Human. And this is the solution!

Between Yin and Yang is *jen* (that means "person" in Chinese). Between man and woman there is the center, the Human, whose vision cannot be clouded by a "male" or "female" way of looking at things because otherwise their relationship will not only be constant pushing and pulling but become *inhuman*. Such relationships are usually only good in bed and even then, not for all that long. A long-term relationship needs both parties to be able to speak as humans.

I can also take a look at *myself* from the center of my soul. But I cannot do this impersonally. It is as if I wasn't me . . . as if the whole thing wasn't happening to me . . . as if I was not a participant but an *onlooker* to my own life. A person who has managed to find the center of their soul has found themselves; they see, know, and do what is correct and precise.

A marksman doesn't pull the trigger until he has found the target with his eye and aligned his attention with the center of his soul. It is only then that he is at his most calm, his most confident, and most precise.

The message of chung in the I Ching is to find your Center Point. Watch out, you have lost your balance, don't take another step; otherwise you will fall over or be pushed over. Before you act, retreat to the Center and create your balance.

5. Listen to Your Better Self

How often do we say, "I knew but I didn't listen to myself"? Naturally, we listened to ourselves at these times—not the "self" who knew, but the one who didn't know. We have a self who knows what is good and we have a self who *thinks* it knows, but it doesn't know.

We often speak of a person by saying that they have a "better self" when we are describing a person who more commonly shows their "worse self." The I Ching refers to our better self as *chun tse* and to the other, ignorant one as *hsiao jen*. You know both of these within yourself.

Hsiao jen is the ego who thinks that it only lives once, there is no such thing as immortality, no such thing as God, no spirit, and its interests are the only things that are important; it lives for itself, it collects for itself, and it is in a permanent state of stress because it is frightened of suffering and frightened of death. It is the one who doesn't understand the wisdom of the I Ching and pays it no heed. The literal meaning of hsiao jen is "little man." It is translated in many ways; sometimes it appears as "common man" as well as "mass man" or "low-ranking man." Mass man because he is the product of society and, for the greatest part of his life, he displays all of the foolish habits, beliefs, expectations, fashions, and fads of the age in which he lives. He is a man of the moment and does not see beyond the material world and neither does he want to see beyond it.

In my Oracle, I use the Buddhist translation that is closest to the original meaning, "a person who is not yet fully grown." This person lives in us all and rules our fate with virtually unrestricted power; we are living in the age of people who are not yet fully grown and we are the same ourselves. The fact that we don't see this only proves that we do not have a clear view of ourselves—we really are little people of the moment.

The other self is chun tse. The literal translation of this is misleading as it means "the son of the Chief." This sounds amusing today but there was a time when the Chief represented God on Earth and so the true meaning was "the son of God . . . born from on high . . . he who knows that he is the son of the Sky." *A spiritual person.* In ancient times, chun tse meant "noble" or "chosen one," someone of a higher order who would have been referred to by the Greeks as an aristocrat. This caste has long since disappeared and the term has become worthless.

It is not fully expressed by "higher order," or "high order," or "of noble spirit." The point is that we know who it describes—our real "better self" who knows we are the child of God, knows that immortality exists, and who lives its transient earthly life while looking upward because it has not forgotten its spiritual origins.

Such a person is driven by this inner self, sees clearly, and does not give in to any illusion or deception. It is the one to whom the I Ching speaks and who understands what is said. It is the one who speaks within you in all your good moments. It is the voice of spiritual presence and inspiration. It is the one who occasionally hears the message of the Holy Spirit (shen) because it is related and easily tunes in.

The voice is only ever heard by the True Man not just because he has an ear for it, but because he too is a spirit, a shining spirit; and it is a universal law that everyone resonates together who shares strength and intelligence.

This is not only true of the "other world" but also with life on Earth: the reason we understand each other is *we are in each other*: we recognize in ourselves all that others say to us because they resonate a similar string within us. The reason I sense and understand another person is because they are inside me and I am inside them. This is also why I unfortunately resonate with all negative influences like vanity, ambition, revenge, or thirst for power, because I too am vain, vengeful, and thirsty for power. As a man, the reason that I understand women is because hidden femininity lives within me. The reason that I understand Christ is because something Christlike is within me. If angels whisper, then they are only able to speak to what is angelic within us. That is the law.

The reason that you understand what I am saying is because *you are in me and I am in you*—whenever you don't understand me, whenever you don't feel what it is that I want to say, that is where we are not inside one another and that is why the circuit of understanding cannot be completed. The only reason I mention this is because establishing a connection with the Holy Spirit always means a connection with our own spirit and so, if it is established, it makes a nonsense of the question, "Did he say that or was it me?"

The Holy Spirit (shen) is also the spirituality of the True Man (chun tse) and that is why the materialist approach, which does not believe in the supernatural world, responds to such inspiration by saying, "The whole thing played out in your head! You never heard any kind of Holy Spirit—just yourself—and you claimed to have heard it from the outside!"

There is really no point in arguing about this because if what you heard was true, then it doesn't matter who said it and where you heard it from. A higher voice is always resonating on a higher frequency and is not alien information poured into our heads through a funnel. However, the source is above and not within our own ego. Buddha said, "To wish for all people to know that 'I am the author' is the thought of a person who has not yet fully grown."

The point is that *each Oracle Sign is a fate situation*. It is a chapter in the drama of your life. On each and every occasion, the Oracle communicates how the True Man within you would respond. In other words, the divination tells you what is "good." But it will often warn you that you will get into trouble if you are directed by the person who has not yet fully grown.

The question is, who do you listen to within yourself?

6. Attend to the Quality of Timeliness

The I Ching often advises patience. It also tells you how to wait: drink, eat, enjoy your present state, and don't ruin things by impatiently tapping your knee and looking to see if the postman is coming with a check.

You should know that fate is never in straight lines but is woven in cycles. It leaves, it returns, it stops, it starts—it begins to look as if nothing will ever come of anything, then suddenly something really does happen. Fate, you see, is not only your fate but the fate of many and in order for an event to come about, it requires *coincidence*. Others, as well as you, must have reached a point where they are ready for it to happen. And when I, you, he, she, it, we, and they are ready, that is when it happens. And still nothing is certain as there is still a chance that it will all be abandoned, but at such times the air is full of change—this is the moment when something may happen.

Chinese people liken this to "gathering clouds": things reach a point when a storm is sure to follow. It is *fulfillment* when "it starts to rain." During sex, ejaculation is described as "the clouds release their burden of rain." This is the point of no return, it just has to happen. At times like this, everything coincides and the event takes place on the earthly plane.

There is another and more important coincidence: the divine, spiritual idea has to coincide with its accepting, earthly, material form. That is the Great Coincidence. If it happens, then the world will be fertile—if it doesn't, then nothing happens at all.

When you read about an Oracle Sign that conveys "the spirits are not working with you and they have not given their blessing to your plan," it means that you are trying to force something from life that is not in your fate. Your efforts are in vain. Plans like this can never succeed. One of the most important things that I have learned in my life is that there is no dedication, will, belief, magical power, or miraculous spiritual exercise that can make something happen that is not in my fate. As it is, I need enough "faith" to be able to solve my own fate—but it is impossible to step out of it because it was created on a plane over which I have no control.

God himself cannot step out of fate—Christ, the miraculous healer, does not come down from the cross despite the taunts he faces; this is his fate. Fate is called *ming* in Chinese and this means "mission." We all have our own mission that we cannot escape. But I only mention this as an aside.

Coincidence is when the heavenly fertilizes the earthly and the invisible idea takes shape. If there is no earthly openness, the wedding is cancelled. If there is no need for it here, it doesn't matter that they give it from there. Jesus gives an example of this when he talks about the importance of the ground on which a seed may fall.

If this has become clear to someone, then they understand one of the deepest thoughts in the I Ching—which all farmers know—timeliness. In ancient traditions, time did not mean numbers but rather *quality*. Talking about something happening at half past eleven at night on the twenty-third of next month and all this occurring in the year 2002 would not have meant a thing to someone living according to ancient tradition. Neither would it say anything in the modern world to a shepherd or a farmer if they didn't have to pay taxes or their monthly bills.

That is why the ancient past has no authentic dates. There were calendars, days, years, and hours, but no one was interested in them. There was, however, "dormant time" and "ripening time" and "fulfilling time" and "decaying time" and "planning time" and "doing time."

The Chinese word *shi*—one of the basic words in the Oracle—means "timely." It means the right time. It means living according to the spirit of time. It was the spirit of time that was the important thing and if you look at the shi character, it depicts a temple and the sun, the original meaning of which was "holy time."

"My time has not yet come," said Jesus to his disciples. In nature, everything has a time. There is a time for spring, for summer, autumn, and winter—and the requirements of time differ throughout. The Bible teaches that

> *To everything there is a season, and a time to every*
>   *purpose under the heaven:*
> *A time to be born, and a time to die; a time to plant,*
>   *and a time to pluck that which is planted;*
> *A time to kill, and a time to heal; a time to break down,*
>   *and a time to build up;*
> *A time to weep, and a time to laugh; a time to mourn,*
>   *and a time to dance;*
> *A time to cast away stones, and a time to gather stones*
>   *together; a time to embrace, and a time to refrain*
>   *from embracing;*
> *A time to get, and a time to lose; time to keep, and a*
>   *time to cast away. (Eccles. 3:1–6)*

And so, it goes on . . . We do not know "when" these wonderful lines were written in the Book of Ecclesiastes but it is certain to have been in the time of inspiration and wisdom, because they are beautiful and true.

If you talk to the Oracle, it will tell you what is timely. This does not primarily mean when to act but rather "what and how." It will tell you what sort of action is most appropriate. It will tell you what tactics, what deeds, and what conduct are appropriate to the spirit of the time. This is very much like a meteorological report for a sailor.

Do not forget that we, the people of today, rarely sense the quality of time. That is why we cannot handle ourselves correctly and cannot manage to steer our lives. We want spring and flowers in the autumn, we want youth in our old age, and we want to be older than we are when we're younger than we want to be. We take fright at low tide and are convinced that nothing will ever succeed and we lose ourselves in wild celebration at high tide, while also harboring a dread of running aground.

The art of life is all about never losing your better self in any kind of situation—the True Man—and dealing with and feeling good in the time that you are in at that precise minute.

There is an important thing that I have experienced many times. For exactly the reasons that I have been describing, I was never able to say exactly when something will happen or how long it would last. There are times when a situation resolves itself quickly and there are times when it is a long and lingering process, and there are times when the coincidences simply don't come about—the promise of the Oracle Sign can be postponed for a very long period of time or it can be aborted. How many times has someone waited for something to happen tomorrow only for it to eventually happen six months later.

Never forget: the web of fate is woven by live spirits and there is no official deadline.

7. Let the Magic Work

The sages of the I Ching do not believe in aggressive action. The more egotistical someone is, the more aggressive they are. Since our egos are terribly overdeveloped, we can be aggressive where we would never suspect. The ego is always fighting to get center stage; it dances in the spotlight even when there is absolutely no need at all, and it tries to convince us that we will fail without it. "If I do nothing other than plot, attack, argue, sue, battle, and elbow my way to the front, there's going to be trouble." This is what our ego whispers.

The sages of the Oracle say that it is sure to lead to trouble if your ego plots, attacks, argues, sues, and elbows its way the front. You only have to flip through the Oracle to see how often they advise to wait and be patient and not to interfere rather than undertake forceful and determined action. This can easily appear to be promoting laziness, passivity, and sloppiness and anyone reading it may forget that it was created by one of the world's most wonderful cultures.

Wu wei does not mean "no action" as it is often translated but "no aggressive action." This means going with the grain. It means turning the sails according to the direction of the wind. It means swimming in that direction and accepting the invisible breeze. In higher terms, it means "inspired acts." It means action that isn't what your ego wants but what your spirit inspires. If you have ever been in such a state, you know that you didn't have to struggle or hesitate—the inspiration took the lead. You knew what you had to do and it wasn't difficult to do it. It happened virtually *by itself.*

This is how all lasting works are born. It may happen that there is still a lot of work to do on them but their essence is sent by dreams, moments of clarity, and "angels." This work could be a picture, a sculpture, a piece of music, or a good marriage, help, or a word said at the right time, a healing moment, a brave deed, justified self-defense, a useful intuition, or perhaps a moment that seems completely insignificant but changes your whole life.

How many times are we stunned to realize, as we reweave the threads of our lives, that what seemed like a chance moment of passing inspiration set the shape of everything that followed it—that you were courting Sara but Julia left her bag there and you ran after her, you looked at her and she laughed at you, and afterward you went back and carried on wooing Sara for quite a while . . . and yet, still . . . *that's when everything changed*! This was wu wei. It is if someone was whispering. We don't know. We say, "I instinctively felt it."

There is, however, a "more conscious" version. The reason I put this in quotes is because it does not refer to everyday consciousness but rather a kind of higher vision. This is a more vigilant knowledge, the secret of magical action. If someone uses the Oracle a lot, this is more or less what they learn because if they regularly follow their instincts, they learn how to create this feeling, this inspired state at the right moment—not after having already taken a step, but before it. If you use the book well, it will let you know beforehand what is beneficial, what is the hidden message of our state of fate, and how to deal with it in the best possible way.

In physiology, this is called *making unconscious content conscious.* This is really what all performers do. A concert violinist cannot only perform when she feels inspired to do so; she has to play on Tuesday evening at eight o'clock and with such an inspired performance to suggest that the work was born there and then. In other words, inspiration can be consciously created.

The secret of magical action is that a person sees further than they step. And because all visible reality comes from the invisible and everything natural comes from the supernatural and everything in life, without exception, is born out of thought, spirit, and soul, if someone can see into this spiritual world, they see both in advance. They can catch sight of events while they are still in their early stages, before they are born, when the decision can still be made—shall I bring it into the world or not?

The magician influences events when they are still easy to shape. Where they are still at the level of thought. Where they aren't even energies, just plans. Where they are simple ideas. Today, people say that realization is decided at the information level. The magician weighs up the "codes," the "shoots," and the "information" that feed in to the center of the soul and become reality. Afterward, this all appears as if it were magic. If you don't know what information makes a computer work, it too looks just like magic. (This is all a distant comparison. The "information" in cybernetics or even genetics is nothing in comparison to the magical, wonderful working of the human spirit with which, among other things, the secrets of cybernetics and genetics were revealed.)

What does this look like in practice? You see a shoot of what things will become. Two chess players sit facing each other for hours. The one moving the white pieces says, "knight to F6." His opponent gives in because he can see that after the eighth move, he will lose his queen and the match becomes completely pointless. But this can only be seen by a person who can see the invisible. A person who cannot see the invisible is surprised: "Why did the idiot stop when he really wasn't doing so badly at all?"

The Chinese have their own version of this: "A good general has won a battle before it even begins. A poor general battles in the hope that he will win." This quote is from Sun Tse's *The Art of War.* The great orientalist, Allan Watts, has seen battles take place in China when one of the warriors fell to the floor in defeat without the other combatant having even touched him. He defeated him with his spirit.

What we are talking about here is simply a distant goal.

It is called wisdom.

Hexagrams of the I Ching

1. Creative	2. Receptive	3. Difficulty at the Beginning	4. Immaturity	5. Waiting	6. Conflict	7. Army	8. Holding Together
9. The Collection of the Small	10. Treading Carefully	11. Blossoming	12. Stagnation	13. Fellowship with Men	14. Great Harvest	15. Modesty	16. Enthusiasm
17. Following	18. Work on the Spoiled	19. Approach	20. Clear Sight	21. Confrontation	22. Beautification	23. Splitting Apart	24. Return
25. Spontaneous Action	26. The Collection of the Great	27. Nourishment	28. The Preponderance of the Great	29. Conquering Difficulty	30. Enlightenment	31. Harmonizing	32. Persistence
33. Retreat	34. The Influence of the Great	35. Progress	36. Darkening of the Light	37. A Man's Family	38. Opposite	39. Difficulty	40. Solution
41. Reduction	42. Expansion	43. Removal	44. Contact	45. The Gathering	46. Upward Ambition	47. Oppression	48. Well
49. Renewal	50. Sacrificial Vessel	51. Arousing	52. Calm	53. Gradual Development	54. The Bride-to-Be	55. Abundance	56. Wanderer
57. Influence	58. Joy Shared with Others	59. Dissolving	60. Restriction	61. Truth of the Center Point	62. Advantage of the Small	63. After Fulfillment	64. Before Completion

PART TWO

HOW TO MAKE DIVINATIONS

Practical Advice on Using the Oracle

6

Secrets of the I Ching

There are a total of 64 Oracle Signs detailed on page 54. It is these that I described as being the "thoughts of God"—they are creation patterns filled with fantastic amounts of energy. They express all the possible processes in the world. They are dense and dynamic like the structure of genetic code; they contain the future as well as the present. In terms of our lives, they represent inner and outer dramas, special life situations, spiritual problems, and fate tasks that require resolution.

As you can see, each Oracle symbol is made up of six lines, and these lines are either continuous (they depict positive, Yang force) or they are broken (they depict negative, Yin force).

So, the positive Yang sign is: ▬▬▬▬▬
The negative Yin sign is: ▬▬▬ ▬▬▬

The Oracle calls these "lines"—they really represent forces very much like the positive and negative charge in electricity.

CHANGING LINES, CHANGING SIGNS

Each Oracle Sign is made up of six lines and each of the six lines is capable of changing because of the energies that build up inside them;

they can transform. This transformation is the essence of the whole of the Oracle—that is why it is known as The Book of Changes. All that is needed is for one single line to change and the state described by the Oracle Sign changes and transforms into a different Oracle Sign and a different state.

Adopting the system of Richard Wilhelm and the Chinese master Lai, let us take a look at the 2nd Oracle Sign. The name of this sign is Receptive. It consists of six broken lines as shown below:

The 2nd Oracle Sign, Receptive.

If the bottom line changes—negative Yin force becomes positive Yang force—then, at that exact moment, the Oracle Sign and the state that it describes also changes and it transforms into another state.

The 24th Oracle Sign, Return (Rebirth).

This is now the 24th sign, the Oracle Sign for Return (Rebirth). As you can see, not all the lines need to change; only one force needs to "change over" and the whole fundamental situation has changed. If you look in the Oracle for 2nd, Receptive, and 24th, Return, and read the attached analyses, you will see a fundamentally different life situation has formed. It is like stepping from the calm of late autumn into the freshness of spring.

The transformation depends on the character of the individual lines. When the positive content of a continuous Yang line fills to the point of bursting, it switches over to its opposite and becomes a broken, negative, Yin line. And the same is true in the opposite direction: overcharged negative energies change a broken Yin line into a positive Yang as happened in the above example.

The other lines, in which the forces are balanced, do not change. They retain their state. They remain the same. That is why it is said that when you are interpreting the Oracle Signs, *only read the part related to the changing lines*: these are the fate situations where everything explodes the current situation and changes into another. In other words, the Lines section of the Oracle only deals with the dynamics of the changing lines. These are the situations where "the dice turns."

CALCULATING THE NUMERIC BASE OF THE LINES

The technique I use to create Oracle Signs will be dealt with in the following chapter. It can be done with coins and it can be done with sticks—the point is that the divination has a numeric base that creates numbers that need to be learned.

They are as follows:

The number of the positive (Yang) line: 9
The number of the negative (Yin) line: 6
The number of the residual, inert, positive (Yang) line: 7
The number of the residual, inert, negative (Yin) line: 8

It isn't difficult to remember because there is "too much" odd in the changing positive and "too much" even in the changing negative. These "too much" powers go on to create the *changing lines*. Where the positive and negative forces are not overloaded, the lines remain and do not change. They are calm.

The Oracle Signs, rather like plants growing out of the soil or cells, are constructed from the bottom up. If you look at the example below, the Receptive Oracle Sign was created according to the above number rule:

8 in the last position ▬▬▬ ▬▬▬
8 in fifth position ▬▬▬ ▬▬▬
8 in fourth position ▬▬▬ ▬▬▬
8 in third position ▬▬▬ ▬▬▬
8 in second position ▬▬▬ ▬▬▬
6 in first place ▬▬▬ ▬▬▬

If you succeed in deciphering the message of the Oracle Sign, the 6 in *first position* is really important because this alters the whole state. At the same time, there is no need to take any notice of the unchanged lines, just the general strategic advice for divination.

So, following the change, the Receptive changed to the state of Return (Rebirth) because the first negative (Yin) line changed to a positive (Yang) line.

The 2nd Oracle Sign, Receptive, changes to the 24th Oracle Sign, Return (Rebirth).

As you can see, the individual Oracle Signs are able to change into one another via changing lines. This is how life changes, how fate changes—the task changes as well as the challenge of different situations.

This is the essence of the book: each fate situation has a special task that can be solved well or solved badly. The situation changes as does the task and the tactic. This is where the I Ching offers priceless advice: how to position your sails as the wind changes direction. What is the best thing to do? What is good behavior? And what is bad? The right action brings luck, it brings fortune—incorrect action brings trouble and shame.

Wilhelm says, if a fortune-teller predicts that you are going to get a letter from America, you are left with no other option than to wait and see whether or not the letter will arrive. Fate is independent of you and that is why this type of cheap prediction of the future has no moral significance. However, the Book of Changes trains you "how to recognize your fate and become its creator, former, master." If you are able to recognize the sprouts of processes, you can have an influence on events in the future because it is still easy to shape emerging things—if they have opened up and frozen into dense reality, then you have lost your control over them.

The Oracle Signs and the moving lines are symbols of forces that express the movements and changes of the micro- and macro-cosmos in mysterious ways. Whatever question you may have related to your fate, *you have to create your Oracle Sign* and the commentary, based on interpretation of ancient experience and changing lines, will tell you how to act correctly. *It will tell you what directions your actions are taking.*

The ability to ask the book—says Wilhelm—does not work the same way in everyone. It depends on the quality of a person and their mental condition. You have to be clear, calm, and collected when you ask in order to be receptive to the higher powers that appear during the divination.

The divination takes place with sticks or with coins. These tell you when you are in the energy field of 9, 6, 7, or 8. They show numbers— six numbers in succession—and these form the Oracle Sign, and these also show future tendencies with the direction of change.

According to tradition, the sticks are controlled by cosmic forces. Coins function in a similar way—that is why it is recommended to keep them clean in a little box or in a special little velvet or silk bag. The point is that these are sacred objects as divination is a holy occupation. This means that one should treat one's life and fate as a truly exalted and holy thing. Jung explains this by saying that at times such as these, you come into contact with your subconscious. But who knows where the boundaries lie between states of consciousness?

In the next chapter, I am going to describe divination with coins. The main point to consider, as I have already mentioned, is how we get the numbers 9, 8, 7, and 6 and how we construct the Oracle Sign from six lines. If we have received changing lines (9 or 6), how do we create the Oracle Sign to describe the new state appearing on the horizon of the future.

Buddha said that it is well worth repeating important things many times. This chapter is one such "important thing."

7

Creating an Oracle

The practical part of divination is terribly simple. The first thing that we have to do is to create the Oracle Sign.

USING COINS TO CREATE THE ORACLE SIGN

For this we need three coins of any kind. Let's say that you take 3 ten-cent pieces.

The tails side of the coin is Yin and the heads side of the coin is Yang. The numerical value of tails (Yin) is **2** and the numerical value of heads (Yang) is **3**. The reason behind this lies in numerology that I won't go into now, but you already know that ancient Chinese thinking has many parallels in modern genetics where the female chromosomes are even and the male chromosomes are always odd. So, if you take all three coins in your hand that all have a chance of landing heads or tails when tossed, then you have four possible variations in terms of the total numeric value:

First variation: Heads (**3**) + Heads (**3**) + Tails (**2**) = **8**
Second variation: Heads (**3**) + Tails (**2**) + Tails (**2**) = 7

The number **8** is that of the "young Yin" ancient force. Its sign is a line broken in the middle.

The Yin line (8).

The number 7 is that of the "young Yang" ancient force. Its sign is an unbroken line.

The Yang line (7).

So, these are the first two possibilities. There are two more variations, if all three coins fall on the _identical_ side:

Third variation: Heads (**3**) + Heads (**3**) + Heads (**3**) = **9**
Fourth variation: Tails (**2**) + Tails (**2**) + Tails (**2**) = **6**

As you can see, the upper **9** is virtually bursting with unopposed, unstoppable, and "too strong" Yang energy. This initially forms the Yang line but since, sooner or later, it will switch over to the opposite, we draw a little mark in the middle. This is where it will break up and Yang will become Yin; this is how "male" will become "female." We call this "old Yang"; this will be the changing line.

Yang will break and become Yin.

In the other example of **6**, it wants to pull in on itself. There is so much self-attracting Yin that, sooner or later, it will collapse in on itself. We draw a little mark in the middle; this is where it will stick together and become one. This is how Yin will become Yang, how "female" will become "male."

Yin will connect and become Yang.

We call this "old Yin" and this will be the second changing line. *Change* means that, in time, the force will switch over to become its own opposite: old Yang will be ripped apart by unstoppable centrifugal force and it will become a young Yin.

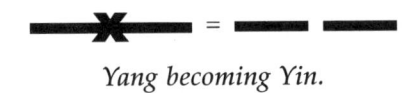

Yang becoming Yin.

And old Yin will be pulled into itself by unstoppable centripetal force and switch over to its own opposite and become young Yang.

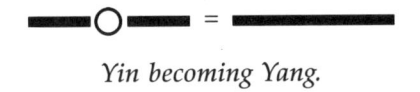

Yin becoming Yang.

This is how Yang becomes Yin and Yin becomes Yang. This is the secret of life and eternal change: everything has to experience its own opposite!

It is important to say again that this is the law that means that all *quantity* change reaches a critical point when it makes a *quality* change. The cells multiply and multiply in a caterpillar while it is in a chrysalis until it suddenly turns into a butterfly. The "Yangness" of Yang builds up to the extent that it becomes Yin, and this results in the Oracle Sign becoming a different Oracle Sign. It is just the same with a butterfly. The quantitative over-strength of the initial Oracle Sign, just like a caterpillar, suddenly changes, and it becomes another Oracle Sign. The butterfly is the caterpillar's future; it has ripened this in itself—but this couldn't be seen at the time of the quantitative change. Only a knowing eye notices what fate will bring.

Now let's look in detail at the rest of the divination process.

❷

Creating an Oracle Sign

An Oracle Sign is made up of six lines starting from the bottom and moving up. Because the Oracle Sign is constructed *from the bottom up*, the first throw creates the first line, the second creates the second, and so on with the sixth throw forming the top, sixth line. Each line can be either an unchanging or a changing line.

- Concentrate your mind on the question and throw the three coins six times in succession.
- Create a line after each throw.
- Note this down.
- After making the sixth throw, place the coins to one side: the Oracle Sign is now before us that we will proceed to look up with the help of the table on page 98. I will tell you how this is done a little later.

This is as much as you need to know about the "technique" of divination.

I will now show you an example.

I take the coins in my hand and I throw them onto my desk. (I have now stopped writing and am creating an Oracle Sign. I will tell you what my question was later.) I got six numbers and I noted them down.

Here is the result, in sequence (from the bottom, working up):

6th throw: Tails (2) + Tails (2) + Heads (3) = 7 ⎯⎯⎯ (6th line)
5th throw: Heads (3) + Heads (3) + Heads (3) = 9 ⎯✖⎯ (5th line)
4th throw: Heads (3) + Heads (3) + Tails (2) = 8 ⎯ ⎯ (4th line)
3rd throw: Heads (3) + Tails (2) + Heads (3) = 8 ⎯ ⎯ (3rd line)
2nd throw: Heads (3) + Tails (2) + Heads (3) = 8 ⎯ ⎯ (2nd line)
1st throw: Heads (3) + Tails (2) + Tails (2) = 7 ⎯⎯⎯ (1st line)

I got the 42nd Oracle Sign, Expansion.

The 42nd Oracle Sign, Expansion (I).

As you can see, the 5th Yang line is changing in it (because it adds up to 9). For the sake of the example, I would have liked to have thrown another changing line, preferably a changing Yin line, but unfortunately this didn't happen. You cannot simply play or experiment with the Oracle because you meet with live wisdom every time. And as I—I now admit—was struggling with the question of *how to teach the use of the I Ching in the best and simplest way,* the I Ching has now provided the answer.

You cannot cheat even if—purely for the sake of the example—it would have been more useful to show not only one but two or three variations. However, this is what I threw—the book knows the answer to my problem better than I do. It really is my job to "expand" your knowledge. This is what the Oracle is telling me, along with everything else that is behind this sign. (Read what is written about the 42nd sign in Part Three.)

The secret is not actually here but in the *change*. If the only change that I have thrown here, the over-tense old Yang on the 5th line, "bursts" and changes into a Yin line, then the whole Oracle Sign will change. It will become a completely new sign. A new "shoot" sign will form out of the old "root" sign—butterfly from a caterpillar.

The new sign will be the Direction Sign, the target that we are moving toward, the outlook. This is how the Base Sign changes.

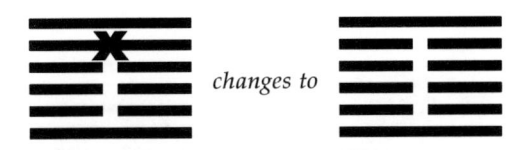

changes to

The 42nd Oracle Sign, Expansion, (I)
changes to become the 27th, Nourishment, (I).

This means that the Expansion sign changes to become the Nourishment sign.

When we reach the section dealing with deciphering the secrets of the Oracle Signs, you will see that this change tells me that I should *expand* your knowledge as simply, understandably, and "digestibly" as possible—while at the same time, it encourages you, my imagined reader (who, now as I write, only lives in my spirit), to *digest* the spiritual nourishment that you read. It will only become your own if you make it your own, as a body makes nourishment its own.

The Oracle Sign tells me to speak clearly, and to "nourish" you with pure knowledge, while you, dear Reader, are to build this into yourself and assimilate the thought.

But that is the secret of interpretation; I apologize for getting ahead of myself, but the opportunity presented itself. I could not have thrown another changing line, even if it would have been better for demonstration purposes, simply because the Oracle spoke to us and it wanted to tell us the secret of Nourishment. This was the important thing.

The reason that I have said this here, before any explanation, is because we must get used to the thought, one that also surprised Jung, that we need to talk to this book as if it were a *living person! It is as if a real sage were standing behind it who does not say what you want to hear but says the thing that is most important.* (The I Ching presented itself to Jung and he describes this experience with great wonderment in the preface to the translation written by Richard Wilhelm.)

Of course, if I had thrown another variation—for example, a 6 on the 4th line—then this would have collapsed into a Yang line and so, with two changes, I get the following sign (or, rather, would have gotten).

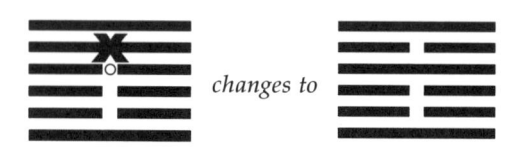

changes to

Expansion changes to
Shih Ho, the 21st Oracle Sign, Confrontation (Biting Through).

We would have ended up with this new sign and this would definitely not have meant the same as Nourishment—that new material should be digested—but rather that "food is stuck in our throat," we need to chew our way through, "bite through" the topic with hard work and dedication to the cause. This is what the 21st sign Confrontation (Biting Through) would have meant. But that isn't the task we were presented with. We were given an easier one.

This is perhaps because the invisible sages of the I Ching thought that if I explain intelligibly . . .

Perhaps.

IDENTIFYING THE ORACLE SIGN: BASIC SIGN OR DIRECTION SIGN

So, let's just run through this again: the Oracle Sign needs to be created by throwing three coins a total of six times. Each throw has a numeric value: Heads is 3 and Tails is 2. Thus, with differing results, if we add all three, we get 7 or 8, but if all three coins give the same result, we get 6 or 9.

Each throw gives one line of the Oracle Sign moving in order from the bottom upward.

If we throw only 7s and 8s, then we only get one sign. I call this *Basic Sign*. (The Chinese call this "root sign.")

But if either 6 or 9 appears, then the line changes: the 6 Yin will become Yang and the 9 Yang will become Yin. Any of the lines can change and sometimes all six. We call these lines the Changing Lines and they play an important role when interpreting the Oracle Sign. If the lines change, we get a new Oracle Sign. We call this new sign the *Direction Sign* as this is the sign that shows the possible direction or tendency of the future. (The Chinese call this the "shoot sign.")

Look up the Oracle Signs in the table on page 54. If there is no changing line, only read the message of the Basic Sign. This does not mean no movement—each and every Oracle Sign is an inner movement—it means that movement will take place *within* this energy field.

If, however, there are Changing Lines, they receive great emphasis when we interpret the sign; they often carry the most important part of the message. So, it is these that must be studied with special care.

Then finally comes the general advice of the Direction Sign (shoot sign). There is no need to read the meaning of the 6 lines of the Direction Sign. It is enough to look at the whole thing to see the whole picture and to know that events are headed in this direction. But not unavoidably.

It also depends on how we solve the Basic Sign. Do we step out of it or not? It depends on us. The Direction Sign can be promise, "Carry on," or warning, "Avoid coming here." Everything depends on us.

8

The Oracle Sign

We have been looking at the Oracle Sign with six Yin or Yang lines constructed from the bottom up. Before we turn to Part Three to look up the sign, we have an important decision to make about the *code structure of the Oracle Signs.*

CODE STRUCTURE OF THE ORACLE SIGNS: DRAMA IN TWO ACTS AND SIX SCENES

Each of the six lines is a fate phase. Every Oracle Sign is a "thought of God"—a special part, a special story in the world drama. It really does resemble a stage drama: each has a fundamental theme or conflict. This theme is also in the name of the Oracle Sign. For example, the 42nd is about Expansion. Something is "growing, spreading, gaining strength, becoming useful" within it. This can be both material and spiritual good.

The six lines are the six dramatic scenes that make up the total work. The first line (at the bottom) is the pre-play of the drama— this is how the play begins. The sixth line (at the top) is the post-play of the drama—this is how it ends, but it also indicates where a new, different theme will begin. The second, third, fourth, and fifth lines describe the different stages of struggle. This is intrigue (both good and bad).

This is important as you often see the danger of collapse appear in one of the lines of a very hopeful Oracle Sign, or the other way around; it is possible to emerge triumphant from a dark Oracle Sign if a promising line switches over. For example, Expansion begins with an invigorating action (1st line) and yet it still ends with punishment. You can get your knuckles rapped for selfishness (6th line).

This really is similar to works for the stage, which is no coincidence as playwrights want to reflect life. A merry operetta may have a deathly conflict between two characters, and a bloody tragedy has moments of light and comedy. The major difference is that, in the Oracle, these moments offer the opportunity for change. You can escape the drama and step into a new theme.

The characters in an operetta cannot fight with one another to the extent that they will not fall on each other's necks at the end—there is no escape from the story. But there is with the I Ching. Here, if the Yang bursts or the Yin collapses because you couldn't or you didn't want to address what, let's say, the line in the second "act" recommended—you instantly step out of the theme and you are no longer playing light comedy but dark drama. This is the mystery of the changes that we often experience in our lives—events can take a sudden change for the good or for the bad and the direction of things changes completely.

As to why there are exactly six lines in the Oracle Sign—six dramatic acts—all I can say is, for exactly the same reason that God created the world in six days.

THE PA KUA TRIGRAMS

The Oracle Signs are not only made up of six lines but also two parts: dramas in six scenes and in two acts. Each Oracle Sign has three lower lines and three upper lines; these three lines represent the Ancient Unit. Each Oracle Sign is made up of two such ancient units. Apparently, there was a time when divinations were made using only the three-line ancient units.

These are the spiritual, cosmic, and energy blocks of Creation. These are the *Pa Kua*; they are also known as trigrams as they are made up of three lines. There are eight such giant, dynamic energy patterns known as Pa Kua. The legend says that King Wen drew these on the wall of his prison cell. As they contain all the secrets of the Universe, superstitious people later used them as lucky amulets.

It would be possible to write a separate book about each one. There is no need for detailed interpretation here, partly because I didn't intend this Oracle for scientific research but for everyday use, and because I have included their most important meanings in the explanation of Oracle Signs.

I will outline their meanings in brief if only to allow you to look up the interpretation of the Oracle Signs at the end of the book. So, here are the eight Pa Kua:

Ch'ien   <u>≡</u>   *The Creative*

Creative spirit. Creative energy. Its symbol is the Sky, its act is enduring and solid, its keyword is "Let it be." In the country it is the king, in the family it is the father. It wants, it does, it rules, it fertilizes—it is the information.

K'un   ☷   *The Receptive*

The receptive material. The mother's womb that gives form to all things and gives birth to them. Its symbol is the earth, it nourishes and serves everything. In the country it is the queen, in the family it is the mother. It is giving to the Will—it receives and forms "information" into life. Creator. It subjects itself to the Will.

Chên   ☳   *The Arousing (Thunder)*

The moment that starts all things, when the force wanting to be sparks. Thunder and lightning. Energy that starts, stirs up, initiates; spring force that shakes nature from its winter sleep. Dynamic, great starter.

Sun   **The Wind (Tree)**

The spirit of the wind, delicate penetration, unnoticeable formation and influence. Gentle but irresistible force that ripens things. It is the meek aggression with which a root finds its way in the dense earth or the invisible wind that moves everything.

K'an   **The Abysmal (Water)**

Water falling into an abyss. Treacherous, risky, dissolves, avoids, and carries away. The kind of spirituality that places in your path obstacles and problems to be solved and dangers that you are forced to confront. Instinctive, subconscious force. (The reason that it meant "danger" in ancient Chinese terms was because it is an enormous, ancient force and yet it is not conscious.)

Li   **The Fire**

The spirit of fire. It gives light and warmth. The power of knowledge and consciousness. The light of intelligence. The strength of expression. Light makes things visible; it makes things understandable; it is also called clinging because it depends on whatever gives to it; it not only separates but also holds together. (Knowledge also analyzes and synthesizes.) Beyond that, the flame depends on the wick and the bright light of genius depends on Universal Intelligence. If it forgets this, it goes out.

Kên   **The Mountain**

The spirit of the mountain. Calm, stillness, completion. Final form of the invisible will. Boundary. Hopelessness and solidity, the end of movement and effort.

Tui   **The Lake (Joyful)**

The spirit of the lake. Open, joyful, friendly, happy spirit. Uplifting words, useful relationships, associations. Good feeling, inspiring speech. Enriching—this really is the life-giving water of the paddy fields. *Joy* is one of the basic words on Chinese wisdom.

*

These eight trigrams or Kua form the Oracle Signs. According to legend, King Wen drew these on the wall of his cell in cyclical form. This is a universal compass that provides an insight into all the energies, qualities, and eternal change of ancient knowledge and the emerging Universe.

It looks like this:

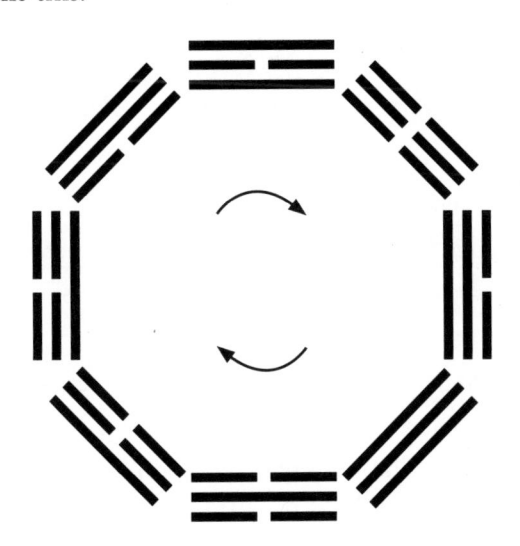

The Oracle Signs are formed by two Kua. There is a lower and an upper Kua. This is how you need to look it up in the table on page 98. (The lower Kua is in the vertical column, the upper Kua is in the horizontal row: where the two lines meet (like F6 or B4 on a chessboard) is where you can find the Oracle Sign that they combine to form.

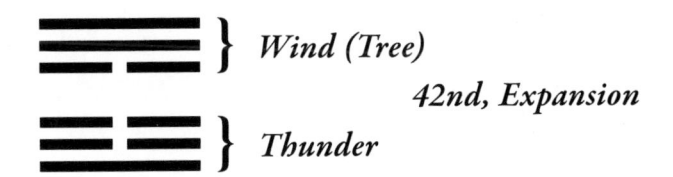

Wind (Tree)

42nd, Expansion

Thunder

Thus in this example, Thunder below and Wind (Tree) above form the 42nd Oracle Sign, Expansion. It is as simple as that.

If you recall from our example, it was our 5th line that changed. A Yang line became a Yin line. This meant that the upper Kua changed from Tree (Wind) to Mountain. This led to the whole six-line Oracle Sign changing from the Expansion sign to the Nourishment sign.

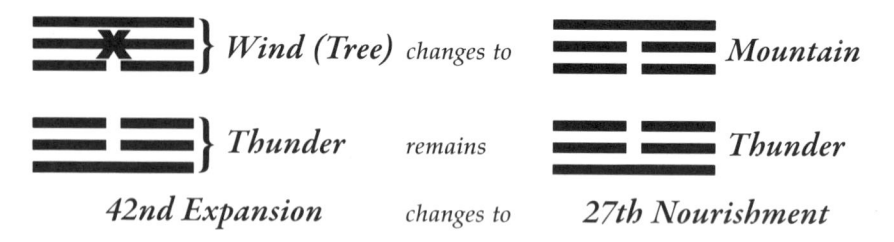

Wind (Tree) *changes to*   *Mountain*

Thunder   *remains*   *Thunder*

42nd Expansion   *changes to*   **27th Nourishment**

It is self-explanatory that if there is more than one changing line, the Kua will change in more than one place and, therefore, so does the final Oracle Sign.

That is all that you need to know about the practical "technique" of divination. There was a time when they only used Yin and Yang. The Yang said, "Yes! Act!" The Yin said, "No! Don't do anything! Let everything happen on its own."

Today we call this 1 and 0 "information." Researchers suggest that the 64 Oracle Signs made up of six lines were known in the most ancient of times.

9

Interpreting the
Oracle Signs

If the sages didn't object to the words *difficult* and *complicated*, I would definitely have begun this chapter with "Interpreting Oracle Signs is the most difficult and complicated. . . ." But the sages of the I Ching hold that what is not easy and simple is not true.

I will therefore try to explain easily and simply.

HOW TO ASK
THE QUESTION

First, I will tell you what I have read about this and then I will relate my own, personal experience. The two do not entirely agree.

The book says that you can ask anything that you think is related to fate. There is no "big deal" or "little deal." But since the I Ching doesn't tell the future but predicts—in other words it gives advice that you can, if you like, use to shape your future—you cannot leave the decision to the Oracle. Therefore, you should not ask questions like:

Should I divorce my husband or not?
Should I take the new job or not?
Should I travel or not?

With questions like this, you should only ask about *one* option:

Should I divorce my husband?
Should I stay with my husband?

The Oracle does not decide on our behalf—it just lights the way like a beam of light in front of us: what would happen if we were to take that route? Then you can also ask the question, "What does the other way hold?"

This is what virtually all books on the I Ching say. And it is used to this day like some kind of heavenly meteorology: "What can I count on if I take a specific route?" (There are similar questions inscribed on ancient runes, so there may be some truth in it.)

My experience, gathered over many years, is completely different.

My experience is that the sages of the I Ching see your problem very well indeed. They know what is in your heart. They know what is really important and *that is what they answer*!

So, there is only really one good question: "Wise masters. I stand here with such and such a problem. Can you see? Look at my situation and give me advice." That is a good question.

You need to form the question for yourself and say it out loud if need be. Not just for the sages but also for yourself. Think it through, take a good look at it, and then open your heart. The spirit world can see better than you where you have become stuck, what hurts, what is hindering you, and what it is that is truly important to you. "If someone asked correctly," said the ancients, "then they would also know the answer. They would have no need for our advice." Take that as your starting point.

Your problem is like the fire lit by one shipwrecked on a deserted island, asking for help from on high. Those up in heaven can see real fire. It attracts helping glances. It also means that you should express your problem as precisely as possible in its stripped-down form. Blow on the "fire" of your problem. The more honest, precise, and merciless you are with yourself and the clearer that you see the Great Question Mark, the better it will be seen from on high and *the better you will understand the question.*

Let me give you an example.

A married woman lived in a hopeless—or at least that's how it appeared—and odd love that caused her a great amount of pain and suffering. She could have asked any of the following questions: "Should I leave my husband?" "Should I leave my lover?" "What are the prospects of such a love affair?" "Should I put an end to it?" Or even, "Should I keep on suffering?"

But I would recommend that she shouldn't ask any such question. She should ask, "Wise Masters, here I stand with this odd and painful love of mine. I don't know what to do. I don't even know if he loves me or not . . . and I really don't know what to do! Do you see? Look at my situation and give me advice."

I will only tell you the essence of what happened. As an answer—with many variations—she received the 48th Oracle Sign, the Well. The message of this sign is the following:

A person can change the town that they live in, but they cannot change the Well. They come and go but the Well remains. If the bottom is muddy, if the rope is short, if the bucket breaks: trouble!

In other words, the woman found her deepest self in this cathartic love affair. The point of a shocking love experience is not always a case of *with them* or *without them* but rather that *we find ourselves* in the spiritually turbulent experience and passion. Lovers come and go but our inner being—the source of our life, the Well—remains. This is what needs to be cared for and looked after.

Naturally, the answer was not about the love affair. It was neither the husband nor the lover—she herself was the point. She became a different person in this cathartic experience. She became wiser, more sensitive, more genuine. She became deeper—like the Well. This was the role of this love in her fate, nothing else. Looking back, you can see that both "Should I go?" and "Should I stay?" would have been misleading. In her fate, this love was not there to "happen" but to wake her up. It was there to bring her back to her real self.

Fate sometimes weaves a cunning web. We often play a catalyzing role in each other's lives. A female friend of mine once said that the reason that she had to meet her first husband *through fate* was to be able to meet her mother-in-law, who introduced her to the secrets of theosophy. It was through her that she came to know Ramana Maharshi (India's saint), the spiritual secrets of Eastern tradition, and the teachings of Paul Brunton and Madame Blavatsky. She became a totally different person over a period of decades. This wise and farsighted woman, who was later known as a great actress, was born for this special meeting. "I got married because of my mother-in-law," she said with a laugh, "I only realized long afterward. She was my first guru whom I simply adored!"

We cannot know what roles we play in each other's lives. This is why questions like "Should I stay or should I go?" and "Will something come of it or not?" *don't get to the point.*

A friend of mine who is an excellent pianist and conductor once asked me why the Oracle always gave a stunningly accurate and wise answer to his first question but not to the ones after that. My answer was, "It is because you opened your heart for the first question but not for the others." And that is obviously why he did not ask good questions later on.

I have often found myself in the same situation. Just as you don't always understand a guru, the words of the Oracle can fall on barren ground. Not only is our ego not capable of asking, sometimes it doesn't understand the answer either.

HOW TO LISTEN TO THE DIVINATION

It is my experience that I am much better at interpreting the Oracle of others than I am my own. I don't have a clear view of myself. Apparently,

Confucius had exactly the same problem and said that the I Ching only once made a mistake and that was when he asked advice for himself and really didn't like what he was told. The divination really was spot on, it is just that the old man—however wise he might have been—was unable to accept it.

This is one of the reasons that divination should begin with meditation. The point of meditation is excellently described by Leo Tolstoy: "Lifting up to a great height from which you can look down on yourself as if you were a stranger, really is a necessary thing. This is the highest act of the human spirit." If this doesn't happen, you are bound to misread the divination. You will be driven by obsession, even fear—you will make a mistake.

You will not hear the warning—to use the words of twentieth-century Hungarian writer and philosopher Béla Hamvas, "You do not apply it to yourself"—and you see your situation as being worse than it really is, or you are too shocked and say that it can't be true. Only the True Man understands the divination and the little man, "who has not yet fully grown," never understands. The book teaches us to dare to think bravely against ourselves because this is the key to victory. *A person who cannot see their mistakes is unable to make them good, they do it again and again, and end up worse off.*

The Oracle also sees how obstinate you are. The Chinese Oracle words at the end of each line speak about exactly this. I will tell you a few here, but there is no need to learn them as I will repeat them when I deal individually with the Oracle Signs.

Chi means "blessings" because you listen to what your master tells you. *Li* means, "You will be fortunate because you are open." *Wu chi* means, "You follow the way of your fate and you make no mistakes. If you do, you always put them right." *Lin* means, "You do not recognize your mistakes and even if you do, you do not correct them and that is why you can be ashamed." *Hêng* means, "You achieve success by making sacrifices." *Hiusing* means, "You are heading for trouble, come to your senses." *Hui* means, "You recognize the mistakes of your past and you regret them." *Hui wang* means, "As you have recognized and corrected your mistakes, your trouble and regret have gone."

There are obstacles that are not of your own making; fate has placed them in your path and you have to deal with them. *Wu Yu Li* advises you not to set any goals and don't act at all costs because your efforts are not timely. *Wu Pu Li* means everything is advantageous. And what has held you back up until now can turn to your advantage.

These are not final judgments, just warnings. There are life situations in which we are more obstinate, when our ego is more tyrannical than usual. In such turbulent and troubled times, when we lose balance, we tend to retreat into selfishness rather than to God. We turn into a cul-de-sac and instead of turning around, we step more heavily on the gas and go blundering forward.

We are deaf and we do not hear good advice. This is how heroes behave in great tragedies. It is what the Greeks call *hubris*. My mother used to say, "He's following his own, stupid head!"

10

Reading Your Oracle

So how should you read Oracle Signs? There are two options. The first is that you have not thrown changing lines, only 7 and 8. You have created a Basic Sign. Read the name of the Oracle Sign, the symbolic meaning of the Chinese character, the general description, and the "Thoughts" section, all of which you will find in Part Three.

My interpretation of the individual Oracle Signs began in meditation with one single momentum. If I wrote an interpretation, I read it through again the following morning and added further reflections, the kinds of things that I thought were important but that had somehow been left out. You will find these under the "Thoughts" section for each and every Oracle Sign.

Most authors say that you don't have to read any of the individual lines when none of them have changed. I agree with Jung, it is well worth reading the lines since we understand a book better if we read it all and not just the list of contents. But you don't have to take the lines into account when making a divination. That's all you need to do. Then meditate on the answer.

The situation is different if one or more of the lines change—where you have thrown 6 or 9. This is when these lines change and you get a new sign. The Basic Sign will become another Direction Sign. In this instance, you have to read the general message of the Basic Sign and the Thoughts; the message of the changing line or lines in the Basic Sign;

and the general message of the Direction Sign and the Thoughts.

You do not have to consider the lines of the Direction Sign (but it is still best to read them; they do not impact the divination but they help to explain the drama of the new sign). This is all you need to know about this process.

THE SIGNIFICANCE OF BASIC SIGNS, CHANGING LINES, AND DIRECTION SIGNS

The Basic Sign carries the archetypical dramatic situation of the question that you are in. This is the decider. Its theme determines the whole of the divination. This is the river that you are swimming in.

The changing line or lines are the overripe situations that force you to step out of the Basic Sign. These are urges. These are over-strong or over-weak points where the forces can switch over and a *quality* change can take place. These lines are key scenes in the drama. These are the rapids on the river. This is how the Direction Sign is formed.

The Direction Sign means probability, the direction in which the events are leading—or the opposite, events that are approaching if you follow this direction. The Direction Sign can say: What will happen? What is possible? What should I watch out for? Which way should I go? What is approaching? What can I count on? What should I avoid?

You could compare the Direction Signs to the satellite weather forecast: it isn't certain that the storm will hit this spot but the chances are strong. The Direction Sign brings the scent of the future to us. It brings opportunity, warning, and promise.

Let's take a look at an example from theatrical drama. Hamlet's Basic Sign—his real drama—remained until the murder of his uncle and the collapse of a regime. This was quite probably the 36th Oracle Sign, Darkening of the Light—but events don't come to an end here. Fortinbras arrives and a new regime starts up on the ruins. This new world is the Direction Sign that has lived in "coded" silence in the events and Hamlet's life up until this point. He suspects or senses something, but he doesn't know. If Prince Hamlet had asked the I Ching, "What should I do?" he would have received a divination that hid behind his struggles all along. His present was burdened with this future. This is why his struggles ripened. This would have been reflected by his Direction Sign.

In my own experience, the process, as with the weather, is terribly simple. Light and shadow follow one another. A sunny sign may become stormy and the opposite is also possible: a cloudy Oracle Sign may change to sparkling sunshine. Peace can become war and war become peace. A broadening life phase may follow a narrowing and dry fate situation.

If I accept the advice of the I Ching, I can do exactly what a good sailor does on the sea: I can look for the path of the sun, the calm waters, and with clever maneuvering, I can even avoid the storm . . . but not always. It is at times like this that the Direction Sign warns to make the most of this still period in your life—it won't last long. Prepare for the storm. Or, hang on through the troubles, more peaceful times are approaching, keep your faith.

I will now demonstrate this on our familiar example. You are sure to remember my question from Chapter 7: *How should I teach the use of the I Ching in the best and simplest way*? I received the 42nd, Expansion, Basic Sign. As you recall, the 5th line of this was changed, giving us the 27th, Nourishment, Direction Sign.

But what would have happened if I had thrown it so not the 5th but the 6th line changed?

The 42nd, Expansion, changes to
the 3rd, Difficulty at the Beginning.

You can see that if this had happened, the Direction Sign would not have been 27th, Nourishment, but 3rd, Difficulty at the Beginning. The basic sign is still the same: "I want to expand you."

Read the Oracle to see the many things that this sign still hides. Then read the message of the changing 6th line. The 6th line of the 42nd, Expansion, says the following:

1. The ancient Chinese text: "You are not expanding at all. Perhaps you will even be punished. Your unfaithful and wavering heart is the reason. Trouble!"
2. My experience of this: You are in a situation when you should give but you don't give. You need faith and you are crippled with doubt. Your selfishness isolates you from the world and you bring out antagonism in others. If you carry on like this you could get your knuckles rapped. This is expressed by the chi character (punishment).

This would have all pulled in the direction of the 3rd, Difficulty at the Beginning. If you read the general message of this Direction Sign, you see that I would have ended up in a situation like someone who had failed at school and I would have had to start the whole thing again from the beginning. If I had received that changing line and that Direction Sign, it would have forced me to great self-examination. It is possible that I would have stopped writing for a time.

In itself the 3rd Oracle Sign, Difficulty at the Beginning, does not mean failure, but if an author receives it after writing a book, when approaching the end of a piece of work, battling with initial problems is obviously equivalent to failure. Also obvious is the need to start the thing all over again from the beginning. (This has happened to me. I have torn up a stage work that I had completed and written it again differently, with other inspiration.) This is to say nothing of the 6th line that would have given me very serious and indigestible criticism about my spirit and my approach.

More precisely, it is a warning. If I accept and process the strict judgment on that line, I loosen the knot of my selfishness and regain my faith in the work, it is possible that I will be able to avoid the dangers of the Difficulties at the Beginning Direction Sign. *The "direction" of the Direction Sign is not fate—it is just an indication, warning, advice,* opportunity. There are times when you can escape in much the same way as when someone takes good advice and makes fundamental changes to their plan.

If the Direction Sign is dark, it can mean two things:

1. Prepare yourself.
2. Try to avoid—in other words, try to stay in the Basic Sign.

INTERPRETING AN ORACLE SIGN BOTH INWARDLY AND OUTWARDLY

I would like to share a few of my experiences related to interpreting Oracle Signs. If I only received a Basic Sign (meaning I threw lines with no changes), it did not mean that the situation remained unchanged. Each and every Oracle Sign has enormous dynamism; just think, we can ask the I Ching what sign your child is born in at the minute of their birth and this one single Oracle Sign can contain a whole life!

There are 64 cosmic ancient patterns; there are an infinitely large number of tasks within these. If I create a particular sign, it means that *my question is currently moving in this energy field.* The electrical circuit of my problem contains not only me, but everyone else with whom I share the same fate in relation to this question. Dramatists refer to this as a "situation" or a "dramatic scene." Chess players call it a "stance." Soldiers call it a "position."

These are terrible dynamic energy fields that boil and move even without any changing lines. At times like this, it is worth reading the unmoving lines; so many things are crammed into a situation that appears to be static.

Whatever I asked, I asked about my fate. It is at this point that I had to understand the ancient thought that is terribly difficult for a modern person to understand with our quality of consciousness: *others are also in my fate.* I ask for a divination for myself but everyone who is connected to my question, however distant, will also be included in the divination. We are not isolated and solitary beings in the world in the same way that the coding in a tiny cell contains the characteristics of a whole person and all the cells in their body. Not only can our own history be read from our souls, but also the histories of anyone, however distant, who is connected with ours.

I have already spoken about the links between the I Ching and genetics. Both work with archetypes. This is why even a single cell contains the familiar characteristics of a whole person or their every cell, and even provides information about the genes of their grandchildren—and this is why your whole "outer world" can be seen in one single Oracle Sign.

At times like this, *the same archetype is operating on the inside as well as on the outside.* This sentence becomes important if you ask the great question, "Am I at fault or is it someone else?" Or, in other words, "Is the world mistaken or is it me?" The I Ching will not, and cannot, respond to this great question. It will simply place the ancient drama in front of you that may contain you as well as others.

How do you decipher this?

People today automatically and self-explanatorily blame the world: "Others are the idiots, the evil ones, the sinners, and the criminals. I am just a victim. I am a victim of my circumstances!" People were raised differently long ago. "What the True Man seeks is within him—what the common man seeks is in others," says Confucius. The True Man blames himself first, he works on himself and he improves himself. According to the ancient Chinese view, the transformation of the world does not begin with me stirring up revolution in sinful society but with me making fundamental changes to myself. If I become a better person, my family will be better and if my family is better, the society in which I live will improve.

There is no reverse! As we have already experienced a number of times, you cannot clean up the world with grimy souls.

If you receive a divination, look for it first in yourself. Accept the advice of the Oracle Sign first as speaking about your spirit, your emotions, your thoughts, your spiritual state, the relationship between your conscious and your subconscious, your battles, your fears, your anxieties—the relationship between your Higher Self (True Man) and your ego (the person not yet fully grown).

For example, the 36th, Darkening of Light, paints a dark, hostile, and, in many ways, harmful world around you—and yet you still have to look for the solution even though you cannot see clearly. The light has darkened within you. Your vision is clouded and you look at the world through blurry spectacles. The light of your consciousness has been lost in the mists and you judge your situation badly.

The first message of the Oracle Sign speaks to your self-knowledge. When you have cleared things within yourself, then you can turn outward. If you are no longer darkened within, you can look outward and understand the world in which you live. If you are light within, you know what tactics to employ against the dark tools of a dark life situation. But if you, yourself, remain dark, then not only will you not recognize the nature of the anti-forces but your blind attempts will leave you unable to battle well against them. (This is, by the way, the main command of martial arts.)

The second message of the Oracle Sign will enrich your life awareness. It will also show you the other players in your life, your surroundings, and the situation that you are in at that present time.

According to tradition, the spirit follows its own path and that is why there is no situation for which it is not responsible. If you cannot see its cause, look for it in your past or in your distant past. The fruit that we eat today may be the fruit of a tree that we planted in childhood or even a previous life. The relationships of other people to us is often fate.

Thus, it is recommended to first apply the Oracle Sign to yourself. Firstly as psychological insight and secondly as fate advice. The two are always related.

DIFFERENT MEANINGS OF THE ORACLE

An important issue belongs here: the Oracle Signs can have many different meanings. I have described a good many but you have to discover the rest in such a way that, with time, you develop within yourself the ability to interpret the symbols.

So, for example, each Oracle Sign has a psychological interpretation. The whole thing plays out in me, in my mind. Even signs such as the 37th, A Man's Family, can reflect the state of my own spirit as the *family*, and *community* may be a faithful mirror to the various forces of my soul. If the forces of my soul are in order, then my "outer" family will also be fine.

Confucius and Richard Wilhelm reflect this with the same social and political images. But even this has to sometimes be translated to the language of our spirit as we have a "king" within us—our Higher Self—and there are spiritual forces within us that serve the king or topple him, we have order or anarchy within us; in other words, society is a true mirror of our souls.

There are some who compare the I Ching to dream interpretation. I don't agree with that—the I Ching is much more concrete than that. But you have to get used to its many meanings.

Let me give you an example. The 18th, Work on the Spoiled, describes a situation that has been ruined and has to be restored. Several lines speak about the "sins of the fathers" and the "sins of the mothers."

The first reading of the Oracle Sign speaks about well-known childhood traumas. But not just about that. Perhaps the situation only recently became infsted, you ruined it, or others did, and in order for you to put it right you have to recognize the source of its ruin. Here, the *sin of fathers* means Yang sin: abuse via control, power, and authority—aggressiveness. The *sin of mothers* means Yin error: the faults of weakness, softness, cowardice, powerlessness, and selfish love. There is no need to go back to childhood, you only need to decide, have I sinned or have others? Or all of us together?

I hope that the often charmingly humorous and often highly poetic Chinese characters will inspire you.

PREDICTIONS NEAR AND FAR

When I receive a divination, I spend a long time turning it over in my heart. I meditate on the answer.

There are times when I instantly understand, I had suspected as much. It is as if the answer lay dormant within me. Sometimes, it took weeks for me to realize what the sages wanted to say. And, unfortunately, it was also often the case that the message of the Oracle Sign only became apparent eighteen months later, when the event had already happened. I spent a great deal of time thinking about why this was the case.

In the first case, I think that the reason it happened the way that it did was because the message was virtually conscious within me. Only a thin membrane covered the recognition in my subconscious: the divination broke through the membrane and the advice became conscious within me. It is also possible that the event that the Oracle Sign predicted was already at a visible distance . . . a storm was brewing and that is what I could feel.

In many cases, the truth lay buried deep down within me. I didn't know and I didn't want to know about it. I call this "obstinate suppression." But in most cases, the predicted situation was still far away from me. Only the sages of the I Ching saw that "I had become pregnant from desire" . . . and that the event was inching toward me from my future. There was still no sign in the here and now. The sun was beating down and I didn't have the faintest idea that there was a storm around the corner.

At such times, the truth is not only deep within us but also far in front of us. There were occasions when events could be read from so deep down in my soul that they were only able to materialize years later. These divinations lack the *aha* sensation.

11

Meditations on Chance

The I Ching is a holy book. Its advice can help in the spiritual development of a person at the mercy of their fate. It speaks to you from three places.

Firstly, it speaks to you from your own subconscious world. Your suspicions and feelings that live below the surface of your consciousness are given a voice and they speak to you. Others are also present in our subconscious because our fates are intertwined and we create them together. That is why the divination that speaks to you may also include us, you, and them. The surface of the sea is still your "private sea," but the depths of the sea are shared with everyone else. It is possible that I make a divination for you as you are the one sitting in front of me, but the fate of your child or your spouse appears in the divination. It is just like a dream. Sometimes we dream the future of others.

The second source is your genuine Self or the True Man who undertook this earthly life.

And thirdly, your helping spirit or "guardian angel" may speak, call it what you will, who does not send suspicions but consciously provides concrete information—of course this is only in a general form—that you have to translate from the Oracle to the problem current in your life.

PREPARING FOR DIVINATION

You have to approach divination in a meditative state, read the Oracle Sign, and try to "listen" to its message in a sensitive frame of mind. Do not forget that the I Ching is a holy work and long ceremonies have always preceded its use.

You have to bring yourself into an intuitive state. *Intuition* means "taught from within." It means inner hearing and this requires silence and, primarily, attention. You should pay attention to all that goes on like a hunter in a hide.

The secret of real attention is that your consciousness should be empty. It contains no desire, imagination, hope, fear, or thought. It is empty like a photographic plate that bears no image. It will capture what appears. It should be unhindered by all forms of expectation, emotional code, or "Oh, let it be like this!" and "Oh, don't let that happen!"

You should read the divination as if you were simply an eyewitness to your life and not a participant. It should be as if the whole thing is happening to someone else. This is meditation.

Prepare and Throw

I will share here the steps I take to prepare and consult the Oracle.

- I keep the three coins in a separate box and I always wash them before the ceremony, especially if they were previously used by someone else. Objects retain the "spirit" of those who used them. (Seers are able to say an awful lot about the traces of spirits that are left on objects.) It isn't only washing that is important; I warm the coins in my hand for a considerable period for them to "adopt my vibration."
- I light incense.
- I have a large notebook that I use to enter and analyze

the divinations. This is important because frequently the divinations only become "real" two or three years later. (The Oracle that you hold in your hand has been written largely from such collected notes.)

- Then I meditate. The first thing that I do after completing meditation is to ask for protection so that I can clearly receive the message free of any other spiritual interference.
- I place a little red velvet cloth in front of me now and I throw the coins onto this six times, one after the other, with a short pause between throws. **It is very important that none of them should ever fall on the floor.** (I have had bad experiences with coins that have rolled away and repeated throws.)
- I record the result of every throw in my notebook.
- Then I look up the Basic Sign in the book . . . and if there are changing lines, I also look up the Direction Sign.
- Then I decipher the Divination, if I can . . . there have been times when the real message has only come to me days or weeks later.

There have been occasions when I have asked my spiritual Master by other means whether or not I successfully interpreted the message. He is happy to help and gladly corrects as well—he helped an indescribable amount in the writing of this book—but he never interprets the Oracle Sign for me. This has never happened and neither is it likely to ever happen in the future.

Each interpretation is a small awakening to ourselves. It is a discovery, the victory or failure of which should never be taken away from anyone as then there is no advancement.

Neither should the ritual before using the Oracle be seen as empty "mystery" any more than prayer. Prayer has no scientific meaning either. But this is the shame of science and not of prayer. Really great scientists know the significance of prayer.

WHY DO THE COINS FALL THIS WAY
AND NOT THAT WAY?

And finally, the unanswerable question: why do the coins fall onto the table as they do?

Jung responded to this question with his great theory of synchronicity. The great, archaic sages responded with the subject of analogies. But if you were able to ask any medium from the distant past, they would say that the Great Spirit is present at the divination and doesn't allow the coins to fall in any other way. I will tell you what my own experience has been, and it includes all three of these.

A birth horoscope will establish where a person will suffer injury. Some are destined to be injured in the head, the eye, the knee, the ankle—for me it is the thigh and the hip. I was shot at several times in 1956 and only ever hit in the hip and thigh. These were the exact points detailed in my birth horoscope.

We are slowly starting to accept that our illnesses have spiritual origins: it has been proven that inner conflict can lead to a stroke, an ulcer, high blood pressure, or even a heart attack . . . this is all accepted as it takes place inside a person. It is, however, a little more difficult to accept that accidents have a psychological cause and that they affect certain parts of the body and organs—because they come from the outside.

What do we have to do with that? A person's inner and outer worlds are completely isolated from one another, surely. We live in this false belief that we are not one with anything and that everything is *separate* from us, and we are only linked if something touches us, or—a more refined thought—if its force transmits to us and influences us. We only have anything to do with a metal rod if it hits us over the head. Everything that is outside of us is just like a mirage. It belongs to another universe.

Such a person is trapped inside their body, has nothing to do with anybody, and is alone; not only does this person not feel links to the outside world, but they live *against* everything. For them, the universe is a machine that is directed by unconscious, mechanical laws—and they are a completely separate and painfully sensitive part of this clinking, clanking, self-making, and self-breaking machine.

This "sense of separateness" leads to humans destroying all life on Earth without a second thought, feeling no more connection to it than they would to a hotel room. It doesn't matter if other people die—the main thing is that I should live.

The ancient view looks at things in a very different way: the Universe is not a meaningless, clinking, clanking unconscious machine but a very Conscious world that was created and occupied by Perfect Intelligence. Even atoms have modest sense, memory, sensitivity, and they too imitate something—a thought, a pattern, a law of energy—that all leads to the creation of a crystal, a mountain, a star, a plant, or an animal.

What remains invisible is the unfathomable pattern, strength, and spirit that influences everything and forms an integral part of all existence. The truth is not what we think, that we are clever humans living in an ignorant universe. The reverse is the real case; we are ignorant and foolish humans who not only live in an intelligent universe but are, in fact, an integral part of the whole where everything is linked to everything else. We do not live on a stage set that is separate from us; we are one with all that surrounds us. Nothing is separate.

The coins can fall no other way than the way they must. This is because everything is alive and living things are linked in quality, strength, law, fate, will, thought, and spirit.

We have materialistic words that really have no equivalent in the Chinese language. It is often hard to find words that are even similar.

Our word *chance* is represented by two words in the dictionary. One is *ou* and the other is *p'eng*. These two words were considered to be the best fit for what we "barbarian Westerners" refer to as "chance."

But if you read an ancient dictionary, you would find words like *association, unification, connection, linking, pairing, interdependency,* and *similarity*. These are the things that happen if you throw the three coins. You tie the invisible to the visible. Your spirit, your fate, the fate of others, and the fate of the coins are all linked. This is what the Chinese mean by "chance."

This is now being looked at by what is commonly referred to as "chaos theory." That is really all there is to say on the subject.

Perhaps the only thing to add is that you should talk to the book like an enthusiastic researcher who has some doubts, rather than a blind believer waiting for a miracle to happen. The truth will endure doubt and it has to be there for genuine discoveries to be made. Blind faith is only needed for things that are not true. That is when it is needed the most.

You can now set off on your path and the I Ching will be your guide. All books have a soul. If you read Tolstoy, you talk to Tolstoy. It sometimes takes a while to get to know one another and sometimes not. It is hard to get used to the idea that a live spirit lies behind the dead letters.

Ask it questions. It doesn't matter if your question is great or small but whether it is worthy or unworthy. You can use it every day, but you must always remember that you are interrogating your fate. Read it through, over and over again, and reply as if it was written to you personally. Treat it like a mysterious message that you have to decipher.

I have tried to express that each Oracle Sign has a main theme— this is the basic answer to your question—and it also has several pieces of important, strategic advice that I have highlighted with italics or bold lettering. Try to place your burning question in the energy field of the Oracle Sign. Your question will draw the answer from the sea of text that is meant only for you.

Lao Tse says, "The longest journey begins with the first step."

Bon voyage!

Oracle Signs

Upper trigram / Lower trigram	Creative	Receptive	Abysmal (Water)	Fire	Arousing (Thunder)	Mountain	Wind (Tree)	Lake (Cheerful)
Creative	1	11	5	14	34	26	9	43
Receptive	12	2	8	35	16	23	20	45
Abysmal (Water)	6	7	29	64	40	4	59	47
Fire	13	36	63	30	55	22	37	49
Arousing (Thunder)	25	24	3	21	51	27	42	17
Mountain	33	15	39	56	62	52	53	31
Wind (Tree)	44	46	48	50	32	18	57	28
Lake (Cheerful)	10	19	60	38	54	41	61	58

PART THREE

ORACLE SIGNS

1  *Ch'ien*

Creative

*Character: The life-giving force of the sun
dries up the mist.
The shoots emerge from the earth.*

Six Yang lines form the 1st Oracle Sign: Ch'ien. A doubling of the Sky trigram (Kua).

This is not only the purely spiritual but it also symbolizes the greatest force that creates everything. When we say God the creator made humankind in his own image, it means that we were also given the gift of his own supreme quality, *the ability to create*. We all create! We do this with our spirit, with our soul, with our body, with our words, with our thoughts, with our desires, and primarily with our faith.

Ch'ien is when our spirit fertilizes the world and the image dormant within us becomes real. Ch'ien is when a sperm cell runs into a passively waiting egg cell, passes on endless commands—or, in more modern terms, information—(including the gender of the future being) and from here on in, this is served by Time: it forms that which it has created.

The Creative is primarily spiritual. Information is even more determining than the biological process. Secondly, the Creative is the purest *energy*. It is the creative Force that forms visible reality from an invisible idea. The Creative is *persistent*. It not only initiates its work but sees it right through to the end. It doesn't want once; it wants for a long time. Time works for the Creative.

That is why the view attached to the Oracle Sign says, Creative (Ch'ien): *juan, hêng, li, chen*. This is a magical formula. In ancient times, these were the four sacred words of the royal divination. In this case, it not only means "exalted success, persistence" but also that the creation has to pass through the "beginning" (juan), the "ripening" (hêng), and the "harvest" (li), so forming into its "beneficent" (chen) meaning.

I could also translate it as "Look back to your Sacred Origin" (juan), "Sanctify your creation with your sacrifice" (hêng), "Yours will be the gift of blessings" (li), "I speak to you, to the High Spirit, who understands the divination" (chen).

The thing that is important from this is that **there is no result without sacrifice, only that creation can be beneficent that one does not create from selfishness for their own benefit but for the glory of God.**

The symbol of the Creative is a Dragon floating in the Sky. It is the symbol of the Sage and the King: it means a person who is in constant contact with the Sky and the "land of the Heavens." If Jesus had been born in China, he would have worn the symbol of the dragon on his robe as he was in a continual state of creation throughout his life. Even before his death, he said, "Let your will be done, Holy Father, and not mine." This is the key phrase of this Oracle Sign.

There is no higher gift than creation—and there is no greater sin than for one to selfishly exploit this gift. We can turn the earth into a blessing or a curse: a selfish, greedy, godless creature wants to grab its part so much that it pulls it all onto itself.

While we are talking about higher thoughts, respect for our ancestors is not the same as the duty we show to our dead today. Neither is it the same as the duty with which we respect the deceased prominent figures of our nation. This was *divine service* in tradition. My father and my mother only stayed such as long as I looked upon them with the eyes of a child. They really were divine spirits and it is possible that, following their death, they both regained this high, sovereign dignity. Today, the believer should respect the divine in others and even more so if the other has already departed. We do not know, after shedding an earthly role, what spiritual dignity waits beyond.

If you throw this sign, you become creative. No obstacle can divert you; the future is yours. What is invisible will become visible because of you. You bring it into being. It doesn't happen instantly and this is why you need to be persistent. A creative person not only takes strength from themself—they also move universal energy.

You are the Yang in your affairs; you are the determiner. You also inspire others. What lives in your thoughts and in your imagination comes into being. The same is true for bad, so beware! God's first creative words were, "Let there be light." Only want things that are light, beneficent, and good—not just when you start something but to the very end of the realization. Creation is not only about making a child, it is about taking that child in your arms, raising that child, and taking responsibility for that child until the day you die.

Prepare yourself for a long process!

THOUGHTS

The tactic of the Creative is *wu wei* or "no action." This means that our ego moves to one side and all that happens is carried out through us by a higher Will. Unfortunately, our ego is so cramped that we do not know such marvelous spontaneity.

If we say, "Let God's will be done," we do two things afterward. The first thing that we do is to wait: let God do it without us, on his own. It is, after all, God's will—we shove our hands in our pockets and stand to one side. The second thing is that we secretly do not trust in God and, where we can, we gently or aggressively "lend a hand."

The secret of "no action" is preserved by the Eastern martial arts where pupils are taught to become instruments of the universal, divine forces. Such a person neither stands aside nor "helps" but serves with continual vigilance.

This is what we learn in the sign of Creative. This means that only he can live with wu wei where the *5th line* is changing and the ego waits for all the others: the Dragon will be either too weak or too aggressive, or—the biggest problem—it will become intoxicated by its own power.

In a divination, it means an active or even hyperactive time in which you are the creator.

KEYWORDS

Lightly

Loosely

With love

Unselfishly

Persistently

LINES

1. Immersed dragon. Do not act!

You know from the Bible that, before the creation, "the spirit of God floated above the water." If you combine this with the Ch'ien Chinese character, you see that here the creative sun has already risen high in the sky and is drying up the water. In this line, the Dragon is still living, immersed in the water. *Its time has not yet come.* It is there but it does not yet create. It would be untimely. Either you are still immature or the other conditions are. Wait. Do not listen to any kind of encouragement. You still don't see clearly.

2. You now see the Dragon in the field. It is desirable to see the "great man."

The creative process has begun. The "field" is the symbol of manifestation—the field of Life. The great man (*ta jen*) is primarily within you. He is your better self who concentrates on the goal, makes sacrifices, and is humble. This is where his greatness hides. But since you are a "beginner" creator, the "great man" can mean all those who give concrete help to the completion of your work. The "great man" often means your role model whom you have to follow.

3. The Higher Power creates all day long. It is uneasy by evening. Trouble—but not mistake.
Confucius says that real Creation is light. It is inspired and spontaneous. It is the totally selfless action that comes from deep within. But this is not the case here. Ambition, impatience, and lack of faith still interfere. Have I hurried something? Is there something I didn't do? Was I aggressive or too compliant? You are starting to know the art of the beneficent act. But your ego keeps on interfering. This is why you cannot sleep at night. One who does the will of God sleeps peacefully. Your action is still not pure; it is confused. It still contains more will than faith. It isn't a problem if you recognize this and move on.

Practitioners of martial arts learn about stillness after a deed. They call this *zanshin*. It means that after a life-threatening act, a warrior cuts the thread of the memory of the previous moment in order to step into complete silence and a state of vigilance free of all thought. They do not take a single vibration of terror, fear, or passion with them. Zap! And peace returns to their heart.

4. It is possible that you are leaping over the deep. Not a mistake!
This line is described by the "leap" (*jue*) character. The bird has legs and it has wings; it can walk if it wants, it can fly if it wants. You also stand at a crossroad. If you go to the right, you work on your-self and if you go to the left, you work on the world. You can carry your plan to the end and you can start something else now. Just play, don't want. This line says relaxed spiritual state. Your heart will decide which way you should go. It is easy to grasp the right moment with a light hand.

5. *The dragon takes to the air. It is beneficent to see the great man!*
Spread your wings. Build, create—you can experience the joy of bringing something into being. The attraction of like spirits is decisive—but realization needs a central will. The notes now become music; its quality is in the hands of the conductor. The conductor is in your heart. Fulfillment!

6. *The domineering dragon flies too high. Regret.*
There is nothing higher than the Sky. A person who wants to get high plummets to the ground. We know this line. The disciples also asked, "Who is the greatest in heaven?" We become dizzy with power—not only in politics but even in a conversation it is important that I assert my power; I should be on top and not them! This ambition is what caused ancient rebellion (and also the downfall of the spirit). Me! Me! There is no one who is free of this great *self-cramp*. If not, they wouldn't live here among us. And there is no one who will not pay for this self-cramp sooner or later.

2  K'un

Receptive

*Character: Earth—and the sign of
"territory" and "space."*

K'un, the 2nd Oracle Sign, is formed by six Yin lines: A doubling of the Earth trigram. K'un is the Earth, the Mother, Mother Earth, and Nature.

The Sky is the place for all invisible ideas, where everything is in the "I think," "I want," "let it be" stage, in the fourth dimension of time—in order for it to *come into being* it needs the devotion of the mother's lap, the patient, forming strength of the mother's womb in which the seed forms into a body and the thought takes form; it needs the strength of fidelity, the strength of devotion, and the strength of adaptation. The Heavenly needs the Earthly.

Wherever you look on Earth, whether it be in plants, in trees, in mountains, in rocks, and even in a handful of soil, you see the *Work of a Mother*. This is what she made out of what the Heavenly Father wanted; she brought it into being, she formed it into shape and space.

The message of the Oracle Sign is just as "fortunate" as the previous one. Receptive (K'un): *juan, hêng, li, chen*—but all this is achieved with the devotional persistence of a mare. The horse is the symbol of the Earth. So is the stallion. The reason that the mare is mentioned here is because the ancient view is that if a stallion sets off, all the mares will follow. The other thing that is important is that a mare can carry a much heavier load than a stallion.

Following is the essence of the sign: "He informs and I do" (like being led in a dance). K'un realizes what Ch'ien wanted. It creates abundance, beauty; it grows, nourishes, and multiplies. If it loses its humility and wants to direct, the process fails. Beauty becomes distorted, achievements are aborted, and cancerous growth replaces abundance.

The immeasurable strength of K'un is through **devoted following.** Its strength lies in bringing thought into being. All the conductor does is to wave a hand—the musician is the one who creates the notes, the melody, and the music by following mute will.

The Oracle Sign of K'un advises **don't follow your own head.** Listen to your intuition rather than your mind. Don't push to the front. Don't try to direct. The more giving you are, the more successful. Creation is not your task—realization is.

KEY PHRASES

Be patient.

Be simple, tenacious, sober.

Trust in your inspiration.

Follow your star.

Bringing into being.

Pay attention to "real" processes.

Set your feet firmly on the earth.

THOUGHTS

The "Eternal Female" is the deepest symbol. Unfortunately, we do not understand this today as the dignity and character of the sexes became hopelessly tangled in the dark age. There are no real women and neither are there any real men.

God is one—but manifests as two: Creative and Receptive. We are all Creators and Receivers—irrespective of our individual gender. In the same way that we breathe in and out, our life has Creative and Receptive phases. We sometimes play one role and sometimes the other in our community lives, irrespective of whether we are mothers or fathers. If we pray, then we are all Receptive—Jesus was the same; he followed the will of his Father in all he did. He was Creative for his disciples, like a true Master.

"Male" and "female" roles and phases of being are continuously changing.

The essence of this Oracle Sign is that *I have to follow something but I don't exactly know what it is.* I don't understand it. It has still not sunk in. I have to give myself for something—not because I know but because I have faith. The higher order progresses first by being confused and then fulfilled. *Devotion* is the essence of this Oracle Sign. Maturation is led by processes that are mysterious, instinctive, much deeper, and more elemental than knowledge. You do not understand what is going on and this makes you uncertain. You know in the end what you didn't know because you give birth to it.

You ruin the whole process if you imagine you know that which you don't know. You claim ignorance to be knowledge and you begin to lead yourself. We all do this. Instead of faith, dedication, and waiting, we take our fate in our own hands and ruin everything.

If I look back, I am stunned to see how much spiritual help, good will, opportunity, and beneficent achievement I have ruined because of my own willfulness and by impatiently interfering in the invisible maturing process. I called this feeling "fate panic" that repeatedly demolished the beneficent achievements within me. When all I had to do was to wait, believe, bear it, and go about my work, all I felt was that *nothing is happening, I have to take my life into my hands!* I snatched my life out of God's hands and it could find no worse place than in my hands, just like grabbing the photographic paper out of the developer too quickly—there's no picture and the whole thing is ruined.

This is the largest danger of this Oracle Sign: playing master instead of pupil; taking power through aggression, obstinate will, false reasoning, and false "manliness" where humility would be beneficial, along with waiting and quiet work. The fruit of the K'un Oracle Sign—if we live it well—is valuable. It is here that we learn to watch others, accept, and understand many different kinds of people— good and bad alike. *The broad being of the noble of spirit contains all spirits.*

Philosopher Chuang Tse said, "The life of things is like a galloping horse: there is no movement that does not bring change and there is no moment in which they don't alter. *What should you do? Leave everything to form for itself!*"

This is the secret of Receptive.

LINES

1. Frost sets in. Hard ice comes. Initial doubt leads to total disbelief.
The "frost" is a doubt. The "hard ice" is a crucible of disbelief. Let everything take care of itself? Won't that lead to trouble? Shouldn't I take control of my own fate? It is from these transient and uncertain thoughts that trouble is born. Nip them in the bud because if the thought freezes into reality, it will already be too late. Keep on being a faithful mare. Follow your heart—not your mind.

2. Each of his sides is straight and large. He doesn't practice and yet still he completes everything.
Things are going well all on their own. The symbol of Creator is the circle—the symbol of Receptive is the square: this is symbolized by circular Chinese coins with a square hole in the center. Squaring the circle: the realization of theory. This is what is happening now. It is happening by itself, naturally and automatically. It isn't your rowing, but the current that is making your boat speed through the water. It is also your faith that you are being carried in the right direction.

3. Be persistent and hidden beauty will manifest. If you are serving the king, do not strive for victory but fulfillment.

Don't concern yourself with your vanity. Forget what people say to you. Don't be interested in recognition. You serve a king and not common people. This is Béla Hamvas's line: he did not strive for success but for "glory." According to his concept, this means recognition that comes from deep within and high above. This is the line of every good mother who has brought a child into this world. The reward for a true deed is with God. "I do not take praise from people," Jesus said. With vanity I not only mess up myself, I also mess up my human relationships. Now all you have to do is to work "precisely and nicely"—the reward is in the future.

4. Tied sack. There is no mistake. There is no praise.

Avoid any confrontation for the time being. You are lacking strength (Yang) to break through and your passivity (Yin) is still weakness. Do not collide and do not give up—do as a hedgehog would.

5. Yellow inner robe. Exalted blessings.

Yellow is the color of earth and the color of the Center. Now you wear it hidden. You do not show your qualities and no one knows about them. Fortunate processes are also taking place hidden. And this is how it should be. Continue to be discrete and tactical. It doesn't matter if you are not valued. The result is maturing.

6. Dragons do battle in the meadow. Their blood is black and yellow.

This is a power struggle in which both parties will lose. The ego gets fed up with second place. It rebels and tries to push to the front and order collapses. This is a familiar situation: it is the image of most divorces, failed revolutions, and unsuccessful rebellions. In martial arts, it means that the warrior fighting in the sign of K'un abandons the soft fighting style out of fear or aggression. They want to defeat Yang with Yang, and they are beaten. Boxers simply use the phrase, "Don't stop to brawl!"

3 ☵☳ *Chun*

Difficulty at the Beginning (Sprouting)

Character: A succulent blade of grass
victoriously emerges from beneath the soil.

The lines of Chun, the 3rd Oracle Sign, are the trigrams Water above Thunder—the obstacle. All beginnings are difficult. Sprouting, shooting, birth, and beginning a new plan or a new form of being are all very difficult. This is also the most difficult moment of creation: to form order from chaos, harmony from noise, living beings from thoughts. Something is starting to happen.

The sages see this as being encouraging and they say the magical formula to this Oracle Sign is *juan, hêng, li, chen*. All this means here is that the sweet fruit of effort becomes ripe after germination, growth, and blossoming. It also means that the process will be long since it will pass through all four stages. It also says that this is a test. It mainly tells you to remember what children used to write in the first page of a new exercise book: "I begin in the name of God." All beneficent deeds are born out of sacrifice.

The beginning is difficult because you have to defeat great resistance. Think of the drama of the heavy, hard, and dense earth and the shoot. It is not only weak but also inexperienced. It gains its strength through bitter struggle. Those who live upward are strengthened by troubles, problems, difficulties, and struggle. Those who live downward are weakened and broken by the very same things. Live upward! Think of a little baby who is learning to walk: he falls over a thousand times, bumps himself but stands up again and again and eventually can walk.

The Oracle Sign advises you **do not concern yourself with your distant goals but struggle with your present.** And ask experienced helpers who are experienced in the struggling practice of "sprouting." Listen to good advice and accept help.

The Oracle Sign is encouraging. The beneficent result will only be missed if you take fright at the difficulties, if you feel sorry for yourself and see yourself as weak, and especially if you are disorganized and you give yourself over to confusion. The True Man creates order. He relies on the solid foundation of tradition. This means that he has unshakeable faith. The Chinese image linked to this (*lun*) shows that the Great Man weaves many threads into a plait. Here, order means that many small things come together in a single whole. It is just like cellular growth. Collection is also important here: the many struggles of the quantitative process that give birth to new quality.

THOUGHTS

The situation is difficult. It is difficult because I am still too immature to solve it. If I were mature, I would know that difficulty doesn't exist for the sage. Everything is easy for the sage—this is the basis of Taoism. The sage fulfills the difficult via the easy, the large via the small. The things of the world begin with the easy and that is why the sage never affects things that have become great; that is how great things are created. The giant tree grows from thin roots.

This is really about magical knowledge. The origins of all visible things are in the invisible. This is where shoots are along with thoughts, desires, spiritual ideas, and the genetic ancient images of deeds and fates: *it is easy to have an effect here and not later when the struggling process of realization has already begun.* I can easily exchange plans for a statue in my mind—but later, if my theories have already solidified into material, I can only chip away the excess slowly and with difficulty.

The fundamental principle of the I Ching is *light* and *simple*—this means that the person who preserves the knowledge within themself that the manifest world originates in the unmanifested, that all things material are a reflection of the spiritual, finds everything in this world to be light and simple. Even miracles.

"The only victorious army is that which has never fought," said Lao Tse, and in ancient times it was not seen as a miracle that unapproachable masters managed, without a sword, to ward off their opponents with their "supernatural" powers. The gospel healings also belong here; these all went lightly and simply. And they still do, to this day. Magic means to affect the Spiritual Seed of something. This is the seed from which everything comes. The Chun sign is about this wise ability having been lost (or not yet gained) and that is why I have to battle my way up slowly and painstakingly in order to gain this sacred knowledge. It isn't the task that is difficult—it is I who am weak. It isn't the world that is chaotic, but me.

Recovery is difficult because *I have to make myself suitable for it.* The sage lifts a weight with the tip of his little finger that would crush me—but he is wise and strong because the experience of countless bitter failures and reassuring victory in the sign of Chun awake him to his own strength.

You have to collect strength in Chun. It takes patience. You have to accept help. And one more thing: do not try to force your own ideas onto the future. Let things develop according to their own nature.

"If the Great Founder," says Chuang Tse, "melts the metal, and the metal starts to jump around and shouts out, '*Make me into an ornate, ruler's sword!*' the Great Founder judges it to be inappropriate metal." And he adds, "If we consider the world as an enormous melting pot and the creator-transformer (Tao) as the Great Founder, then what can he form us into that *would not be beneficent for us?*"

The problems of Chun not only stem from some new life cycle

beginning where the tried and tested strategy no longer worked—but mainly from the fact that I do not have sufficient faith in God's will. The situation is too chaotic, difficult, and unknown for me to believe that there is an Absolute good will behind it. "Do not be afraid," says Jesus to his disciples as he walks on water.

LINES

1. Although it is motionless like some pillar, it is desirable to persist. It is desirable to find helping companions.
The superficial advice of the line: do not be frightened off by initial difficulties. Be solid and steadfast and especially sufficiently humble, because you can only fight the battle with the help of those who are "lower" than yourself. A deeper advice comes from interpreting the Chinese symbols: the stone pillar (*pa huan*) means a "tombstone." Persistence (chu) is replaced by "stay in place" and helping companions (chien) is replaced with "the poor, the looked down upon, the undervalued." The meaning is the following: insistence of physical and spiritual roots can be of immeasurable value when in the middle of initial problems.

A person gets enormous strength from their cultural and religious roots. If you look at the character for the Oracle Sign that shows the blades of grass emerging from the earth, the roots are much longer than the fresh threads working their way to the surface. Its new stability and strength is deep down. It lies in tradition. It is in the roots.

"Stay in place" does not mean that you shouldn't take anything on now but **stand with your feet firmly on the ground before you distance yourself and draw your strength from tradition and the treasury of your subconscious.** "Helping companions" are not only other people but also as yet unknown or not sufficiently valued abilities of your own being. This is your hidden knowledge, instinctive strength that appears in difficult situations. We are sometimes taken aback—in tight situations—at all that was within us that we were not aware of. This comes in the form of courage, daring, strength, instinctive knowledge, and toughness.

2. He would grow but he is incapable. Like someone riding around and around. He doesn't meet with enemies but escorts. The girl would rather wait for a whole time cycle to pass before giving her hand.

The situation appears to be standing still. I suspect an enemy in everyone in difficult circumstances; I project my fear and failure onto others. I suspect them of being the cause of my problems. First advice: my own weaknesses cause my difficulties. Second advice: don't run away but solve it. Do not accept the offer of those who only offer a way out. It is better to wait until the solution arrives, until my fate is mature outside and inside. Don't rush it even if the process is very difficult. Don't blame others.

3. He who hunts deer thoughtlessly loses his way in the forest. The Great Man prefers to stop for a short time to catch his breath as going on would lead to shame.

The goal has appeared but you are still too immature to reach it. You are not driven by vigilance but by impatient instinct and the blindness of "I want it now!" You thought that it was already here—but it is still far away. The goal has disappeared, you blunder into an even denser forest and, according to another Chinese character, you are led by just *chins*: untamable, wild birds. Stop. Take a breath. Calm your impatient shrieks. Everything comes in good time—but not if we hurry it. Then— like the deer in the dense forest—it simply evaporates.

4. Riding around and around (stagnate). Aim for unity! It is beneficial to go. Everything has a helping effect.

This is not about external obstacles but inner inhibitions. This can be any one of a number of things: lack of faith, shocking experience, loss of hope, underestimating myself, prejudices, perhaps arrogance or pride that stops me accepting help. The one who is faithless doesn't believe in a miracle even if they touch it for support. Look into yourself: why don't you believe? Work it out. Defeat it. And act!

5. Protect the oil! A little persistence is beneficial, great persistence: trouble. The outside world does not yet value your inner values. It does not matter that you would like to share your light: there is no one for you to shine it on. Not only you but also your surroundings need to mature. There is a lot of indifference and uncertainty—you are not being appreciated for your real values. Get by with less.

6. You are riding but not getting anywhere. Tears of blood are falling. Don't allow this to last a long time!
"It won't go. It's too hard. It's too tough. I can't stand it any longer!" This is the thought of the dead point. All efforts and all struggles have a dead point when we feel as if we can't keep on going. Something really does die at the dead point—either faith dies or lack of faith dies. If faith dies, you give up. If lack of faith dies, you keep on going and win the battle! Remember the Hassidic tale: the rabbi's car gets stuck in the mud. His pupil pushes and pulls with all his might and finally gives up. "I can't do it!" he pants. "You can stand it," says the rabbi, "you just don't want to!" We can only solve difficult situations by using our secret reserves.

4 ䷃ *Mêng*

Immaturity

Character: Tender climbing plant
that hides and covers something.

The lines of Mêng, the 4th Oracle Sign, are the trigrams Water in the Mountains. The situation is stormy. It might be difficult and anxious. But this is only because you don't understand it. You have to solve something that you do not know, something of which you have no experience. The task is a new one: you are not mature enough for it yet, like a child for life. The key to the solution is understanding. If you get to know it, you will easily solve it. If not, you will ruin it. The situation only hides one real danger: if you think you understand where you don't understand at all!

The Oracle Sign is about the learning process and the correct behaviors of the master and the pupil. It is about how to attain the power of knowledge. It is as if the I Ching were speaking about itself: **Immature youth can be successful. I am not seeking him—the immature youth seeks me. I was enlightening him with the first Oracle Sign. But if he asks twice or three times: things remain misty. There is no good advice in mist.**

"Mist" (*tu*) is the mist of ignorance. Knowledge makes one master of their fate—it places the key to solutions in their hand. *A person who is shrouded in the mist of ignorance is laid open to trouble, whim, chaos. They stumble through the mist and make mistake after mistake.*

Whatever it was that you asked, the answer now is **understand your problem first and then you can solve it.** Ask for help and advice. Ask experienced people to show you the way. Be a pupil. The first thing that a pupil needs to know is that he *doesn't know.*

You are faced with a task that requires you to grow. At first, it may appear to be large and frightening and perhaps you will stop short in front of it—but this only lasts until you understand it. Understanding means maturing.

THOUGHTS

In ancient China, it was accepted that a person does not get knowledge from the outside but that it is hidden deep within. An uneducated child was referred to as *tong mêng. Tong* means "child." *Mêng* is the name of this Oracle Sign and it means "hidden" or "covered." Teaching of a child was called *ki mêng,* which means "the discovery of that which is hidden."* The character of the Oracle Sign also expresses this hidden or covered knowledge. The knowledge of all things has to be revealed—the veil of mist has to be slowly pulled away: this is the mystery of education. It is making the unconscious conscious.

There are two types of not knowing. One is innocent and childlike. The other is blind, arrogant, and unapproachable. Lao Tse says that if someone does not know and yet still believes that they know, then they are sick. What is more, they are incurable because they do not seek out the cause of the problem, since the poor unfortunate thinks they know.

One is sick who is not satisfied with the precise advice of a master and asks for an Oracle Sign over and over again, wanting more and more answers. The book only talks about two or three questions but

---

*The word *Mongol* also comes from *mêng.* It means an immature, uncivilized people, a young people that need to be further educated.

there are people who just keep on asking, and they never understand the response—because they don't want to.

As the knowledge is hidden within you, the first answer *needs to touch you!* Even if it is unpleasant and you had hoped for something else. If you are open, then the "Aha, I suspected as much" should light up inside you. *This is how you should turn to the Oracle: with an open and innocent spirit.* Otherwise, it won't be able to help.

The Mêng Oracle Sign answers a question in which you are still inexperienced. You are ignorant. Perhaps this is not true of thousands of other questions in life, but it is in this one. This is the blind spot within you. The secret of your success is to see. Learn to see. This is your task now. It is still too early to act.

LINES

1. Discipline is required for the education of the immature. But ties are not needed. To carry on like this leads to shame.
There is no advancement without discipline. But it has limits. We don't really know this now—not if we educate ourselves or if we educate others. If life is educating you now, you should know that the hard tests will benefit you. But this is only if you have beneficent goals. If you don't, then discipline is pure slavery, meaningless drudgery. Don't stand it. Confucius says, "The best teacher is not words but the *role models*."

2. Wisely bearing the immature: beneficent. To take a wife: beneficent. The boy has become the master of the house.
This line is not about the pupil, it is about the teacher. It is about how we treat our own immaturity and—the same thing—how we treat the feebleness of our fellow man. The character for "bearing" (*pao*) shows an embryo in the mother's womb that she not only bears but also protects, nourishes, and develops, the unselfconscious little being who sometimes even gives her a kick. The "boy" (*tse*) is he who has already grown within us. You have grown up enough to solve the problem. Now

you raise yourself and your surroundings. Do this with patience, understanding, gentleness, and strength. Solve your problem this way. You know what you have to do.

3. Keep a distance from the helpless woman who, if she sees a strong* man, loses herself.
A person who is immature—having no sense of self—may be tempted by the illusion of money, success, and power. The fault of servility also belongs here. Never follow anyone whom you follow out of weakness. Do not listen to your siren voices. And if you are tempted by your surroundings or by others, keep your distance. The false principles of today's world want to keep people in slavery. Do not take a single step forward. This is not your path.

4. Restricted immaturity: shame.
A person who believes that they know when they do not is shamed. A person who cannot be educated does not listen to the word of the master and is raised by hard knocks. This is the last warning: things are not as you think.

5. Young immaturity: beneficent.
A person who knows that they do not yet know is open to knowledge. They can be educated. Your self-knowledge is developing, you can be led—and you will receive spiritual help. God can only help the true believer—because they are open. Openness means, "Give me, Lord, what is good for me. You know what that is and I will also know in time." This spiritual behavior is the key to solving your question. In martial arts, the "principle of innocence" means openness and the ability to be inspired. It contains no prejudice, fear, or confusing thought.

---

*The other meaning of "strong"—*chin*—is metal and gold. But, in the *Book of Songs* it means attractive.

6. Hitting the immature. Holding back illegal aggression: beneficent.
Releasing illegal aggression: problem.

Discipline is required now, but aggression is not. Aggression will not solve the conflict, it will just intensify the problem. The problem is caused by your own immaturity or the immaturity of others (often both). This can only be stopped with strength. True strength is understanding. It wants to raise and not to hurt, not even in thought. The sage knows that it is really good to avoid sin. If we have already done it, we should not make things worse by intensifying it further with passion, revenge, or anger. The same is also true of the "sins" of others. "Forgive them, Lord, for they know not what they do." Forgiveness does not mean lack of discipline.

5  *Hsü*

Waiting

Character: Ancient, magical rain-making ceremony.

The character shows a situation where rain is needed—but the dense clouds only continue to gather. The need is great, the "must" is tense— but fulfillment still does not arrive. It has obstacles in its path; the conditions are not yet right. You have to wait.

The secret of waiting is *patience*. The secret of patience is to do everything that I can within my power and entrust fulfillment to the power of Universal Providence. I desire something and then I let it go. If I want something very much and the hunger and thirst make me impatient, I ruin the whole thing. Watch, when you continue to really want something, you don't get it. In fact, constantly wanting something can hold back or ruin the maturation process.

The man "who is not yet fully grown" is impatient, "Lord, give me rain!" The True Man waits happily. The character says that he eats, drinks, and does lots and lots of enjoyable things. In other words, he happily enjoys the moment of the present. He does not look at the sky with bitterness and dissatisfaction, because he has entrusted fulfillment to the heavenly providence.

The Hsü sign is about doing everything within myself, but knowing the completion is not my problem but God's. We receive what is ours in due time. What we do not receive is not ours. You can "force" something, but it isn't worth it.

THOUGHTS

Our fate is not solitary but a community process. In the big board game, we only live our own role and we are unable to understand what is happening to us, to say nothing of what happens to others. Karmas are linked; in order for something to be fulfilled, it requires all the role players to be ready for it. Sometimes we are left behind, sometimes the others—this is when you have to wait because the moment that we call *coincidence* is late arriving. When this comes, it can only be seen with divine eyes, with the eyes of the Great Director to whom everyone is important and who sees the maturing processes in everyone.

You will ruin the whole thing if you are impatient. Fate cannot be forced with your pushiness. This is not only about the deeds that you carry out but also about the ones that lie within you—desires, hopes, thoughts. These cannot be hidden because they radiate out of you— we are all connected on the invisible energy level of the spirit. If we as much as project our desires onto someone in thought, and that person is not yet ready, then they will run away. One who hunts fulfillment down makes those who are unready flee.

It is only possible to wait well with faith. This is not easy as the three Yangs on the bottom really want and the Water Sign at the top places an obstacle in the path of fulfillment. And this means that tension and restriction are both operating at the same time. As with any other problem, it can only be left by moving **upward**: your real self, the True Man lives above doubt and hope, and happily so, as his home is in the Eternal Now. He is not dependent on the future. The key phrase for faith: *Your heavenly Father knows well what it is that you need.* We do not know. We really don't know. Looking back, many people experience fighting for something tooth and nail only to see it ruin their lives. ("The mouse chews on a mouthful," says Kálmán Mikszáth, "until it eats its way to the cat!")

Like all magic, rainmaking works with the community praying with the shaman for rain. He sent his desires and hopes to the invisible spirit world and then forgot about the whole thing. He happily danced and sang and enjoyed life. This was called "release of desire."

It then started to rain.

LINES

1. Waiting in the meadow. It is desirable to stay with the lasting. You are guiltless in the situation.
Don't worry about tomorrow. Whatever comes, be calm and solid. Don't go ahead. A person who waits badly cannot be happy with what is. Only the dreams of a person who finds themself in the present are fulfilled.

2. Waiting on the sand. Little words. It turns to blessings in the end.
Doubt, uncertainty. Disturbed inner voices torture. A person who is without faith looks in many directions. It is also possible that they are judged by the little ones around them. But these are just powerless words. Listen to your heart.

3. Waiting in the mud. He encourages robbers to approach.
"Mud" is doubt, lack of roots, lack of faith, worry. Mud is illusion and wishful thinking that has no reality. A person who lives in such things gets stuck. And others exploit this. The situation is not final but a warning.

4. Waiting in blood. Getting out of the hole.
"Blood" means dark passion and hate. In final embitterment, one becomes one's own enemy and the enemy of others. The "hole" is false belief that everything and everyone is against you. You should not act now because you cannot see clearly. You cannot fight like this but just flail around and there is no sense in that. (The line can also mean the

danger of material greed. This is also hidden in the Chinese symbol for "blood.") The advice does not encourage battle but immediate removal from the situation.

5. Waiting with food and drink. It is beneficent to hang on.
This is how a sage waits, enjoying the gift of Great Now. The joy of the present makes the signs of lacking disappear from his spirit. One commentator says, *"chung cheng,"* which means that it is recommended to create balance within ourselves and to concentrate on the center of our being. What you are waiting for is still not here. But it isn't missing at the moment. You should collect strength now and especially inner joy. Now you understand the advice; don't worry about tomorrow.

6. End up in a hole. Three unexpected guests arrive. Respect them and fulfillment and blessings wait at the end.
Everything is in vain: what you waited for, what you so desired and wanted has not happened. And so—in this state of total failure—there will still be something. It is like a deus ex machina on the stage, something suddenly happens. It is different from what you imagined and so surprisingly and shockingly different that you even forget to greet it. Perhaps you don't even have to in the first moment. Perhaps you receive it with anger: "I didn't ask for this. This isn't what I prayed for!" Don't forget, Fate's paths twist and turn. What appears as a step back may also be the start of a great leap forward. And what now appears little is the seed of a lot. Treat it well. If you look back now, you will be surprised to see that the greatest events in your life started off as sorry and insignificant little shoots.

6  *Sung*

Conflict

Character: Litigious mouth and publicity.
But perhaps better still: the mouth shouts to the world—
with the character of depute next to it.

The message of the 6th Oracle Sign is: **This is a crisis. Be true. Don't be surprised by the situation! Turning to the central point: beneficent. Taking it to the end: failure. To see the Great Man: desirable. It is not desirable to cross the Great Water.**

The situation is debatable. It is as dramatic as a lawsuit in which two opposing views (interests) collide. You are already in it or you are just about to enter it. The I Ching has the following to say: **There is only one real crisis: conflict with ourselves.** Inner war. Bounty. When we believe and when we don't. We want something and we don't want it. We say something and we regret it. When we do something only half-heartedly. "Obstinacy is the death of the deed."

When I am daring out of fear; when I thrash around out of blind faith and I dare not open my eyes because I am afraid that I am not right and I cannot come to terms with my bloody victims; when I do not agree with myself deep down in my soul—this is the fundamental situation of people today, the conflict between the conscious and the subconscious. The conflict between the ego and the Higher Self.

The essence of the ego is to argue with everyone and everything. Conflict is the ego's element in which it bathes with desperate pleasure.

The I Ching says: Chung! Return to your center point. There is no conflict or doubt there—there is only Unity. And resist taking your battle to the bitter end because, in the end, whether you win or you lose, only trouble awaits you and you will make the conflict eternal. The only way that you can free yourself from the whirlpool is to hold your nose and dive down to the motionless central axis, but you will surely drown if you thrash about and swim to where the waters are the roughest.

The Chinese way is to spurn argument. "He who argues," says Chuang Tse, "does not see deep down. . . . If he tries to argue with words, he achieves nothing!" No one has ever solved a single thing by arguing. "Through Tao," says the sage, "all that is contradictory merges and becomes one." Do not look for your own truth; rise up to boundlessness! You first have to resolve the conflict in your own head. If you are "together with yourself," it is easy to resolve the outer conflict.

The Oracle Sign says: **The worst thing is if you attempt to solve the conflict with aggression. Don't do anything at all now because there are too many contradictions. Wait for the best moment and prepare to reach compromise.**

THOUGHTS

The I Ching advises you not to enter into conflicts. And if you already have, you should get out as quickly as possible. This advice falls far from our own approach as we see it as cowardly withdrawal, and this requires explanation.

The first syllable of the Japanese word *budo* (meaning "martial art"), *bu* means "to silence the weapons of destruction." This is how Master Ueshiba teaches, who says, "The essence of budo is harmony and love. Everything is one and belongs together."

This is the sum of a samurai's creed and nothing more. There is no belief, denomination, religion, opinion, interest, philosophy, party, or policy for which he would strike with his sword. The only philosophy for which he would give his life is peace and quiet. And he applies this philosophy to himself first of all. Zero conflict—inner peace—is not only his religion but also his spiritual state. He is the "meek who will inherit the earth," as Jesus teaches. Conflict is only in those who attack him. Then the samurai draws his sword and he only does this to put a stop to the conflict of others and to restore harmony as quickly as possible. His opponents will become the victims of their own conflicts—this is all that happens at such times and nothing more.

Jesus worked in much the same way. He never argued with anyone, he never fought, and he never wanted to defeat anyone, and when Peter drew a sword on him, he warned him of the law of karma: "He who lives by the sword, dies by the sword." Jesus lived in unity (in love) with people. People did not live in unity with him—in other words, the conflict was not with Jesus but in the spirits of the people and is to this very day. We are incapable of appreciating that we should love our enemy and if they strike us, we should turn the other cheek and not resist evil but allow it to be eaten up by its own conflict and to be consumed by the belief that "I am right!"

Religious debates are meaningless. It is the essence, the spirit of love that has been abused for thousands of years: it is obvious that truth is not on either side. The "principles," according to the words of Hamvas, are "covering theories" and there simply to conceal the original cause of the conflict: the opposition of views. You cannot win in a conflict, just rise above it. Religious debates are just as endless as blood feuds.

A conflict does not last until you win or lose but until you step out of it. This is what the Sung Oracle Sign teaches in the symbol meaning, *The True Man brings his hidden contradictions to the surface before he begins anything.* This is how conflict can be avoided.

A vigilant mentality—like a good chess player—sees the consequences of each move before it is made. They play the match out in their head and that is why they are not surprised later on. It is also possible that they decide that it is not their game and they don't play at all. It is a good decision when the sage within us—before stepping onto the path of realization—runs through the whole story mentally beforehand. If the conflict is still only in bud, don't ripen it!

Sung advises **caution**: consider who you associate with, what you plan, and what you commit yourself to do and how. Examine what is "true" for you. The obstinate, quarrelsome "truth" that leads to conflict knows that you also have a much wiser truth than this.

If you are already in conflict, do not listen to your ego but wait for the solution to come from the center point of your being.

LINES

1. Don't make the matter permanent. A small exchange of words (judgment) and go!
Don't turn a little unpleasantness into a conflict. Perhaps the matter has nothing to do with you, and perhaps it can be solved with just one word. Don't jump straight away. Let it run off and don't watch it go.

2. You cannot control the conflict. Come back to your sense (tsuan) and retreat back to your strong city! In this way your people and hundreds of homes will remain free of trouble.
This not only points to the danger of being outnumbered in the situation but also that you would battle recklessly. (Arrogance? Passion? False sense of self?) The Chinese Rat symbolizes wise adaptation and sense. The tsuan character appearing in the text depicts a rat that retreats into its hole and, in so doing, it saves itself and its own.

3. Take nourishment from the strength of old tradition! There is danger but there will be a beneficent end. If you happen to be serving a king, don't strive for your own work!
The lines can be interpreted in many ways. The important thing is, as with the 3rd line of Kun, the 2nd Oracle Sign, that service is important

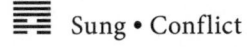

and not individual recognition. If you want to make yourself independent, you will create a conflict. The essence of the old traditions is that the power and the glory belong to God. The danger appears when you protest against this. The key to the situation is not to break out but rather to respect what is.

4. Don't get caught up in a conflict. Turn in the direction of your fate. Peace and self-denial will open up a path for you.
What you have to deny is impatience, stubbornness, aggression, and the self-deceiving thought of "I am fighting for my truth." Your true fate is on the side of peace and not on the side of war. Do not attempt victory even if your opponent is weaker. If others challenge you, do not take up the gauntlet. (Fernando, the bull in the children's story, could not be enticed to charge with any kind of red cape because he was happily smelling the scented flowers in the arena.)

5. Conflict ahead: exalted blessings.
A believer says, "I entrust God with the decision." A common man says, "I will only trust an impartial judge." The Tao sage says, "You see and do what needs to be done in the center of your being (chung)." The line does not talk about what the decision is: struggle, waiting, or peace. Only a person who has freed themself of ego is capable of restoring the harmony of truth. This is the goal. You can reach it.

6. Maybe you will be awarded with a leather belt. It will be pulled off you three times before dawn.
A person who struggles against fate may win passing battles but will end up losing the war. A person who stubbornly takes a senseless struggle through to its conclusion achieves momentary glory but will be continuously shamed after that. Do not be an "arrogant dragon" because the pleasure of your victory will only last a short time, but you will carry the karmic load of your shame for a very long time.

7  *Shih*

Army

*Character: A crowd gathering
around the center point.*

Order needs to be brought to chaos. Order is required because we cannot live up to the challenge. Life is struggle. And winning the struggle is only possible with a gathered spirit, organized powers, and good tactics. Chaos may be within us, on the outside, or in both places. A lot of voices, a lot of wills, a lot of desires, urges, feelings, thoughts—a conductor is needed who can restore order in the disharmony with the appropriate amount of force. Similarly, in world drama a mob cannot win a battle, only a well-organized army.

The Oracle Sign looks at this: you stand before a challenge. Now you need your strong, seeing being, your inner "captain" who organizes your life with persistence and strength. What are the characteristics of a good general? The first thing is that they should be able to see the future goal and make others see it. We can only struggle if we see the reason why. This is because each struggle is accompanied by sacrifice and we can only make sacrifices for a cause that we see the sense of in advance. The cause motivates.

Secondly: strength is needed. The general is stronger individually than the whole army; others also take their energy from this leader.

Thirdly: the general needs wisdom in order to know the secret in the hearts of the soldiers and the struggle in every situation. This also requires understanding so that the general can engender love or respect in order not to be followed out of force.

The sign sometimes just says, **Pull yourself together**. At times like this, the crowd represents the many different voices in our spirit and the chaos in our heads. But it more commonly means that you are facing a challenge that you have to live up to. *Sort yourself out*!

The Shih sign is translated as "army" but some Chinese academics disagree on this point. There were no regular armies in ancient China, only peaceful peasants who could be organized into armies in a matter of minutes. They only fought wars in two cases: in self-defense or if a dictator needed toppling. However, they did not keep an army because it was felt that where there is a military army, there will be war.

A real general avoids battle but is invincible if attacked. The true general is peaceful, should know discipline and moderation, and is listened to and obeyed because he has managed to make everyone understand (feel) that he wants good.

You stand before a task and for this you require functional unity. "Will," says Nietzsche, "is to want something for a long time." Who do you listen to within yourself? Who is the most important within you? Do you follow yourself? Do you make your conscious or semiconscious urges inferior to your life plan? If not, you will fail. You will fall apart. You will be defeated. You cannot live up to your undertaking.

This Oracle Sign says, "Blessings! Faultless!" In other words, it sees the "conductor" within you; it sees the general. Victory is not certain—nothing is certain in the I Ching—because it depends on you, but you have the opportunity.

THOUGHTS

We want a lot of different things all at once. In this Oracle Sign *you have to act and the deed can be nothing other than obvious*. This is about solving a fate task. The danger in the task is that our powers are disorganized and we are not clear in ourselves. Here—as in every fight—collective strength is required. First, we have to pull ourselves together and then—if that is our task—we have to bring others together.

The Oracle Sign has only one strong line: the 2nd. This is not the sign for the king but the sign for the captain. A captain also serves, not himself but the boat and the affairs of all those aboard the boat. Call up the captain within yourself! This is the one who can, who believes, and is forceful if necessary and understanding if required. The stormier the sea, the more the captain is needed.

We can only achieve a goal that everyone wants. This is the other message of this Oracle Sign. If you believe one minute and not the next, lack of faith will extinguish the strength of faith. If you are confident in victory and yet you still fear failure, you will lose. If you say "I know" and still have doubts, you take a false step.

The Shih Oracle Sign describes the danger of *doubt* and the victory of *unity*. **You stand before a life situation that you cannot solve if you are disorganized.** Neither can you do it if you are impatient. You need persistence.

LINES

1. The army needs to parade in order. If there is no order, misfortune threatens.

There is no order if there is no shared goal and shared faith in the worthy goal. Many interpret the *lü* (order) character as meaning "musical rhythm"; in ancient times, military maneuvers were accompanied by musical movements. Music creates a higher level of unity than common principles. In the Eastern martial arts, the movements have rhythms and the battles have a mysterious beat. But whatever the fight, even if it is a business meeting or political debate, a sense of rhythm is vital. It is a far-reaching thought that says *that which is without music falls to pieces.* Here we are talking about the fundamental meaning of the whole Oracle Sign because something is started and all beginnings are decisive.

2. The army general's heart is in the right place. Blessings, no mistake. The king presents three fate gifts.

It was rather a loose translation of mine to say that the general's heart is in the right place. This means acting from the center. Such action is unselfish, pure, fate-like, and blessed. It is fulfilling. The "three" means a great amount that provides for everyone. It is good for musicians to follow the signals of a good conductor. Beneficent result. Good fate.

3. The army transports corpses in the cart. Trouble!

You stand to be defeated if you do not take the advice this Oracle Sign offers. The same is true if you have no general or if your general's heart is not in the right place. If you listen to your fears, your aggression, your bad memories, your instinctive urges from the past: trouble! A campaign with no leader may end in defeat.

4. The army retreats. Not a mistake.

It is wise not to collide now. It is not timely. Retreat is not defeat and may even be the first step of a future victory. Don't allow yourself to be forced into a fight. Deliberately avoid it. Do the same even if the opponent comes. (Think of the bull and the movements of the matador: it makes no difference that the angry bull charges.)

5. Wild game in the field. Catching them is desirable. Watch your words. There is no fault in you. The older boy should lead the army—the younger boy transports corpses; it is trouble to be persistent in this.

This is the turmoil of struggle. Each word counts—there is no hesitation. Either yes or no! The true command: precise and to the point. At times like this, there is a danger that urges and instincts will break out: trouble. Preserving a clear head, moderation, and calm in struggle: beneficent but difficult task. Panic and rush can only lead to trouble. In peace it is easy to silence the ego. But it breaks through in dramatic situations and it can't be slowed. A trained warrior battles like a good surgeon operates: they see, know, judge, and their hand doesn't tremble.

The opposite is true of an untrained fighter who loses their head. It comes out in this line how much of the whole Oracle Sign was successfully realized.

6. The Great General fulfills fate. He establishes a town and homes. Don't employ a common man.

This is the realization phase. Be careful not to fall at the last post. More things have failed in victory than in defeat. There are few who would not be ruined by power and who would retain their humility after a victory. It is then that most parties and good causes start to rot. Who do you listen to within yourself if things are going well for you?

8 ䷇ *Pi*

Holding Together

The character has two interpretations.
The first: two, together as if in a dance.
The second: someone stops, looks around, and examines.
He compares.

It won't work alone. We look for companions. This is the job of the Oracle Sign Pi. You have to find those with whom you can get along and with whom you can sail in safety on the sea of life that is often so treacherous and stormy. The reason I use this common comparison is because it is doubly valid. In the 8th Oracle Sign, the Earth is below with the Water above on which sailing is not without danger: the water is deep. Secondly, the condition for safe sailing is not only a devoted crew but also a captain who is wise, strong, and persevering in times of trouble. (This is the 5th line of the sign.)

The message of the Oracle is, **Togetherness is beneficent. Take another look at the divination to see whether it contains faith and perseverance. If yes: faultless. The ones anxious in their hearts gather from all sides. A person who joins too late will have trouble.**

The condition of every gathering is that someone should stand in the center point to whom everyone can relate. It could be a king. It could be a conductor. It could be a captain on a boat and it could be someone in you who is strong, directs, and to whom all your powers can relate.

The reason people today are incapable of creating a true community is because they are missing their own center. They are ruled by a different whim, desire, passion, ambition, and mood. One minute they attract, the other they reject; now they love, then they hate; today they hurt, tomorrow they regret, and they hurt again the day after that. There are many within us, but others cannot relate permanently to so many because if they approach us, they do not know who is in power at that exact moment: Beauty or the Beast? Have you got a center? If you have, they will gather around you. If not, you need to find like souls who have not been gathered by attraction and repulsion but by some kind of "director."

There can be many kinds of community. *Pi* originally meant "village community." But it can be any kind of collective that has come together as the result of a shared fate, plan, or spiritual connection. Hamvas says, "Our abilities intensify in real communities." And the same is true in reverse: our abilities deteriorate in sick communities. But however sick the world may be, and however incapable we are of creating and running a normal community—you still should try because it won't work alone. The Oracles Sign asks a lot of us, people of today, because we are community-incapable. It's what we long for but we are incapable of creating.

Togetherness is still in the early stages. Perhaps you will become suitable for it—but only if you give your love can others love you. Only if you find yourself can others find you. So, the first thing you have to do is to be "together" with yourself. It is now easier with others because inner harmony is strongly attractive. People happily join the strong. Everyone instinctively runs away from the weak.

It is time to get in tune. Because they don't let people into a concert who arrive late.

THOUGHTS

This Oracle Sign asks untimely things of us. It asks us to *love* one another. The word is not as Jesus used it but in a more modest fashion: show solidarity, stick together, harmonize with one another. We are people and this means that we do not knock together like objects, but we meet in body, mind, and spirit; all relationships are *spiritual relationships*, even those that concentrate solely on material matters and business.

It needs to be above the level of interests: moral, respect, admiration, togetherness, and trustworthiness—if this isn't there, then it is *inhuman*. The I Ching asks us not to be inhuman. Togetherness is beneficial. It is very rare nowadays.

Pi means an ancient village community. You would be hard-pressed to find a village like that now, where the neighbors don't envy or despise one another. There are few harmonious families or teams that would not be blown apart by interests or temper. Parties and sects can only survive for relatively short periods if they turn the energy of unreleased tempers outward and hate others. As we know from psychology, *they create an image of the enemy in the interest of their own cohesion.*

The hate of others is the best glue. The herd spirit is strengthened by the sense of threat. It is at times like this that those "come together" who have nothing to do with one another; if it transpires that there really is no enemy, they are at each other's throats in seconds. This is typically what happens to revolutionaries after revolutions. They fight shoulder-to-shoulder against the joint enemy but when the smoke clears and there is no one left to fight against, they are shocked to discover that they do not share a single ideal and that they actually desperately hate each other.

This Oracle Sign expects the strength of togetherness not from outer warring but from inner dignity and the recognition of our genuine humanity. This does not pass. Faith and persistence last longest in life.

LINES

1. The Honest and the True stick together. There is no mistake. The clay pot virtually overflows from it. It becomes more beneficent as fulfillment draws closer. The relationship weaves shared spirituality. This attracts great energies to itself. "Honest, true" (*yu fu*) means that there are no background thoughts; we also see each other with our hearts. This is the attraction of the center point. In the ancient sense, such association is supported by the high spirit world. Deeper collaboration can only be formed if the spirits are purified beforehand. The same is also true in physical reality. Before you join things together, they have to be cleaned—otherwise they won't stick.

2. Togetherness comes from within. Blessings. Persistence.
True coming together happens by itself—it doesn't need to (and can't) be forced. The inner connection is more important than any interest or superficial emotion.

3. You are together with those who are not worthy of you.
The need to belong somewhere sometimes gets you into unworthy situations. This is not your quality; it is not your community! If you have to remain among them, be guarded. A good relationship makes people better. A bad relationship pulls them down.

4. Also look for togetherness on the outside. Blessings. Persistence.
The 2nd line means "intimate" faith and this is public declaration. Here, togetherness is with the leader of the community. Not because of their power but because they are valuable and a human. It is common now that when people lose power and wealth, they lose "good friends" as well. Don't be subservient. The true sign of faithfulness is if one declares it in front of everybody.

5. Togetherness becomes public. The king only allows beaters from three sides on the hunt but leaves the game free to run ahead. The town's inhabitants do not need to be warned to comply. Blessings.
Only one who comes voluntarily belongs to you. No form of influence (cajoling, promise, threat, temptation, spiritual "influence," preaching, etc.) is appropriate. This is how a real community comes into being to which everyone belongs and in which they keep their own identity.

This is the secret of a complex harmony. A person who doesn't belong here should leave. "If you cannot love," says Nietzsche, "keep on going." This is how a good leader thinks about their community. The spirit world forbids aggressive influence. Béla Hamvas would say that a real community stands in the sign of freedom. This is true of a nation, a religion, a friendship, a marriage, or even a good football team. It is true of any good relationship to which a person belongs because they can give themself voluntarily.

6. Togetherness, without a head. Danger!

This needs no explanation: without a head a herd of cattle would drift apart. It would flee heedlessly. Projecting illusions, self-deceit, fears, ambitions, images of desire, or nightmares onto others—in other words, not recognizing that a situation is "headless." It is impossible to stay in relationships that have been cobbled together because they lead nowhere. You are shocked to find that you are sitting next to a driver who can't drive. If you are the driver, stop now! If someone else is driving, get out immediately! In psychological terms, this is a situation in which you have lost your head. If you do not see others clearly in a relationship, then you have confused illusion with reality.

The analogy that you can use now in every area of life is *without a center, everything spins out into nothingness.* Stars, atoms, plants, and animals all know this. The cells in a body know this as well if they aren't cancerous. The basis of the solution to the situation is try to find the center.

9 ⚏ *Hsiao Ch'u*

The Collection of the Small

Character: The Tiny—and the fertile earth
that collected from the mud of the river.

Hsiao means "collecting and taming." The thing that needs to be tamed is ambition and "I want everything right now!" The goal is already in front of you but it isn't quite as close as you would like. First of all, you and your surroundings have to become appropriate for it. Be tame, careful, and adaptable. You are driven by momentum, will, and the desire to create—but you need to tame all of these. Your strength is still too raw and especially too selfish.

The advice of the Oracle is **Avoid applying your strength as it would only be aggression and roughness or even worse, hysteria.**

Learn humility. The other meaning of *Hsiao* is "collection." A lot is made out of many little things. It is made out of perseverance. It is made up of what appear to be insignificant parts. "Even the longest journey begins with the first step," says the sage. Value the little things. Learn that the outer form is important, not only the inner spiritual. Take one step at a time. Your tactic should be soft, not hard. The certainty of a distant goal should not make you reckless.

This is a time of preparation. Be ready for everything.

THOUGHTS

A person who doesn't appreciate the little things, doesn't deserve the big things. The disciple greets a single plate of rice as if it were God's greatest and most marvelous gift. And that it is. The Mature Spirit knows that there is no "big and little"—everything is great. There are no negligible moments in life. Only the ambitious think that Life and Glory are at the peak and not in a march that takes one step at a time.

Before the creative forces take form, they go through slow and divine cell-by-cell growth. This slow maturation and gradual emergence are the essence of Hsiao Ch'u. You should not impatiently interfere with this process, although the inclination is there to do so. The great Yang forces need to be held back because they are still not balanced and are still arrogant, selfish, vain, and ambitious. All they can do now is make the situation worse and gather mainly bad karmas with the impatient greed of "I want." You still don't have confidence in this sign that God gives, and you say, "I'll take it instead!"

This is the sign of great preparations and great preparers; it is the sign of Moses who led his people to Canaan but he could not go there himself. And he knew that this was how it should be. It is the task of this sign to merge into the Tao, into the will of God.

LINES

1. Return to your own path. How could this be a mistake? Blessings!
When something doesn't turn out the way our ego would like it to, we feel an immediate urge to take the direction of our lives into our own hands. But we still hear the sound of our heart and we still know that the hardest road is our own. Our own path is the biblical "narrow path." You can only move forward on it by taking little steps, with humility and modesty. This takes you toward divine happiness.

2. They pull him back and he returns to the path. Blessings!
A person who is loved by God is kept on a lead. The lead can be many things: obstacle, shocking event, the example of others, a sign—"Not over there. Over here." It can also come as an inner voice that defeats temptation. What is temptation? In this sign, it means that somebody wants more and bigger—not what they deserve—that would be beneficial for them. We sometimes receive this and the previous line sooner than the temptation appears in our fate.

3. The spokes on the cart fall out. The man and the woman don't look at each other.
We underestimated the external obstacle or we overestimated our own strength. The secret of beneficent action is self-awareness and life awareness. This is what is missing here. Also, the experience of defeat does not force self-examination but self-blame or passionate self-accusation. Do not add to the mistake with a new mistake: do not take your bitterness home with you and do not project your mistake onto anyone else. Not onto yourself either. If you have aborted something, then work out the cause and make things better. If not, accept your fate.

4. Honest, true. The worry and anxiety cease. There is no mistake.
The first two words (*yu fu* in Chinese) do not only mean that you are honest and true. The ancient meaning is "united experience," the uniting of the conscious and subconscious, the outer and the inner; mainly that you have earned the trust of the spirit world. It means that you are open to the truth. You are not overshadowed by selfishness, self-deception, or ulterior motives; you are willing to help and ready for action. Ancient Christian tradition calls this "faith." It defeats all obstacles. Fear and anxiety only survive while their causes are in darkness. Darkness evaporates in the light of truth—a person who trusts is trusted by others.

5. Honest and true. Holding hands. You are rich in companions.
Here, yu fu covers others. Nothing is yours, it's all shared. We live for one another and not for ourselves. Here, the "collection of the little"

means sharing; the taming power of the sign tells us that there is no "mine" but only "ours." Life is not a monodrama but a game with many players. All together. It is a rare moment when not only we, but also others, realize that we live for one another and salvation is only in cooperation. Finding a companion or companions in the dark is the greatest mercy. Give yourself—this is the first step.

6. The rain begins and stops. The power has collected. If the woman stubbornly continues: trouble. The moon is not quite full. If the noble of spirit continues: bad luck.
The result has been born. The little has been collected. Be grateful and satisfied. If you long for more, then you will lose what you have received already. A person who forgets about modesty in the moment of victory and hopes for much more than they received will lose themself.

10 ䷉ *Lü*

Treading Carefully

Character: Someone in shoes takes careful steps.

You are advancing on the path of your fate. You fulfill something step by step. *Lü* once meant a pair of shoes in which one "took steps" toward their higher goals. But how? The 10th Oracle Sign has the weak Lake Kua above the strong Creative—what is more, there is only one single Yin line in the whole of the Oracle Sign—and so the advice here is directed to the weak on how to behave in the face of the strong and the powerful. *Behavior* is decisive, although instead of such a passive term, I would prefer to use the word *self-direction*.

The Oracle says, **He treads on the tiger's tail. It does not bite. Success.** It is from this sign that *courtesy* was born, which is a term that is hardly known today. It means that everyone has a "court" that I do not blunder into. I am tactful, I respect the other person's social and human rank, I do not want to force them out, I do not want to take their place, I do not want to "tread on the tiger's tail," and not only because I am frightened of it but also because I respect it. Be careful, tactful, and respectful.

In the world of qualities, genuine ranks do exist. Today's world is full of careerists and usurpers—these are the tigers. They are not the noble ones but the bloodthirsty kind; there is nothing more dangerous than if your superior notices that you also want to build a career. There is no more courtesy in today's world, only a smile forced onto our faces.

It is rare today to possess the inner conviction that I do not look up to someone because they are socially high up or they have more money but because I consider their human spiritual value to be greater than my own. You can only follow someone with this approach. This is on the condition that you want to be more and to be more valuable.

If you only want to make a career, then—according to the I Ching—you will tread on the tiger's tail and it will bite you because you do not represent higher values but only your puffball ego, and this attracts ugly karma. You can only upset world order for a short time; it has a self-purifying law that pulls the climbers to the deepest depths.

THOUGHTS

The reason that the Oracle Sign encourages caution is because there are great, creative energies at work. Other meanings of *Lü* include "fulfillment," "happiness," and the track that the stars follow in the sky—also there is the joy of the one who follows their own path; this can all be interpreted *if you can handle great tension*. It is like working an electrified system; you have to be aware that your situation is *not without danger*. The knowledge of danger does not mean fear but rather caution. In fact, you only have something to fear if you are not aware of what it is that you are getting involved in.

You can insult a lot of sensitivity, respect, self-awareness, and even arrogance, conceit, and vanity now simply out of a lack of caution. That is why it is advisable for you to learn to recognize not only what lives in who, but also what you are doing with others. Insult, hurt, condescension, humiliation—you can inadvertently do all of these things if you overstep the boundaries of courtesy.

According to the ancient approach, each human being has a "court" that they live in the center of. Approaching someone well not only means not rushing into their estate but also not going to the boundaries of my own "court" either. Current law states that you should not plant a tree within a certain distance of your fence. Divine order is very much the same. The secret is not about keeping to the set distances—this is just formality and false courtesy—but that *I respect the being and the spirit of the person who lives in the center of the court.* Not that which they have made (we hardly have any "merits" that would deserve respect), but that which hides within and about which they may not even know. Respect of another person is respect of the God that abides within them. The basis of courtesy is self-awareness. You have to first value yourself—my behavior does not depend on what others deserve but on what my norm is.

In martial arts, your master would advise you to play. You should preserve your relaxed, flexible, playful movement—do not be afraid and do not make your opponent think that there is anything to fear in you. It would be too early. You have to apply disciple tactics: this is the only chance that a warrior has when faced with a stronger opponent.

If you apply the appropriate tactics of the Oracle Sign, **you will become stronger and stronger.** You will also become a "tiger."

(I once asked my spiritual Master to send me a message. He sent me this Oracle Sign with no changing lines. Its meaning: "Follow me like a weak man follows a tiger. A good pupil is a rare thing nowadays. They lack respect, devotion, the desire for knowledge, and childish joy. You all imagine that you know better and you step on the tiger's tail. If you want to be a tiger, do not drive right over me, but follow in my tracks. Follow me.")

The Oracle Sign says, **be careful, do not leave the trodden path, and put up with the "bad nature" of others. Move one step at a time with joy in your heart. The weak will defeat the strong.** The Oracle Sign promises success.

LINES

1. You are advancing simply. No mistake.
There is no ambition, dissatisfaction, or agitation within you. Your inner being leads and that is why the size of your steps is not important,

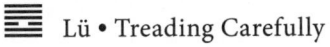

and neither is it important what other people say; the important thing is that you are following the right path. You are taking little steps in the right direction. This is no problem if alone.

2. *You are moving forward on a smooth, straight path. Persistence brings salvation to the lonely.*
If you live in the world, it is as if you don't live in it; the dark and troubled powers of society do not affect you. You follow your own path. You do not give in to temptation and vanities that would cause unnecessary complication. Keep following the middle way.

3. *You can see with one eye; you can walk with a limp. You tread on the tiger's tail and it will bite. Trouble! You fight like a soldier who fights for his great general.*
You are also weak and you badly estimate the situation; this can only lead to embittered struggle. You cannot see yourself or your surroundings: do not collide! It is better that you should collect your strength. Also see more clearly. Upliftment is not the same as overconfident struggle to the top.

4. *You tread on the tiger's tail. Defend yourself and you will finally achieve salvation.*
The situation is difficult but you already know that you do not have to win with force but with understanding. You are already strong within but don't take advantage of it. You can reap victory by being soft, wise, and compliant. The way to defeat a tiger is to tame it.

5. *Determined step. Persistence in the knowledge of danger.*
This is not a moment for recklessness but for brave deeds. The mind and the eye are clear now; you know what you face, what you are risking, and what you want to achieve. You have to act here. You know what to do. The only thing you have to remember is precise timing—not too soon, not too late, but exactly then.

6. Inspect your progress, successful if you follow the path of your ancestors. Exalted salvation if you return.

Today's meaning of the line is perhaps this: you can know a tree by its fruit and a person by their deeds. You can already see what has only been ripening up until now. The situation promises fulfillment. The original meaning of the line is different: The True Man follows the path of the ancestors. This is a path leading upward. If you follow this path, the blessing will return that once blessed your ancestors.

Today, the common man panics in frantic attempts to shake off the past, forget the old, and deny the ancient—and wants to start something completely new. Only a religious person feels—if indeed they do still feel—that the deeper one looks into the past, the more genuine is the faith that they see. Dedication, devotion, truth, and transcendence were at one thousand degrees in the time of Christ and since then they have been getting cooler, fainter, and hardening into an increasingly empty form. Ancient man saw encouragement in this line that he had not become unworthy of his great ancestors. What he received in return was not something new but something ancient: fulfillment returns again and again at every turn of the spiral.

11 ䷊ *T'ai*

Blossoming (Harmony)

Character: Man swims in the flow of Eternal Change.
In harmony with the Tao.

Everything blossoms in time. When the Creative and the Receptive are in harmony with each other, the signs of blessing appear in all areas of life: plenty, peace, fulfillment, prosperity, achievement, and good health. There is a blessing on all who attain **harmony** with the will of God. At times like this, we do not struggle against the flow but merge with it and swim together with it. As in a fast-flowing river, the riverbank seems to fly past; we only need to take one stroke and we cover great distances because our power is in line with the power of the river.

Harmony occurs when your deeds are helped by heavenly Power, the spirit world—in fact, at times like this, the human world isn't hostile either. This is the time of blossoming in nature. The Oracle says, **Blossoming. The little leaves, the large comes. Blessings! Success!**

Today, we become intoxicated and rejuvenated by spring blossom; we awake and are overcome with vibrant joy and enthusiasm—even the blood runs more swiftly through our veins. In ancient China, blossoming meant prosperity and the quiet calm of **peace**. When we swim on the waves of Tao, nothing happens because nothing is ours: everything belongs to the Tao; we belong to Tao, body and spirit; success

151

is not ours either and even the flowers ripen the fruits of the Tao.

Kuo tai—ming an is a proverb that is many thousands of years old: "If there is prosperity in the land, the people are peaceful." "Prosperity" does not mean the cancerous wealth that we know today but the prosperity of the blossoming cherry trees. This is not individual greed but the result of the endless flow of heavenly bounty. *Tai* means that you are now "together" with yourself; your subconscious is with your consciousness. Your ego is gradually softening, giving way, and moving further back. It does not demand, it does not implore, and it leaves you to receive what you truly deserve.

In your first flush of delight, you think that your plans are working "all by themselves"—it is easy to become lazy in this force field— and that is why all of the lines encourage you to work on harmony. Peace needs to be preserved—and since we are people, and everything is transient, we need to create the state of harmony over and over again. You still need to "swim" in the current of the Tao. Your inner harmony is also reflected in your human relationships. Harmony has magical power. The mere presence of the harmonious personality purifies, cures, orders, and creates.

I feel that **this person doesn't want only for themself.** More precisely, what they want they also want for me, for themself, and for everyone all at the same time; they want what the Universal Spirit wants. It is possible that something new is beginning in your life. It is also possible that you will find new allies. Not only internally, but you also meet with external and stimulating surroundings.

THOUGHTS

T'ai is one of the most promising Oracle Signs. Still, we commonly experience this as if nothing were happening—and it is only years later that we recall it being a beautiful period in our lives. In today's topsy-turvy world, agitated and insatiable people associate happiness, well-being, and success with the roar of an orchestra or posterlike life situations: millions, billions, houses, holiday homes, cars, popularity, lovers.

T'ai means "peace." As Jesus said, "Even the greatest riches of King Solomon are unable to compete with the lilies of the field." Behind the beauty of the lily lies the work and the blessing of the eternal, divine being. Solomon's riches are hard; they are the transient riches of the human condemned to death. True happiness is when we don't even notice it; it is just like health, clean water, beautiful landscape, a laughing baby, a gentle and well-intentioned smile. Happiness is natural.

In Chinese, *T'ai* means "more, the most." There is nothing more than this. God loves you and provides you with what you need. And it is as if the din has grown quiet around you, selfishness and aggression became tamed. Appreciate it when people are showing you their better side. Don't keep bitter judgments within yourself.

Practitioners of martial arts unanimously claim that they are significantly stronger when in the state of Tao than at other times. They become mediums to universal forces. Modern athletes use the modest but true term that they are "in form." This naturally needs to be made the most of, such that neither aggression nor arrogance shatter the harmony.

You should know that what you now possess is everyone's. We can only use the wind wisely if we know that it doesn't only blow for us.

LINES

1. If you pull out a strand of grass, similar ones come out with it. Embarking is beneficent.
Mao is not a common blade of grass but a dense grass with which simple and pure-spirited people roofed their houses. This is not time for turning inward but a time to act. You find companions. The darkness lifts and like-minded people recognize one another in the first light of dawn.

2. Bear the uncultured. But cross the Great River and do not postpone your deed even if your goal is distant and you are left with no companions. Yours is the glory if the Center leads.

This is the time to act. You have to set off and in order to reach your distant goal, you have been given the following "tactical" instructions. Let your efforts be directed by the attraction of the goal and not because you want to escape from your current situation. Do not create the impression that you consider unworthy the bank that you are now leaving. Your goal is far away. It is important that you divide up your faith and strength well. Many are left behind on the path of your fate and you are joined by new companions. There are some who go and there are those who stay. Your compasses should not be desire or ambition but the view of the Center; let the calm and certainty of living your fate be your guide.

3. All flat stretches are followed by inclined slopes. All departures are followed by returns. A person who is persevering in hard work: faultless. Don't worry; the visible and invisible world will help. Don't lose your faith; there is blessing in deterioration!

One who is led by the Center cannot be swayed by the intoxicated joy of success or the bitterness of failure. Carry on going even if it is hard. There is blessing on your efforts and help is at hand. The line speaks to the person who starts to lose their faith in repetitive, hard, and mundane work. This period is also referred to as spiritual low tide. You should know that this is a regular phase of all fulfillments. It is the low tide that comes before high tide.

4. Fly, fly. He is still not rich: perhaps in time with his fellow man. Not a warning. Follow your heart's desire!

The lines have numerous interpretations. This is the image of a bird flying from the nest that still doesn't dare to fly free. There are those who say, "You are too much of a dreamer, stay on the terra firma of reality." There are those who say, "Lean on your companions if you are still too weak." There are those who say, "Don't boast but share what you have." This is what I see in it: "You are stronger than you think. Trust in yourself and in spiritual help. Better late than never."

5. *Emperor Ji gives his daughter's hand in marriage. Blessings and exaltations.*
This motif returns in the 5th line of Kuei Mei, the 54th Oracle Sign. The emperor gave his "Fulfilling" daughter's hand in marriage below her station but he commanded her to look up to her husband and give him the respect due to a husband. It is from this wise modesty and humility that the dynasty was born that went on to create China's golden age. This sign not only includes Taoism but also the essence of Christ's wisdom.

Follow the example and your desires will be fulfilled. He who is down rises—the great man's place is *down*. Today people don't understand that *modesty* is not simply a form of conduct that can be chosen at will but perhaps the largest *upward force*. It is invincible. Unbeatable. Unshakeable. Fundamental. There are no modest people today and humility is nothing more than hypocritical role play. This is why we do not know the real, cosmic strength of humility.

6. *The city walls fall back into the ditch. There is no need for an army. Make the proclamation in your city: what happens is fate. To carry on is shame.*
Accept that this is now your fate. Do not rebel or object because this will only increase the problem. Trouble can take many forms—you should know that it is fate. Your own "city" is the inner part of your spirit that is impenetrable. Retreat to this place of safety while the storm blows over.

12  P'i

Stagnation (Disharmony)

否

Character: A mouth saying, "No!"

P'i is the opposite of the previous Oracle Sign, T'ai. T'ai is blossoming, fertile, and harmonious—Yes. P'i is stagnant, barren, and disharmonious—No. The two Kua—Sky and Earth—move away from each other. At such times **things get stuck, stop, and start to rot.** Nothing works that is beneficent, noble, or good. This is the time for the worthless and the bad and all that breeds in the dark with no spirit. The worthless are above and the valuable are below. Historically, this is when the reign of terror of the lower ranks becomes complete: in all this bad, the only thing that is good is that everyone is corruptible. This is not the time to implement noble plans.

The message of the situation is, **Stagnation—because of inhumanity. The test of the True Man. The large leave and the little come.** Don't do anything at all now, just preserve yourself. Your only task is not the realization of your dreams, your plans, or your ideas but that you should protect yourself. From what? From the loss of your faith, strength, and stature as well as depravity, corruption, and corruptibility. The present situation does not favor humanity.

If you want to achieve something now, you will greatly regret it later on. You would have to sell your soul to the devil. It is better to wait.

Be careful; if you can, seek links with those who have also chosen to preserve their humanity and have no relationship with the "order" of the current world. This would only be an interest group but of the bad kind: the mafia. It is sometimes called a "party" or a "sect." The previous century offers numerous examples of what the world will become if it is ruled by bad people. I say this because the meaning of the Chinese terms *fei jen* and *p'i* is "evil, bad, ignoble, and unhappy."

There is rarely trouble with principles. The problem is with the people who serve them badly. If a person is not "good," the most sacred of principles will rot if such a person represents it. Tradition judges based on the essence: the "ism," the religion, the principle, or the doctrine you describe yourself as following doesn't matter, **but what kind of person you are. Good or bad? Dark or light?** Darkness rules in the time of P'i. You should not get used to it or adapt to it to any great degree, because the darkness will pass and you will be left dirty, unhappy, and lost.

The Oracle Sign wants to save you from unsuccessful conflict and especially from later blaming yourself. Wait for the atmosphere to change. In the meantime, familiarize yourself with this Chinese proverb, *P'i zsi T'ai lai,* "Blessings come from misfortune; Blossoming comes from stagnation."

THOUGHTS

The time of P'i does not favor any form of realization. The Oracle Sign gives advice on how to deal with this state. Its answer is a radical one: do not take part in it. Wait. Preserve yourself. It is hard to do this nowadays because if the period lasts for any length of time, we are forced to create some kind of deal with the system in the interest of survival. The question is to what degree. The point is that humanity should not be hurt. If you can, do not take part in anything and if you can't, then at least do not give your soul to anything. The atmosphere is tempting, deceitful, and restricting. It is definitely fate. Continue to quietly mature your plans and wait for better times.

Practitioners of martial arts avoid conflict at such times. You are also told that your opponent who has been "abandoned by the spirit" uses base and underhand methods. P'i has no morals.

LINES

1. Pull out a blade of grass and similar blades of grass come with it. Steadfastness brings blessings and success!
Companions also appear in negative periods. There are others who are preserving themselves and waiting for better days. Take their hand. These are meetings that will ripen the future—they are behind the scenes for the time being. There is another piece playing on the stage.

2. Carry what you receive, hidden inside yourself. Only the route of common people is open—there are obstacles in front of the True Man. Success!
"Carry within you" (*pao* in Chinese) depicts an embryo in the womb. This is the blessed new arrival that quietly hides and ripens within you. Wait. Leave swift success to the common people. This is their time.

3. Bearing shame.
Do not take a step because you will regret it. Think it through again and clarify the cause of the confusion, uncertainty, and doubt. *Pao* means inner "carrying"; it has nothing to do with anybody. The times do not favor shared feelings. *Hsiao* (shame, regrets, and guilt) means that the questions within you or in others have slowly matured to the point where the mistake is recognizable. This means a slight "reserve" after blindness and inhibition—and this is the precursor to change. Don't break a stick over others, nor over yourself.

4. A person who fulfills his fate does not make a mistake. The careful nurturing of fate leads to radiant fulfillment.
The deed has arrived. The outer and the inner coincide: the worthy are helped. "Nurturing" (*chou*) means something similar to when a person

tends a garden. It is not a one-day job. To go from stagnation to blossoming is a process.

5. *The time of disharmony slowly passes. Blessings for the True Man! He doesn't forget that everything is transient! He ties himself to a mulberry branch.*
The true man is the most careful in the moment of success. The mulberry branch (*shang*) is the symbol of inner peace and calm. In the same way that loss does not break it off—victory does not blind one who acts from the heart and fulfills the will of fate. Success is only long-lasting if we accept it wisely.

And another thing: all difficulties that we experience only have meaning if we preserve their lessons within ourselves. Trouble is not just there for us to escape from but also for us to experience its secrets and the outer and inner tactics of defeat. The common man does not learn from individual or community tragedies, and that is why he constantly repeats them.

6. *Disharmony reverses! Stagnation passes—joy appears.*
Blossoming begins. Jung recognized and used the ancient thought in his healing; when something reaches its peak, it switches over to its own opposite.

13 ䷌ *T'ung Jêng*

Fellowship with Men

*Character: Mouth in a house, under cover. This is the sign of
unspoken agreement. And the picture of "man." We speak of
a village housing a number of souls, in Chinese it is measured in the
number of mouths. The principle of community comes from here.*

This is a time to be with others and to be together. The fate task is shared and this requires a whole . . . a community to be created. The advice of the Oracle is, **Fellowship with men in the open: success. Beneficent to cross the Great Water. The persistence of the True Man is beneficent.**

There are many types of human community: nation, family, joint business, army, party, religion, town, society, and so on. But whatever form of "union" comes together in the "diversity," the ancient teaching says, **"The foundation of all genuine communities is communion with God."** If we have no shared reference point above, then below, "horizontally," we cannot agree with each other for any length of time.

Animal herds are held together by instinct, but a community of people is only held together by the Spirit—and if this isn't there, the whole thing disintegrates all by itself and is destroyed by uninhibited selfishness. It is no surprise that shared faith is the strongest cohesive force. Nations are born together with their world of faith. If the strength of this world weakens, then they also lose their contact with God, the community dries out, degenerates, breaks down, and eventually disappears from history. Relationships based on interests are perishable and short-lived.

This Oracle Sign says that your fate task has to be solved with others (shared life goal). It is possible that others sense this too. You have to come together. Harmoniously. If this is successful, your powers will combine and even the most daring undertakings will be successful.

The first secret of creating harmony: you have to sense and you have to recognize what you have in *common*. What is the same or similar; what is spiritually and philosophically alike? This is the point at which you will resonate with each other, where your strength will multiply and this is where you can retreat in the event of disharmony or initial discord, like a safe island in a storm. All real communities contain a sold **center**, a "touchstone," where, if we touch it, our hate vaporizes, our selfishness quietens, the peace of togetherness returns once more. This is the **Love Point.**

There is always something in the other person that can be loved, and if we rediscover this, like a magnet, it pulls us together from disintegration and the whole can be created once more. In essence, all true communities are based on love—the musicians in an orchestra have to love one another, at least for the time that they play together. It is possible they hate each other after the concert—but while they are in the music, the music is in them . . . they have to be together like lovers. They love music and each other. Music is a shared "god" for a good orchestra and if musicians create communion with it, they will also be in harmony with their fellow musicians.

"If two of you come together in My name: I am with you!" This is the mystical, Christlike meaning of this Oracle Sign. If there is no shared spirituality, a real community is not created. The other secret sounds like this: **Burn along with the Fire: this is the image of human community. The True Man classifies nations and differentiates**

between beings according to their nature. In other words, the other secret of Unity is **Diversity.**

It does not mean kneading everyone into a mass dough (as communism imagined the world) but preserving everyone's individual face, dignity, character, abilities, beauty, and individual and special talent. No two leaves on a tree are identical and yet—and that is why—it grows so large. Where we are all the same, we will be strong; where we are all different, we will be rich. This is also true of a good football team: there is a shared team spirit, a shared goal and an "all for one and one for all" faith—and this is accompanied by eleven players of completely different character and talent who would perhaps not get along at all if they were to meet in everyday life.

The psychological goal: **the creation of our inner unity.** People are more volatile, more passionate, and more hysterical in this sign. All the Yang forces can only be brought together by the light of self-knowledge. Nothing instinctively, everything consciously. The forces of the spirit are brought together by recognized life goals. A person who has no goal falls to pieces. But everyone always has a life goal; at worst, they are not aware of it.

THOUGHTS

"Today's man," says Béla Hamvas, "is not mature enough for a community. . . . The titanic 'I' in every man does all that it can to break down community." We experience this every day. Our ego is overdeveloped to the degree that we are incapable of genuine community life. Yet this is still your task. The answer to your question is to *cooperate with others.* You have to recognize that this is about something shared. We have to come to terms with each other's fate.

The Oracle Sign is encouraging. It offers success and tells us to get stuck in because the situation is promising, but that is only if no one has an attack of egoism and breaks the unity. And something else, the human community in question is beyond all group interests.

For people to meet "in the open" means that neither interests, nor prejudices, nor worldviews, nor religious affiliations come into play. God is not a protestant God or Jewish God, but the Eternal One, the Tao. And that is what I relate to and that which *I can love* in all other human beings. The fact that two people are the same religion does not mean that they would be able to live in a genuine and sustainable relationship with one another. This would only be possible if they were to meet one another at that point where no type of interest or "conviction" of the ego operates.

The story of Romeo and Juliet is about how a genuine communion of fate is created between two people in a world that is completely incapable of forming one community. This is not necessarily a love story. I experienced a number of incidents in World War II and the 1956 Revolution when people held hands who would have possibly been enemies in everyday life. They also often die side by side like Shakespeare's heroes.

What we have to realize in T'ung Jêng is that **this is about shared fate**. It is about a task to which not only I but also others have to contribute: **the goal is shared**. The individual lines deal with the extent to which the ego (selfishness, individual stance, formation of factions, and lack of openness and devotion) is able to obstruct harmonious cooperation.

LINES

1. Meeting beyond the gate. No mistake.
You have to open it. You have to step out of your closed world. This is the first condition for you to be able to meet companions.

2. Meeting (tsung) with clan spirit. Shame.
The word *tsung* originally meant the interest alliance of a tribe, family, or race. But it can also mean that certain doctrines or beliefs bring people together. Self-interest always lies behind the workings of such

"communities" and that is why, sooner or later, they are shamed. Such "clans" always live in opposition to others. Whatever lies they may tell, such groups are not led by the Spirit (the Tao) but greed and the instinct of the "Darwinian human beast": taking from others so that I (we) can have. It is here that egoism forms factions and divides the community. It also often deceives itself saying that it has a right to do so—because it is right. It isn't right! Just like a human spirit, a community can also assimilate with itself. Typically, everyone loses but especially the one who initiated the assimilation.

3. He hides his weapon in the undergrowth. He climbs a high hill. He does not rise up for three years.
This is a familiar situation in party politics: distrust and cunning try to topple the strong leader. It is too weak for this but it succeeds in dividing unity for a prolonged period. Commentators call for calm. Don't rebel.

4. He climbs up the high city wall but can't attack. Good luck!
This is the chance for making peace after the successful revolution. Dividing walls still exist between us but there is no longer any war and this is an opportunity to create harmony. Neither aggression nor cunning will upset unity; everyone knows where their boundaries lie and they do not step over them. They perhaps even respect the boundaries of others, and this is a great thing. There is need for an ideal community for self-defense and self-defense by others.

5. Those who belong together first cry and then laugh as the soldiers of the army are brought together by the bitter battle and the joy of victory.
It is a common theme for many a folktale that the boy and the girl come together after a long, hard struggle. There is a need for the struggle. We realize afterward that it was fate. You have to struggle to achieve true harmony. This line says, "Fight because it is worth it." And even if you sometimes despair, do it anyway. The joy comes from the recognition that "we belong together."

6. The community in the meadow. No regret.

All communities that are not based on universal love are mere shadows of their genuine counterparts. But this has to be accepted. Nothing on the Earth is perfect. Something is always missing: the "golden age" that has sunk to the depths of our soul. All of our relationships only work on certain planes. This is the same. No problem.

14 ䷍ *Ta Yu*

Great Harvest

Character: The "Great" Sign and next to it a hand that wants to hold the moon.

This is the time of great harvest. It is the time of great deeds, great achievements, great energies, great "ownership," abundance; it is the realization of everything that has become ripe. The strength of the Sky is below and the intelligent light of Fire is above; the enormous power advances consciously and solidly toward its goal and it reaches it. Today, *Yu* means "to bear, to own, and to be"—but its ancient meaning also carried the warning, "Do not let the wealth and glory go to your head, you cannot hold the moon." *Yu* also means "harvest." *Ta Yu* means "Great Harvest." This is the sign of great success. The secret is that you should accept it with humility and not get intoxicated if your dreams come true.

The advice of the Oracle is, **Fire in the Sky. The image of the Great Harvest. The True Man defeats the bad and helps the good. This is how he fulfills the glorious will of the Sky.** The Oracle Sign does not, however, give advice on how you should achieve your goal. It considers that you can do this and that you have sufficient energy.

The True Man knows that blessings come from the sky and although he does everything he can, he knows it is not only for him. Fulfillment (success) is the moment of self-awareness. The "bad" (*wu*) that has to be defeated is a character that shows a cramp in the heart and a man's innards become all twisted and tangled because he has eaten far too much. Be careful if you achieve success because you may become ugly! Avoid greed. The Sky ripens the thing you desire, but the most important thing is that you too should be ripe. If you are ripe, you know that nothing is yours. Earthly life is not yours either.

You now receive in abundance—accept with humility. Remain calm and do not lose your clear vision.

THOUGHTS

When a person knows what to do, and has the strength to do it, all that has been ripening so far comes to fruition. In martial arts this is the Great Action. It promises victory as long as you "don't fall in"—this means that you think you are terribly strong and you forget self-defense, relaxation, the fundamental gentleness of your being, and you fall into the trap of aggression. This "falling into the action" is certain loss. Begin but do not become hot-tempered. Head for your goal but keep your head.

If your fate presents you with something, you should know that you have become "well off" and **now you can do for others and for everyone.** A person who shoves their hands in their pockets commits a sin, primarily against themself. A person who receives but does not give, "the well-to-do who does not do" but instead "pockets" the blessing, prepares their own fall.

My greatest recurring fault is that I always become helpless in the moment of success. It was often taken from me.

LINES

1. He has no connection with the harmful. No mistakes. If he prepares for hard and difficult work, he will remain without fault.
The beginning of a great undertaking. If you count on difficulties, you will be successful.

2. Take it with a Great Carriage! Go toward your marked goal. No mistake.
You are carrying a lot and traveling far. Your task is great. This is about spiritual treasure and the reserves of benefit. We have some values from which we live throughout a lifetime. Such is a faithful companion, a dependable friend, or the knowledge that we have gained.

3. The prince makes an offering to the Son of the Sky. The common man cannot obstruct.
The good, achievement, and success that you gain is not yours—it is God's. And since you know that, you have no selfish, ulterior motives; no bad will can stand in the path of fulfillment. Do not listen to anyone and don't allow anything to divert your efforts. We want to pull down the great—this is the instinctive intention of the small and untalented. They cannot hurt the truly great—only where they too are small.

4. Do not exploit your power (peng). No mistake.
The peng character shows that someone is beating their drum too loudly. This is about temptations that come from the vanity, arrogance, and the will to win that say, "I am right!" Let others shine. One who is truly strong sees clearly. Clear vision is the foundation of modesty and modesty is the foundation of true greatness. So that you understand well: modesty is not only an attractive human characteristic that is terribly disadvantageous from the aspect of victory (as it is seen today), but also the manifestation of the greatest Power. The other advice of the line is do not wish for too much. This is for others.

5. Your inner truth and dignity affect people. Blessings!
The line promises success. You radiate from your center, the spirit world supports you. And this is felt by those with whom you share fate. Chinese commentators also say that you should not overstep the center; if you are too friendly or too direct, you lose your dignity, which may not only damage you but also the matter in hand. The other advice is keep your spirit relaxed so that you are prepared for a sudden change of

events at any time. Do not prepare for anything in advance—you will solve it if it comes.

6. *You stand under the protection of the Sky from the very beginning. Blessings and great good fortune.*
There is a blessing on you and on your work. We tend to see this as the ripening period of our earthly life but it means more than this: it is a shield against the dark forces of the dark world. The meaning of this line would be clear to us if we could see the wonderful work of the invisible world. Be grateful for everything.

15 ䷎ *Ch'ien*

Modesty

Character: A mouth—and a hand that unites and divides
stems of wheat, equally. Its meaning: man justly measures his
internal affairs and this manifests itself in his outer life.
"The mouth speaks from a pure heart. I show myself as I really am."

The *Ch'ien* name is only similar in sound to the 1st Oracle Sign, Creative. Here it means "modest" "humble," "respectful," "selfless," and "obliging." Your task is now to become **selfless**. Whatever you asked, you can **solve it with modesty**. People don't really understand this today and they didn't much understand it a long time ago either.

"You, wash my feet?" a surprised Peter asked Jesus. And then he shouted out, "Never!" And Jesus answered by saying, "What I do, you do not yet understand, but you will understand in the fullness of time." Peter took the pattern of Greatness from the puffed-up ego. He thought that the Master, the Head Priest, God was "up above" and like an earthly emperor, shone in unapproachable pomp. He could not imagine a true king kneeling before him and washing his dusty feet and drying them with the fabric of his own clothes. He did not understand that "who is the greatest among you should be like the smallest." This thought is not only alien to us but we see it as unabashed hypocrisy.

What we do not know about real humility is that Selflessness (humility) is a magical act. The amount by which a person ends the rule of the ego within themself is the degree by which the atomic force hidden in their spirit begins to radiate, and a lonely, little person will become a divine being with cosmic power who lives with the power of the Whole and glows with its light.

If Jesus had been the slightest bit arrogant, he would not have been able to fundamentally alter the history of humanity, and no one would be speaking of him any longer. A person who humbles himself is exalted. This is the basic teaching of Christianity, Taoism, and the I Ching itself. In martial arts, the selfless person is literally invincible. This is not only because they see clearly and are led by intuition but because they are powered by the atomic force of the Universe rather than their "own battery."

What you see today is false modesty, false humility, and hypocrisy. The puffed-up, vain, and power-hungry cunning game of the ego not only deceives the world but also itself because it wants to get its hands not only on the money, the power, the success, and the recognition— but it also wants the type of glory reserved for "good people" and saints. While it stuffs the money in its own pockets it tells you that modesty is strength. While it stomps on your head, it tells you to stay nice and humble. Uninhibited selfishness likes to appear in the guise of modesty (Pharisees).

The Ch'ien Oracle Sign is about **genuine selflessness**. Here, a person is completely clear about their own merits. Christ, while washing Peter's feet, knew and even said that he was the Son of God and that greater glory awaited him. The modest and the falsely humble are differentiated by genuine self-awareness. A modest artist, if he is dedicated to his art, dares to announce that he wrote his works into the cultural history of man and that "I am going to teach my whole nation." But I have to add that a person who is truly modest does not consider it important that their name should survive.

The Oracle Sign advises you to **stay down and you will rise up**. If you are up, do not celebrate yourself, always step back and down—if you are down, find deep meaning in service. Get to know and value your own values—be neither servile nor your own unjust judge—and do not expect recognition from anyone. If you should happen to receive it, say thank you and that is all.

Do not take glory from people. They are not able to give what they don't possess in the first place. All praise is empty. That is, unless it comes from God—but this praise comes from within. The greatest things are born down below in quiet, deep, and humble devotion. Modesty is the birth mother of the greatest achievements.

Many famous and over-celebrated, fashionable "world stars" have said that they owe their values to the modest and conscientious period of their lives. Their success ripened in the deep and if they are not careful, if they are blinded by the bright lights of success and lose their modesty, they will deteriorate both spiritually and artistically. This is not a moral question but the fate-like workings of the dynamics of being. It is called karma in the East.

THOUGHTS

The Oracle answers your question by advising you to **work modestly, "selflessly," humbly, and conscientiously; in this way you will reach a shining future in silence. This is not time to harvest but time to sow.** The problem lies in the fact that we do not know what genuine modesty is. The word is surrounded by lies—it needs to be purified. The sage says, **Mountain in the Earth: That is the image of modesty. The True Man reduces what is too much and increases what is too little. He measures, considers, and balances them.**

If you are modest, you do not fear failure and victory does not intoxicate you. If you are modest, you do not concern yourself with the reward for your deeds; the deed is a joy to you in itself. You serve not like a servant, but more like a king; you do this not out of weakness, cowardice, or helplessness but out of courage, strength, and talent. You give your all if need be—but you will not allow yourself to be exploited. You give strength to the weak and you break the aggressive. You are not humble when you allow yourself to be humiliated but when you stand up for the cause with which you have been entrusted.

No one is born humble (selfless). You can only achieve this with a great deal of work as well as self-awareness, life awareness, and with the continuous yoga of "consideration." Consideration means that there is puffed-up arrogance, the desire for power and selfishness on one side—and on the other side, there is humiliation, servility, and hopeless exploitation. **Humility is in the exact center where there are none of these things**, only dignity, freedom, and the sense of divine unity. In the final analysis, humility was lost by everyone in the Garden of Eden and left there along with happiness and the Eternal Tree of Life—and that is why it is the most difficult thing to understand.

If you do not want it for yourself, you will receive it. When? If you really are modest, you know the answer: when the time is right. Let me give you an example: A mother asks how she should relate to her daughter who she really loved and was constantly worrying over because she had a difficult life, full of struggle. Furthermore, her daughter never took her advice.

The advice that the I Ching offered was the 15th Oracle Sign, Modesty—with no changing lines. The interpretation: Be *selfless* with your daughter, put an end to the selfishness in your love, do not fret over her and allow her to follow her own path. You gave birth to her, but she is not yours but God's. Entrust her to him. Love her—not with the smothering embrace that keeps her a prisoner of "you are mine" but *modestly* and *selflessly*—with plenty of love. The mother took the advice. This not only changed their relationship but also the girl's fate. Her wings really did grow.

The ultimate meaning of Ch'ien is **that is yours which you place on the altar of God.**

LINES

1. The modesty of the True Man is also modest. He crosses the treacherous Great Water. Blessings!

Do not look for reward or loss, just do what you do "precisely and beautifully just as a star moves in the sky." A person who swims in the flow of Tao, has no obstacle before them—because the Tao will either avoid or overcome it. Whatever you are in, whatever you have begun, keep on going with selfless, pure faith. Obstacles only pile up in front of our ego—not in front of God. If you preserve your selflessness, the difficult will appear easy.

2. Manifesting modesty. Steadfastness is beneficent!

Out of the abundance of the heart the mouth speaks. The religious meaning of the line is that your prayers are heard; you ask for good from a good place. Its everyday meaning is that your surroundings react to the message of your feelings, thoughts, or unspoken words. The *ming* (manifestation) also means the "crowing and chirping" with which birds call and recognize one another from long distances. Say what you want! Give voice to your feelings and the thoughts of your heart. The crowing of modesty can be heard at the greatest distances. And they answer it.

3. The True Man completes his most difficult task with humility. Blessings!

The first meaning of the line: however severe and difficult your task, carry it out because you will reach your goal. If you are a True Man, they will help you. The forces that radiate from you will also mobilize others. The other meaning of the line refers to unselfish conduct that directs the True Man: what he wants he does not want for himself, and this radiates from him. This is why others help him and stand alongside him so that he may help them to fulfill their own fate tasks. The divination is only valid for the True Man within you.

If you are only motivated by self-assertion, then you can count on something else.

4. Appearing modestly. Nothing obstructs advancement.
The situation is favorable. It is a fertile period. Selflessness can make a person "invisible" but their deeds are visible. If you have to wait, keep on waiting, and if you receive, give thanks to God and keep on going. A truly *selfless* person acts for the sake of the act itself rather than for the result, being happy that they can do this. This is why they are not impatient and the praise doesn't go to their head.

5. If you are not able to do it on your own, do it with others. This is now the time for action, struggle, and discipline. Nothing can stand in your way!
A person who is falsely modest dares not act because they are really weak and afraid. A selfless person, on the other hand, who does not act for themselves, is capable of enormous acts. This is about false and genuine humility—because the situation can only be saved with genuine humility; *this is not submission but conquest.* The humble also fight sometimes and when they do, the Sword of Truth gleams in their hand. Gather strength if you feel weak because you have to act. The answer to your question depends on you. Grow up to the task!

6. Manifesting modesty. It is beneficent to set off on a campaign and to create order in the city after the victory.
Here, as with the second line, the cock is crowing to give a sign to his companions: the moment of the great deed has arrived. Order is not restored and darkness does not pass all on its own: *you have to fight for it to happen.* The "capital city" (*i kuo*) can be your own spirit where you have to break the rule of your ego with self-awareness and self-discipline. But it can also be on the outside. For some reason there is need for action, for shared effort, and a "crusade" for the good and the beneficent to appear.

In martial arts, this is the moment of togetherness before the final victory. The battle has not yet been won. Whether you finish by "stepping forward" or "stepping back" is insignificant. The inspiration of selflessness whispers and tells you what to do against the dark forces of the dark world. The meaning of this line would appear before us if we were to see the wonderful work of the invisible world. Be grateful for everything!

16 ䷏ Yü

Enthusiasm

Character: One hand reaching out and giving something—
and a dancing elephant.

Spring is on its way! Lightning breaks out from under the earth—devotion finally gives birth to the long-awaited liberation. This is the birth of Joy. All joy is "liberated" joy—at times like this fear, hopelessness, and the anxious cramp of "I" falls away. You become enthusiastic and you enthuse.

Opinions are divided as to the meaning of the sign of Yü. There are those who see it as meaning Enthusiasm, Joy, and Self-abandon. Others see it as meaning Enthusiasm, Preparation, and Care. The double meaning of Yü apparently stems from the image of the elephant. According to Master Huang, in the southern part of ancient China, elephants were reared to bear heavy loads—while at night they taught the elephants to dance to give joy to people with their jolly tricks. (Apparently, King Wu very much liked the elephant dance.)

The sage says that the ancient kings praised God with music in the sign of Yü and gaily celebrated with their ancestors. Music was sacred in ancient China; it was also strictly restricted. It was forbidden to play music that would have broken the universal harmony. Only that was allowed which was directed upward. Because **it is only possible to**

enthuse in a positive direction: upward. Not downward, because that is recklessness, intoxication, chaos, and loss of self.

I think that both views of the Yü sign are true. Invigorating emotions do lead to great things. Shared joy and ecstasy bring people together with each other and the invisible world. It is the miracle of music, dance, and theater that it brings us together. We step out of the armor of our solitude and experience joy together and our problems and fears evaporate and leave us floating, and it seems as if everything is possible. It is in such an inspired state of "holy madness" that great deeds and works are born. In the psychological sense, this is about combining energies that reinforce one another and the strength of overflowing emotions.

What are missing at such times are foresight and the calmness of the head and the mind. The music not only makes you happy but also *light-headed.* It makes you irresponsible. When we are enthusiastic, we can throw ourselves into anything without having given it sufficient consideration. Dictators, success-hungry politicians, and artists as well as advertising people know this only too well; they long for devotion and that is why *they want to influence.*

The devil offers the same thing as the angel: "I will liberate you from your fears and fulfill your dreams." This is why the sign of Enthusiasm warns you to employ Sober Foresight. **You should know to what and to whom you give yourself.** Enthusiasm is a great thing. There is only one thing that it lacks, and that is wisdom. That is why it can lead to great works, great achievements, and shared successes as well as failures, scandal, and shocking events. The *Ninth Symphony* was born out of enthusiasm as were many revolutions with noble aims—and millions have also been murdered and sacrificed their lives for false beliefs; they have sent people and driven themselves to extinction while marching to anthems about which they blindly enthused.

This is why Yü advises to **call helpers so that your armies may gather.** Prepare for the dance. Gather your strength and knowledge so that when life gains pace, you are ready for action—and do not nurture dizzy, stupid ideas.

THOUGHTS

The Oracle Sign indicates caution, but it is encouraging. Joy and enthusiasm come along with something new that you have been waiting for. Either you are attracted to the enthusiasm of others, or others resonate to the enthusiastic joy that comes from you—things always go more easily at such times because the energies combine.

The secret of enthusiasm is that borders that would otherwise divide people burn away in its flame. The shared strings resonate in the spirits of people of various and different habits, approach, educational level, age, and character. It is a fundamental truth that a great theater needs a great audience—this is the teaching of Yü.

A good leader is able to enthuse. This requires knowledge of the feelings that lay dormant within people. What enthuses? The fact that fear and anxiety fall away from you. Or, the same thing, you free yourself from the pressure of mortality. At times like this, you feel that life is not just painstaking, bitter wandering but also *flying*. But where to?

Yes, this is the other secret. You catch a glimpse of the encouraging future. Not with your eyes but just with your spirit, you sense, you feel, and you smell. There is the Shore. I can smell its scent! The promise of a happy future is there in all enthusiasm. This is accompanied by the possibility of liberation, when the tight handcuffs of problems and the everyday fall off you.

You have to prepare for the glorious moment of enthusiasm—like a gardener for the spring.

You have to prepare to fly upward and not be senselessly intoxicated. The aim in martial arts is absolute spontaneous action. The involuntary act—when the tiger swipes with its paw. There is a **risk of thoughtlessness** in this sign. The fact that something is not well thought out does not mean that it is spontaneous.

LINES

1. Chirping enthusiasm. Trouble.
The image of the chirping bird (*ming*) symbolizes boasting, the aggressive message of the ego, persuasion, and self-promotion. It is an influence that does not sense what is going on in the spirit of others.

2. Solid as a rock before the day comes to an end. Persistence is beneficial.
Your heart is in the right place. Before you are caught up in the heat of the moment, you should know whether it will fly or fall. You know if something enthuses you, whether it will be met with harmony or dizzy chaos. It is here in this line that Confucius gives one of the the fundamental phrases of the Oracle: "Knowledge of the shoots is a divine ability." The future can be seen in the invisible, spiritual seed. Before you are carried away by the passion, the fever, the enthusiasm, or any kind of emotion, there is a quiet, meditative moment where you decide "should I get involved or not?" If you are already involved, then it is too late. Here, you are still calm—often for just a moment. And that is why your decision will be correct. You either enter a pleasing dance or no dance at all.

3. Doubting enthusiasm brings sorrow. You will regret putting it off.
Self-confidence is lacking here. You don't know whether it will be good or bad. Should you dance? Shouldn't you dance? Do not wait for your happiness from others—it is within you. Do not confuse the boring sobriety of the mind with wisdom. The sages like to dance and laugh.

4. The source of enthusiasm. You will achieve great things, have no doubt! You unexpectedly find companions.
The source is your heart. You are enthusiastic and you enthuse others. You direct the dance and those gather around you who feel the same. Nothing is impossible for genuine enthusiasm.

5. *Illness. Keep on going, it isn't fatal.*

The situation is depressing. It tests people. Now you need to be led by deep, inner faith rather than enthusiasm. You need to be a long-distance runner. Do not be worried that you have insufficient strength. Don't give up. Keep on going. (Faith is ten times stronger than enthusiasm and one hundred times stronger than Strength of Will—you should think of this when you feel as if you are exhausted and simply can't go on.)

6. *Dark enthusiasm. How far will you go?*

The "dark" (ming) may be an illusion or false belief—in other words, it is not down-to-earth enthusiasm. Return to your own path. Instead of deceiving yourself, live your own fate to the end. It may be difficult; it may be easy. It doesn't matter. You will see in time that this leads to genuine joy. It is called fulfillment.

17 ䷐ *Sui*
Following (Adaptation)

*Character: Footprints following one another.
Master Huang sees a royal procession,
others see besiegers surging,
one after the other up the side of a castle.*

Sui, the 17th Oracle Sign, is the Arousing under the calm and joyous Lake: **follow your star!** If you feel the urge to follow your own head, don't do it. Stay calm and adapt to the demands of the era. "The true ruler serves" is the paradox of this sign.

The "exalted success" of following is in enduring service; it is in joyful service; it is the magic of selflessness. It is the secret of true greatness and effective spiritual action. Jesus Christ washed his disciples' feet. He said that he had come to serve and this is how he became a ruler. Lao Tse says, "Knowing of our strength and being weak, knowing of our greatness and being small is to possess the Power of the Valley. This is how the Spiritual Man rules."

Today, in the age of immeasurable arrogance and egoism, we believe that this is all hypocrisy. We think that the Pharisees deliberately lie and you are stupid if you believe them. We think that the more inflated the ego and the higher someone clambers up the human pile, the more successful, effective, and great they are. This is what dictators think.

We should realize at last that these are all failed lives gone to nothing and drowned in shame!

True greatness works from the **bottom up** and always **follows** something or someone. A great person is always down and looking up. A musician follows a conductor, a conductor follows a composer, a composer follows inspiration, and inspiration follows divine beauty and harmony. If it works in reverse at any point, it will not be art but pitiful and conceited display. Jesus stated that he wasn't acting "of his own accord"; this is how he performed miracles.

Following means follow your principles! Follow the more you have within you. Follow your inspiration, your dreams—but be suspicious when you think that you know everything best of all. Be open upward. New times are on their way; don't let the past pull you back. And be adaptable; know what is timely, where people are in their lives, and where and when they can be called upon.

You do not speak to "simple" people "simply" because you grandiosely condescend to them but because you are no different from them. Do not consider yourself more than God who could turn into a frog, an ant, a blade of grass, a leaf, a docile calf, or Everything. He hid his greatest secret, that the real creative influence works **from the bottom up and the inside out.**

A careerist doesn't believe this, and that is why he fails. A careerist is someone who clambers ever upward over the head of others and is finally confronted by his own nothingness. He reaches the top and bursts. We do not usually see the pitiful endgame of a careerist's life because we only follow that life on its successful upward arc.

Listen constantly to the word of the new times in the Sui sign. You sense what is in the air at any given time and what the beneficial wind direction is and, if you are not self-willed, you also sense what is good for others. Not "commanded" but followed, you can direct events and this means that you can achieve the greatest results with the least stress. The fact that a sailor constantly adjusts the sail according to the prevailing wind does not mean that they take their eye off the goal. Follow your goal and adjust to the fair winds.

THOUGHTS

There are two wills within us all. One is the ego and the other is the will of the Higher Self. One says, "You only live once. Quickly take advantage." The other says, "You are a spiritual being on an eternal path. Do what is beneficent and good." A person who is driven by blind will lives their *life*. A person who is driven by Real Being will live their *fate*. These two wills are in constant conflict in us all without exception. This is the fundamental cause of our agitation, tension, and unhappiness, and a great many mental and physical illnesses.

The Sui sign message is, **Follow the Higher within you. Follow the divine. Follow the spiritual**. We sometimes simply say, "Listen to your better self." A person who does this has all tension cease within them. They experience incomparable calm. This is why the sage says, "The Spiritual Man calms down at dusk and rests."

We can neither calm down nor rest because we would even take our guilty conscience, inner debates, and our fears to a desert island. The secret of peacefulness is to *follow* our own fate. "Returning to the origin is no more than calming down," say Lao Tse. This is returning to the origin or the divine center point. It is only possible to calm down in the will of God. *We call this fate.*

If you do not live this, you will be careworn. Agitation is a certain sign a person has not given themself over to that will. The uneasy eye, the grabbing hand, the disturbed breathing, and a restless mind all bear witness to the fact that *a battle is being fought, a continuous inner struggle, and it is uncertain who will win.* If someone says that they believe and are still restless, then they are tricking themself.

In response to your question, the Oracle Sign says, **you are walking on the path of your fate—follow it**. The success or failure of this is reflected by your state of calm or restlessness. A person who follows the path of fate is calm. A person who follows the path of "self-will" is disturbed.

In this sign, we realize that our fate does not work in a straight line but follows a zigzag path. This is why we need to adapt to sudden turns. The secret of adapting in this way is not to desperately insist on anything, to be able to start anything all over again. Prejudice, fixed ideas, overly clever plans, or established habit does not obstruct from "turning your sail" at lightning speed if needed. In martial arts, this is the tactic of the follower. He does not oppose his opponent but adopts his movements, merges with him, and eventually throws him off balance.

LINES

1. Break away from your office (social situation). Your path is free! Step out of the door to your home and mix with others. It will have a good result.
Something is beginning. You have to break away from old habits, expectations, and positions—especially the false belief that "this is my life." No! Open up to others. Open up to new opportunities, new plans, and new people. Your approach has become outdated. The line describes power change and often not outside but inside, in the heart. If you can do it, you will be successful.

2. He insists on the little boy—loses the man.
You are listening to your worse self, not your better self. You are following the easier path. Instead of growing up, you are letting yourself be carried along. The "man" is our grown-up divine being. He is the creator of fate. He is the strong one. The child is weak, immature, defenseless, selfish, and frightened. Modern psychology says that most people—symbolically speaking—do not let go of their mother's apron strings their whole life long. They do not grow up. They depend on others. They cannot give and they always want to receive and they are not free for one single moment. This line speaks about this problem. "Do not mix in bad company!" says a commentator and this is not social but also spiritual advice. Good should be followed. We should follow our true, strong nature and stop all the self-pity.

3. He insists on the man—leaves the small child. If he does this, he will find what he seeks! Steadfastness is beneficent!

This reverses the previous situation. I leave the lower quality for the higher quality. It is not easy and requires courage and persistence. Man battles to grow but this is the only way to become tall, this is how he fulfills his fate plan. In order to reach my goal, I have to become more appropriate for it. This process is taking place now.

4. You follow something to catch it. Trouble if you continue like this. Follow yu fu, the path of merging into Tao and your meaning becomes clear. How could this be a mistake?

Sometimes, we manically pursue our goal like a blinded hunter after their prey, we don't look around but forward in the direction of our desire—and we get into trouble. We fall into our own trap. *Yu fu* means "merging." It means adapting to life's current. It means adapting to others and to the times. It means adapting to our inner selves, to outer demands, and to the advice of the high spirit world. The True Man lives in unison with himself and with the world. This is yu fu—together with the Whole. This is not tunnel vision.

In the martial arts, the frantic desire of the will to win cramps the combatant. He slows down, his attention narrows, and if he doesn't free himself of his insane desire, he runs into defeat. A person fights more successfully who is more open, a person who is freer.

5. Following the good makes you excellent. Blessings!

The artist who follows their inspiration, the disciple who follows the master, and the person who follows their star will all be happy. Do not want the good, want the best!

6. He finds attachment and holds on to it. Royal sacrifice in the Western Mountains.

This refers to the sage in the absolute sense who rises above the commotion of the world. But he returns and he helps those who respect him and follow him with his advice. This is the helper and adviser with no self-interest. The everyday meaning of the line is realize that you are responsible for others. There are those who look up to you and for whom you are a role model. We are all "masters" somewhere; if for no one else, then for our children. They are always one rung lower down on Jacob's ladder and they can only climb further up if you offer your hand in help. We are sometimes surprised to realize that we live for others. Not in part but completely. We no longer need to live—the reason that we remain is because of others. This is also possible. (My grandmother lived much longer because of our family and mainly because of my mother.)

18  *Ku*

Work on the Spoiled

Character: Maggots in the holy vessel.

This is a halted, rotting, grubby situation—but at the same time, encouraging. The hexagram of Ku, the 18th Oracle Sign, is Wind below and Mountain above. This needs the first five lines to do a great amount of work.

Man has adapted to a bad situation, his true being has been suppressed, his freedom smothered, and he is now helpless because the past has become built into his being and bears down on him with paralyzing weight. Childhood traumas belong here just as much as the other recollections of our past; the psychology deals with these "maggots" in its entirety. The sins of parents continue in their children.

There is a library full of literature on how images projected onto pure and defenseless souls of children turn into characteristics later in life. And not just a parental home but a sick society can also make the spirit "sick"; we adapt in fright to the conditions of life and if they are inhumane, then that is what we more or less become.

The cause of my problem is not fate—it is the result of human error. It is possible and vital to free yourself of it. Not only for myself but—according to the wisdom of the I Ching—also for my parents. If I change myself, I also change them and I liberate them in the spirit world from their already undeniable guilt. The past can be overwritten. That is the magic of the present. What you change now also changes the past. It does not change the event that actually occurred but the oppressive memory. This is burning the "shoots."

Rotting is not met with such disgust in esotericism as it is in the sensual world; it is the condition of all rebirth. The shoot pokes out from a rotten seed. It is bad to experience but unavoidable as an alchemical process. It is only unpleasant while you are in it, while you live together with the old self and the associated rotting memories and are still unable to come away from yourself.

Find the cause of your problem, the oppressive memories originating in the past, the source of the poison that you have imbibed—and free yourself of them. You stand before a new spring, new undertakings, distant horizons. Shed the paralyzing load of your past. The correct strategy is to recognize the "maggots" that are hidden within you. Deliberation before the new birth—and deliberation after the new birth. The first is necessary because it is not possible to separate the rotten old and the clean new just any old way. The other deliberation is needed because the new shoot needs considerate and wise attention.

This is then a forthright and inspiring action. You stand before a fundamental and good turn in your fate—if the alchemical process is successful. Do not make it lost by seeing the situation as hopeless— do not rush the transformation. Be patient with the "deterioration" of others; give them time and do not pass judgment on them.

The thing in the divination to have "spoiled" may be a friendship, a life plan, marriage, spiritual problem, or rotten plan. It is not certain that the shoot of the problem is in you. It is possible that the drama of others is now yours—for some deep reason it is still linked to you and is yours.

THOUGHTS

The present is a magical time. Everything that you once lived, experienced in this life or any one of your hundreds of thousands of past lives, all the way back to the big bang is Now. Your desires, your wants, your plans, who you want to be, and all your future events all the way to the salvation are Now. Now is a window on eternity. A person who awakens to this will be free. A person who does not awaken will be dragged helplessly by their past: their life will be directed by mental and physical "conditional response."

The message of the Ku Oracle Sign is **the age of spring after a dormant winter.** You have to put an end to corruption, paralyzing emotion, and fate-ruining thoughts. Spring shakes up the sleepy, paralyzed states. You have to shed the damaging influence of the past.

You can only begin with a clean sheet. This is true not only of renovation of our spirit but also of our lives, our relationships, and our fate situations. Do not continue to pass on your "paralyzing genes" because of your weakness, obstinacy, and helplessness.

The True Man sees rotting as the encouraging herald of spring, and this is why he encourages and enthuses all around him, like Jesus or the apostolic teachers of ancient Christianity—shed the old man so that the New may be born.

This is a fetid and bad situation in divinations that can not only be improved but may also precede a great future. Better to encourage those around you than to accuse them.

LINES

1. Repair that which the father spoiled. The ancestors of the genuine son will all be immaculate. Danger and blessings in the end.
This is about the patterns that we have inherited from our fathers and the society of our fathers. The list may be one of hundreds—everyone knows what a bad inheritance is that has to be escaped from. Damage, in the wider sense, was caused by either too much or a lack of power, discipline, or hardness. It can be repaired with brave confrontation. The I Ching sees us as not only the victims of our parents but also as their possible saviors, whatever their sins may have been.

2. To put right that which the mother spoiled. Obstinate persistence is not correct. Find the middle way.

Too much or too little love, care, and protection is that which the "mother" may have spoiled. Dependence and weakness results in a situation in which it is difficult to become a grown-up. In a wider sense, this also includes us becoming too bogged down in material matters; we have to fly the nest into the clear sky if the time has come. The home of your spirit is up above. Our real being does not originate in material nature.

If you asked for a divination for an event, find the heart of the problem first. Do not continue—you cannot see clearly. We see a situation clearly if we also see ourselves in it clearly. Too much softness and compliance caused the corruption—when someone "lets" it be so.

3. To put right what the father spoiled. Small regret. Not a big mistake.

The intention is good but the power and the momentum is too much. I can sometimes be insulting, but goodwill makes it easier to forget this impatient and slightly aggressive tactic. You need to work on the spoiled not suddenly but continuously.

4. Putting up with what the father spoiled. Continuation leads to shame.

If you have realized that it is not good, free yourself from it. Living a cowardly, defenseless, and helpless life together with what is not good leads nowhere. Be lord and not slave to your fate. (Unfortunately, as few awake to themselves, most people helplessly repeat the mistakes of their parents. Socially we tend just to change costumes, fashions, and techniques—the "sins" carry on.)

5. Putting right what the father spoiled. Man meets with encouragement.

It is no small matter to recognize the mistakes of the past. But neither is it enough. An image of the future is also required. The encouragement comes partly from others and partly from above. Each little sprout about to be reborn has a "fairy" that helps it open up from the winter slumber. It still doesn't have enough strength, but it gets help.

6. He does not serve kings and princes. He has higher goals.
The "real Man's" goals are beyond the current social, political, or economic goals. The "real Man" serves God. This is not only as a priest or as a monk but as a father, mother, teacher, poet, worker, peasant, or farmer. The Eternal Man awakes in you in this line. Not the "great" but the real, the spiritual. From here on, I do not ask what my father, mother, those around me, or the whole world say to my deeds—but what is said by God, who, the poet claims, "leads from within."

19  *Lin*

Approach

Character: A leader directs the masses.
He supports and makes those below him great.

Good times are coming. The time of uplifting and fulfillment is approaching. **Something significant is ripening**—something new. You see that the Yang force in the Oracle Sign is rising upward—and the dark force of Yin is decreasing. Here the "approach" is happening from the bottom upward and from the top downward: someone *rises up* from below, becomes increasingly light, and gains more strength, ability, power, and opportunity—and at the same time, a person who stands high, *comes down* in empathy, like a good leader who uplifts, loves, and raises those below them; like the angels and the masters who tirelessly help; like the good teachers who make their pupils great.

The message of Lin is, **Approaching has exalted success. Persistence pushes forward. The trouble can come in the eight months.**

The "eight months" means the autumn that follows spring. It is the wilting that follows blossoming. It is the fall that follows a rise. The sage advises that fulfillment is ripening but don't rush it. *Do not be impatient and strive to get to the top too early.* And especially do not allow early successes to go to your head. What you receive, see as a gift.

You are on the right path—in the middle—if you stand above both bad and good. Do not be dizzied by fortune or misfortune.

We achieve success via conscientious, devoted, and humble work. But when we do achieve it, we easily forget about everything. We become arrogant, bigheaded, greedy, and dissatisfied. The ego wants even more, it wants to fill all its pockets like someone who is only able to harvest once. We are nervous that everything will not be ours and it is because of this fear that we lose everything. Don't make this mistake.

God gives and God takes away. You are most probably going to receive but if you trample on the gift, you will lose that for which you received it; you will lose your freedom, your inner peace. Do not become dependent on the outside world. Success is within!

THOUGHTS

The sage says, "The True Man teaches to think tirelessly. The True Man defends and accepts everyone." This is how you should approach others. Good and bad come and go in life. Good comes now and then a worse period may come along, but what is unchanging and eternal is that the True Man learns from everything and continually teaches—even in the moment of his death. Tolerance knows no boundaries. God's menagerie is great and all the beings in it are different but they all deserve love and are all under his protection.

This phrase is often embraced by those leaders who have made their businesses blossom. The obstacle to fulfillment is ignorance and incompatibility. The two are related. A person who understands otherness is wise. The sign of the True Man in you is that you want to know and you make those around you know and anyone and everyone, without exception, come under your wing. First you love them and then you teach them. (Avoid teaching without love. This is just agitation and that is harmful.) When people sense that you understand, love, and protect them (often from their own stupidity), then they happily learn from you and good feelings turn to knowledge. Great achievements need knowledge as well as "positive" feeling. You not only need to feel but also know what and why!

Sometimes, when I accepted people as they are, life blossomed all around me. This is not about tolerance, it is not about putting up with them, but the fact that I *understood* them. There is an enormous difference between putting up with someone and understanding and loving otherness.

Practitioners of martial arts see the chance for victory in this Oracle Sign. That is why they pay constant attention to timeliness. The approaching triumph does not make them grow too bold. They leave it to ripen with a cool head. They do not grow dizzy in the growing positive opportunity, and they wait for the best possibility. And afterward, they do not get lost in the victory delirium. (I have often ruined a promising situation by becoming too enthusiastic too early on!)

The bottom three lines talk about how you can help the result to unfold—the upper three talk about how you can become the master of the ripening situation.

LINES

1. Meeting approaches. Persistence is beneficent.
Things that belong together come together. That which ripens has many planes: cooperation, association, a good relationship with myself and with the spirit world. Ripen yourself and persistently ripen others.

2. Meeting approaches. Blessings. Everything is advantageous.
An inspirational influence, relationship, opportunity is ripening. Bravely take advantage of it. You still cannot see what twigs and branches the tree of your future will have, but the situation is encouraging. If a person lives their Fate, it is not a question as to what is favorable and what is unfavorable—because there is nothing more beneficial than carrying out our fate.

3. Sweet approaches. No direction is advantageous. If you are sad because of this, it is not a mistake!

Sweet on the outside, bitter on the inside. Do not get stuck in the approaching situation however good, sweet, or advantageous it may appear. Even if it is painful, subdue the temptation and carry on. The true goal is much further away.

4. Fulfillment approaches. No mistake.

Pay attention: the peak is approaching. You know what you have to do and do it. You don't do it for yourself. Be open to yourself and to others.

5. Sage approaches. Characteristic of the Great Leader. Blessings.

A wise person is one who is not just led by emotions and intellectual "information" but by the Center of clear-sighted being. They know who they trust and they entrust this person to organize their shared affairs. A "good" leader can be determined by looking at their colleagues and subordinates. You can only be master of your fate if you know what your fate is. You can now reach the point where you want to be, because you can see what is correct and incorrect—you can see the consequences. This is also the point where you can answer for those who were "placed under you" by life.

6. Magnanimous approach. Success. Faultless.

You eventually understand people. You see not only their egos but the divine heart of their being and their fate. At such times, whatever we do is just. You know what you do and you do not do this just for yourself. Fulfillment. Share with others what you receive, whether it is of spiritual, mental, or material value. The magical power of the magician is for others; that is why it is never lost. Do not forget this!

20 ䷓ *Kuan*

Clear Sight (Attention)

*Character: A bird takes a "bird's eye view"—
and the ancient symbol of Vision.*

You have to see what you are doing and why you are doing it before you act. Your task is to see clearly, impersonally, and free of prejudice. See yourself, others, and the formation of your fate as they really are—look as if you are able to see with the eyes of God.

We are always looking through some kind of spectacles. We see through the spectacles of our selfishness, desires, hopes, fears, inhibitions, expectations, subjective prejudices, and mainly our lies and self-deception. This is the time to free yourself of all of these. See Reality before you take a single step. See what it is *really* all about.

Who are you? Who are you talking to? What is the story about? What do you really want and why? Which is your true path and which one false? Look at everything now as if it were for the very first time. This is how you can free yourself of what is now unworthy of you and that you have grown out of—this is how you can set off on a new path on which you will not be led by your illusions but your vigilance. *This path is called Fate.* Before you take a single step, you have to see the *true perspective.* You still don't see it—the Oracle Sign warns you of this— but this is the time for you to see it at last.

The message of Kuan is, **Clear vision. Wash your hands before you bring a sacrifice. He who takes the true path is looked on with respect** (the path of the holy spirits).

In order to see the everyday message of the Oracle Sign, you have to understand its spiritual meaning. A Tao temple is called *Tao Kuan*. This means "Place where I pay attention to the Tao." The secret of Taoist meditation is nothing other than **Attention.** I pay attention to my breath. I pay attention to the flow of energies. I pay attention to my thoughts. I pay attention to my spirit. I pay attention to my life.

Buddha's reincarnation (Avalokiteshvara) was called *Kuan Yin*. This means "He listens to the voice." "Meditation," he taught, "is nothing more than paying attention to the inner-outer voice." The monks rhythmically hit a wooden fish while singing and reading sacred texts. The eyes of a fish are always open. It always Sees and this is the symbol of vigilance.

And now comes the everyday meaning of the Oracle Sign: *clear vision* means that you are not mixed up in the world. You do not identify with anything, you only see. You see like seeing a view from on high, or like the map of your journey. You can see where the paths are, where the obstacles are, you recognize the hidden connection of your fate and from now on it cannot happen that you say, "Forgive me, Lord, for I know not what I do."

The clear-sighted person not only follows the right path but also has a mysterious effect on those around him. He looks from within and his sight is not only pure but also terribly strong. It isn't weakened by any kind of selfish emotion or thought. Whoever he looks at, he can also see their weaknesses. You cannot hide from this. That is the strength of the penetrating stare that has no fear.

This phrase takes us to the martial arts: the first step on the road to victory is to know your opponent and their strategy—and also yourself, of course. The good warrior sees their own faults and strengths in all their glory. However dangerous the situation they find themself in, they are in a constant state of attention. The good warrior sees clearly when they attack and also when they are being attacked.

The Oracle's answer to your question is *take a good look*. Look as if this is not about you, as if the whole thing is happening to someone else. This is all you have to do. Then you can take a step. This is what this Oracle Sign encourages you to do . . . perhaps this is because it "sees" that you cannot see well, and you do not know that you do not see clearly.

THOUGHTS

True attention comes about if you silence your ego. The view of the ego is confused, disturbed by desires, fears, ambitions, and false beliefs. The ego does not see what is there but what it wants to see. This later turns out to be illusion, which is not to say that it doesn't exist but that it is actually very different. The steps and path are not where our eyes project—we see a bridge over the ditch and as we are staring at the peak, we don't see the snake below our feet. Our knowledge of people can be seen as a series of misunderstandings; we are afraid of people we don't need to be afraid of, and we are not afraid of those who could do us harm. Since we do not come into contact with genuine people but rather the imagined version of them along with their prejudiced, idealized image or caricature, our whole method of relating to others is false. We do not speak to the person who is standing in front of us.

Attention is egoless. It is impersonal. I would see things just the same if I weren't in this situation and it wasn't happening to me. You cannot even hold a successful business meeting without clear vision. A person who truly sees is not afraid to see. A person who sees is not influenced by the hope of victory or anxiety of defeat because hope or anxiety would distort the genuine picture. The only one to see what is real and valid is God—it is surely why he is depicted by an open eye in a triangle.

The secret of vision is that it is active as well as passive. One is accepting-understanding vision and the other is flowing-creative vision. The most beautiful form of active vision is *teaching*. Teaching is nothing more than making others see. If you see, you become capable of opening the eyes of others.

And one more important thing: one who sees also knows that they are seen by others. People other than you can be just as good at knowing people. It is just as impossible to hide the secrets within yourself as it is for others. If you are afraid, they sense your fear; if you really want to win, they see that you are hungry to win, and already a person who is less afraid and for whom it is less important to win can move above you. It is always the one who is more relaxed, freer, and sees more clearly who has the advantage!

This Oracle Sign teaches you that a poker face doesn't mean a thing. Only the "poker spirit"—this means that a person is neutral within. They don't show their desires and fears and really are free of them.

LINES

1. Childish vision. No mistake for a common man—shame for a True Man.
If simple people instinctively follow the road seen to be good, this is not a mistake. It is childish vision when we accept something as correct because our parent says so or current social trends require it, or when our feelings link us to a religion despite us not knowing its teachings. This is not the path of your fate. The path of your fate is vigilance. You have to grow up and gain your clear vision. You do not really understand your situation. Your view is still narrow, immature, and childishly ignorant. Open your eyes!

2. Spying through the doorway. Favorable for a woman.
This is about your narrow vision. In the same way a "mother" only understands and sees of the world what is important in terms of her family, you also have narrow vision over short distances—you only pay attention to your own interests. What is beneficent for a woman is "demonic" for an adult man: this is not his Tao.

You do not understand the spirit of others, their feelings, or their thoughts—you revolve too heavily around yourself. A low quality of vigilance is allowable for those whose fate task is narrow and whose spiritual development is not high. Later on, narrow vision—always due to self-interest—can become suffocating. *Chou* means "demon," "possessed by a bad spirit," or simply "intoxicated."

Try to look at your problem with other eyes. This is the advice: open your eyes wider before you act. Perhaps you are not right.

3. Paying attention to what our life bears, we decide whether this is a period of retreat or advance.

Your clear vision is ripening. This means that you see more fully than through the spectacles of your selfishness. You are starting to see the *effect* that you have on other people. The outside world is a mirror. The best self-awareness is that you can catch a glimpse of yourself in the eyes of others. Beyond this, you are beginning to recognize the *sprout* of a situation and you are able to decide whether it should open up or not. Now you can choose. You are on the border of realization. Pay attention!

4. Paying attention to the lights of the city (the interest of the community). This decides whether or not you are acceptable to be a guest of the king.

There was a time when sages wandered from one province to another and they gave advice to the rulers. But they only took this job where they were able to help and where they could serve a beneficent aim. They carefully inspected the community, the task and the goal, and the heart of the Leader—and they only joined the good one. Do not be tempted by anything—only the genuine opportunity. *Pay attention to what they want to use you for.* Your values can make others more valuable—and if that is what they need, then help. But if they want something else from you, do not join because the city will not be light and you will be dark. Pay attention!

5. I pay attention to what my life bears. Blessings for the True Man!

I do not see myself because I look from within. This is the moment when I can take a look at my life from the outside, impersonally, as if this was all happening with someone else—as if I were reading a novel in which the hero had the same name as me. I see what led to here and especially the effect that my being had on people. I hadn't seen up until now. I thought that they "are like that" and that I don't have such a great influence on them.

Now I have to pay attention to how this whole thing works, and if I eventually understand this, I will not blame myself unnecessarily—because I repair where I can and I accept myself (and my fate) where I cannot. The greatest significance of such self-awareness is not that I get to know the hidden qualities of my body and mind but that *I get to know the One Who Sees all of this in me*. I get to know the Seer. From here on out, the key of change is in my hand, because the Seer gives advice and leads.

The response to your question is, **Pay attention and don't take a step! Only move if you can already see and you will not step blindly.**

6. *Paying attention to what life bears. The True Man is faultless.*

Now I see the whole and not only myself. This is impersonal attention. I experience this state if I write a drama. I experience all my characters. I am in their passions, their stupidity, and I experience their feelings and at the same time I see them from above *as if I see them, just a little, with the eyes of God*. I understand the connections, what they want from one another and what the whole shared play is leading to. At such times, the author sees fate's web—but not only the author. Anyone can look at their life like this and they will see what is happening to them and to all those with whom they share fate. You need this uplifted view or vision because you still do not clearly see your path! But you already suspect that this is not only "your path" but a whole network. *Our fate is not individual but a shared undertaking.* Karmas are connected and entwine in one another. If someone seeks the interest of others and not only their own interest, their life can fundamentally change.

21 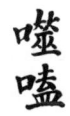 *Shih Ho*

Confrontation (Biting Through)

Character: A mouth and divine divination: man eventually gets to know the hidden truth. The other Sign: three jawbones move up and down like the lid of a pot. Biting through, chewing.

The moment of truth. You have to confront the cause of the problem and put an end to it. All problems have a root. It radiates in many directions and causes a lot of different problems—sadness, bad feeling, and anxiety—yet it all originates from one center of infection. This center is hidden. It is hidden deep down and is hard to find.

In the same way that long investigations discover that your general bad health is caused by one bad tooth—that perhaps does not even hurt—so it transpires that all the problems poisoning your mind and your life can be traced back to *one single root cause*. You have to discover it, recognize it, and put a hard and determined end to it. It will never go away on its own. So, the task is a double one. Ruthless self-awareness digs through layers of lies until it reaches the deeply hidden cause; when you find it, you see that "This is it!" And then you have to put a definite end to it.

The first part of the task is an intellectual, spiritual function: **you have to get to know something.** The second part of the task is a function of will and action: **you have to bite through the thing that is**

stuck in your throat. In other words, you have to reach unison between thought and deed. If you achieve this, then the Shih Ho sign promises success: **Confrontation–biting through: success. The justice system is advantageous (court case.)** The Shih Ho sign is familiar to modern psychotherapy. The ancient comparison says we reach the cause of the problem like chewing on the meat of hidden prey. We bite through deeper and deeper layers—of lies—until we come across the bronze or silver arrowhead that struck the animal.

In order to bite the Ultimate Cause, you have to "chew through" various self-deceits—the cause lies very deep down. The ultimate cause of our problems is that which we least suspect; we dare not think about it. A person does not "hide away" their sins and indigestible injuries in the subconscious because they are so afraid of them! One dares not "look them in the eye."

If we try to avoid something our whole lives, this is the exact drama of this Oracle Sign: **confrontation.** This requires something of which a person is only capable at the boiling point of catharsis—that is ruthlessness (not mercilessness, but ruthlessness). You cannot be "sparing" with an inflamed and rotting tooth. It has to be pulled out. There are moments when you have to judge. Judgment can be clear-sighted, wise, divine, well-intentioned, and just . . . there is only one thing that it cannot be: *it cannot be sparing* because you must not spare the center of the problem.

In the history of drama, this is the point when Oedipus blinds himself. He discovers that the sins causing the problem are not here and there in external circumstances or in his own, insensitive "soft flesh," but like a poisoned arrow, in his heart. This Oracle Sign says to you, "Here, at last, is the moment of truth." Now is the time to look where you have never dared to look before. Do not be satisfied with the truth; there is a deeper truth than this. In fact, **there is a Deepest Truth that you do not dare, or want, to admit to yourself.** Look into its eyes: what are you frightened of the most? And if you see it . . . if you really recognize it . . . then you can put an end to it.

We are happier at the deepest point in our soul—but only at the deepest point! Just a couple of layers up is the arrowhead that secretly stabs and poisons and makes our whole being sick. It has to be pulled out. The "arrowhead" may be a past experience, an unprocessed phobia, a fear, a lack of love, a guilty conscience, childhood love, reincarnation trauma, sins, the meanness or depravity of others. The I Ching does not say what it is, but it tells you that you are eventually in a state of mind and will in which **you can decipher all of this and even solve it!**

THOUGHTS

It may turn out that the obstacle that has to be "bitten through" is on the outside. We do not have to confront the truth, but we have to make others confront the truth. The ancient justice system is based on this sign. It is based on the unity of knowledge and strength. The law has to be *clear and understandable* while the judgment (punishment) has to be *definite and strict*. The point is to be sparing with people and ruthless with sins. There is a divine spark deep down in the spirit of the "sinner" and an originally good and indestructible Spirituality. The "sins" are identification with the darkness, loss of self when someone "knows not what they do." Punishments are for people and not against them.

The first task is clear vision. You have to see precisely what the "sins" are. The second is to find the level of punishment so that it isn't too soft or overly hard. This sign requires *strength*—the only person capable of this is the one who has defeated their own demons and experienced where the border is between compassion and judgment. In martial arts, this is the *iru* moment when a warrior penetrates the opponent's center point and personal force field that is seen as being impenetrable.

LINES

1. His shoes are trapped in stocks and his toes are in them. No mistake.
Small sins, small punishments. Just enough to ensure that it doesn't go on like this. If you nip a problem in the bud, it cannot set down roots.

2. He bites into soft flesh and his nose disappears. No mistake.

This is a situation when someone is too strict. The ancient rule of rearing (rearing yourself) is that overstrictness is not as bad as the lack of strictness. That is why if we misjudge someone, it is worth correcting.

3. Biting into old, dry meat and finding poison in it. The Little is shamed. No mistake.

This is about a question that has been rotting for a long time. You are lacking the courage and strength to put an end to it. The "Little" who is shamed in you is Yin—who would leave the situation to continue poisoning you.

4. Biting into dry and gristly meat. He finds a metal arrow in it. Divination: hard struggle is beneficent. The road stands open before you.

The bad (negative) is the strongest at the root. In order to defeat it, you have to grow up to the task. The battle will not be easy and short, but it is worth it. The symbol also says that you cannot put an end to old, bad habits in a matter of minutes.

5. He bites into dry meat. He finds a golden arrow. Remaining solid in the midst of difficulties: faultless.

A long hard struggle promises "golden" triumph. Do not listen to anyone, follow the middle path of neutral, clear vision, and prepare for a difficult but victorious battle.

6. He is caught in stocks and his ears also disappear. Trouble!

He doesn't hear or see because he doesn't want to hear or see. Do not be obstinate. You do not see well what you see, and you do not know well what you know. If you realize this, you can avoid a great deal of trouble for yourself. Do not stay among those who do not learn from anything.

22 ☶ *Pi*

Beautification

Character: Ornate shell coins—and flowers.

The character is the sign of beauty, appearance, form, behavior, and aesthetics—in other words: **outward appearance**. The drama of Pi is that **appearance and reality are rarely the same thing**. A rose is naturally beautiful—man is not. He needs to "do more to himself" to make himself beautiful, and the question for which an answer has long been sought, from the primitive peoples of the world to the highest civilizations, is how should we appear in the world? What is our outer appearance like? How do we affect one another?

The drama of the Oracle Sign is in the tension between inner content and outer form (or appearance); something can be beautiful and empty or have a repulsive outer appearance. In psychology terms, this is where the Jungian "persona" belongs, the external mask we wear so that the outside world will accept us and also to hide our inner, real being from all communities that are not built on love. Showing our "good side" is not only a lie but the most important law of community life. That which is beautiful, suitable, and harmonious not only has an effect on others but also on us; all women know that if they put makeup on, they change inside as well.

The message of the Oracle is, **Beautification, Success! Follow your**

path but only in little things! Great battles cannot be won with charm, brushes, and kindness. But little ones can. The beautiful, harmonious, and kind is effective. (Charm is also magic!) An artist often affects others with beauty and often with such astounding charm that we do not even look for the deeper truth behind it. It is a rare moment when the beautiful is also true.

This Oracle Sign encourages little steps and cautions against large ones because it is not certain that you are not a slave to appearance and illusion. It is not sure that you see things as they really are. The light of your mind does not shine far, only nearby. Like a fire burning at the foot of a mountain, it beautifies the side of the mountain with warm light but it does not radiate all the way to the stars. Long distance is not the important thing with this Oracle Sign but rather the sheer beauty of the here and now. Make yourself and your surroundings beautiful and harmonious. Meetings, relationships, and community events are not meaningless, but you should know that despite all of the pleasant reactions, illusions are at work within you. You are an idealist. A beautiful love could unfold in the energy field of the Oracle Sign, but a sage would warn you against beginning marriage or entering into a divorce case at this exact moment in time. This example applies to all walks of life where you would like to achieve valid, long-term, deep-seated, and real results. It is not the right time for such things.

It is said that even Confucius blushed when he received the answer to a general question asked of the spirits. The message was the following: even though he had created the Chinese way of life, etiquette, moral, social and political rules—and the aesthetic laws of civilization still in force today—his operation was superficial compared to that of the sages of the Tao. He was not truly deep.

THOUGHTS

Pi is the sign of calm and pure beauty. Its meaning is felt by people rather than known. The outward appearance of all cultures, behaviors, dress codes, appearance, and religious and community life is based on this—an advertisement, packaging, a bird's beautiful plumage, and the picturesque fur of a predator—the whole spectacular world of divine creation.

It is Pi when we smile at one another (or hide our real feelings behind a smile). Pi is the sign of aesthetic or religious appearances and as such, it gives joy—but it is not suitable for battle because it lacks drama, the will for fundamental renewal . . . and **it lacks the deep-seated strength of Truth.** In Hindu culture, this is the *maya*, the illusion, the sign of the magical Appearance—that is the first dream and colored robe of God, the creator.

While the Oracle Sign discourages appearances, it suggests that you should not only try to appeal but also be genuine and true. It also advises that you should aim for beauty, to reflect an attractive and aesthetic outward appearance but also, wherever possible, that your smile should be an honest one.

A modern person experiences the positive meaning of this Oracle Sign when he removes the mass-produced shirt he has worn all his life, his jacket and jeans, and he puts on his best clothes. That which is "divine" should dress divinely. A priest puts on his ceremonial vestments; dressing in a costume is a long and separate ceremony in the Eastern theater—the spirit of the actor is transformed under this costume. The outer appearance is sacred. Your smile is as sacred as is your laughter and your glance. The way you eat is sacred, the way you greet people, and the way you hold a cup of tea. My grandmother sent everyone out of the room just before she died and then she combed her hair nicely.

This is Pi.

LINES

1. He beautifies his toes. He climbs down from the cart and walks.
He doesn't want to appear more than he is. He trusts in his own strength. Modesty and loyalty to ourselves goes a long way just like a

"cart." It might not be as comfortable. The spirit freezes in that life of appearances—it is better to accept the more difficult reality.

2. He beautifies his growing beard.
It is more important what I think about myself than what others think about me. (It is far from certain that they think what I think they think.) Here, the beard is a symbol for appearance. It might be on our face, or someone else's face, or on the face of the situation that we judge based on its external appearance. Look for the genuine content. Look for the truth. The message of the line is encouraging despite all of this: it predicts upliftment. What we create on the outside ripens with time and becomes our own.

3. He becomes absorbed in beautification. Catharsis goes a long way. The way is open.
This is a quiet time in our life full of apparent comfort, good fate, and ease but also superficiality: great temptation. Do not come under the influence of the opinions of others, fashion, or your exterior circumstances. Follow your own path. The picture shows that you are swimming in treacherous waters toward a delightful shore that you can reach; do not allow your ornate but wet gown to pull you under.

4. Where there is beauty there should also be wise simplicity. White horse flying high. Those who arrive are not enemies. They are suitors.
Everyone receives what they see as valuable. There are valueless values, empty joys, superficial society, soulless relationships. A single good friend, an intimate word, or a moment full of love all mean much more than an external success. Your value system is changing. You want the real thing and you will get it. The line warns that a person who has become unaccustomed to the past accepts the new with suspicion. The white horse flying high above is a glorious symbol. (I will not translate it, just imagine it and the picture will touch you.) It should have no bridle or decoration and its billowing mane should be as white as snow.

5. Beauty in the garden atop the hill. Unpainted bundle of silk, impoverished, small. You are ashamed and yet blessings still come.

The deep meaning of the line the "garden atop the hill" is the Ancestors' Tomb to which man, as with the spirit world, can only take the genuine values of his soul. Man arrives in poverty; he has collected rubbish and forgotten to "whiten" the silk. And still the true inner value, the genuine nature of the heart, defeats shame. New circumstances and a new valuable world open up before you. It is more intimate and happier than the one that you have been living in so far. Here, who you really are matters, not who you appear to be.

6. White beautification.

Be true to yourself. The most beautiful is the simplest. Jesus and the gospel are simple—not puritan, but simple. Compared to the Sermon on the Mount, all church services are theater and all sermons are literary posturing.

This line says you influence with your being. You influence with your reality. You don't need to add a thing. You are most beautiful as you are.

23 ䷖ *Po*

Splitting Apart

Character: A sharp tool cuts down a tree, removes the branches, and strips the bark.

There is a cycle in nature: everything is born, blossoms, and decays, and the new is born from the decay. **Something is decaying in you or around you.** This is not your fault, it's the law. Habits, forms, relationships, and survived life situations all decay. They may have been good until now but their time has come to an end. What should be done? Leave it! A lot of dark Yin pushed out the light Yang in this Oracle Sign. The winter is on its way. Your glorious garden looks quite shocking and you forget that this depressing end is the condition required for rebirth. Not only the bad passes away but also what you saw as beautiful, useful, and good. Our immortal spirit finds mortality difficult to accept although this is the case. Don't feel bitter, don't be afraid: what has gone is no longer beautiful or useful and no longer any good at all. *You need to let it pass.*

In martial arts it has been said that "the science of Letting Go is to leave. Not leaving to get lost but to carry on. Not doing a thing." The message of the I Ching is the same, **It is not desirable to go anywhere at all.**

The deterioration happened gradually. Virtually unnoticeably.

You suddenly realize that it is no longer the same. It is lacking the thing that you started it for; night eventually comes for all human relationships, ambition, desire, habit, and prejudice. There is no need to be afraid, protest, panic, or break out. There is no point caring for a rotten tree; it needs to be cut out and trimmed so that a new one can be planted in its place. In order to start something new, you need to close the old. The seed planted in the soil needs to die in order to produce fruit.

The answer to your question is, *you are at the end of a cycle. An old structure falls down in order to provide a place for a new one. Let this process happen on its own. Do nothing for it or against it.*

Remove the "peel" of appearance from the situation, pull off your old costume—do not trust anyone. You are changing as are your surroundings. Someone also dies and is reborn within you who no longer wants to play the old role. The practical advice of the Oracle Sign is **do nothing now**. Wait for the process to come to its natural conclusion.

THOUGHTS

Now is the time that the dark, material forces win over the spiritual forces. The spirit that once created the whole thing now only faintly glimmers: the material helplessly vegetates with no soul. This is aging. At times like this, your mind is full of material worries, earthly problems, and anxieties. You brood on the past; you cannot fly and you have no strength. This is bad "aging" because you have become stuck in decomposing material.

The character shows wood cutting because this says that you should not brood on the past but close it. Gather energy. Create a strong foundation on which you build the new. Don't look back, only forward. The man "who has still not fully grown" has become stuck in all the things that he is used to. He is suffering because he is not free, because he has identified with what is transient—because he has forgotten his immortality and omnipotence. Such a person fears loss of the old and does not believe that there will be new. The True Man is now beginning to write a new chapter of his fate.

Two diverse views collide here: modern people see decomposition in aging while the sages of the I Ching see a move toward the divine. This is why the elderly in China were once treated like gods. It is true that though they were very old, they were happy, liberated, and cheerful. They smiled a lot because they did not regret what had passed. They waited for their future, and this was not death but a new Life. Rather like the clown who has its trumpet snatched away only to cry, "No problem, I've got another one!"

LINES

1. The leg of the bed is rotting. If you do not realize: trouble.
The bed symbolizes a place of calm. It is deteriorating, unnoticed, like a bad tooth that does not hurt. Wake up! Do not rely on it getting better on its own. Do not do anything yet, but know that what has been certain up until now is no longer certain. And it will never be the same again so don't try to continue it.

2. The frame of the bed is rotten. If you do not realize: trouble.
Here the problem is with old companions. Realize! You can count on having to solve this problem on your own—you cannot depend on help. (At times like this, you learn independence—this will be the basis for rebirth.) Do not give in to any kind of negative thoughts. While the framework of your old life is coming to an end, it makes you anxious, so you do not even hear the reassuring voice from the spirit world.

3. No mistake!
What you have outgrown, what is no longer worthy of you, what no longer concerns you: leave there. Step out of it, put an end to it. Don't do this by attacking but by retreating. (Pay attention. If you are silent

for a moment, you can hear supporting agreement from deep down in your spirit. Others don't support you now, but this isn't needed.)

4. You cut into your bed and it touches your flesh. Trouble.
The process of decomposition no longer affects your surroundings: it is close to you. This is the peak of this process. You have to live through the catharsis. All transformations have an unavoidable state when they hurt, when something is pulled away that has grown there. You have to stand it.

5. The queen leads the ladies-in-waiting to the king like a shoal of fish. Everything is beneficent.
Turn of events after catharsis. The joy of rebuilding after destruction. The dark suddenly becomes light and what was against you now supports you, and the desolation tempts you with plenty. The fish is the sign of plenty. The line marks the moment before the full moon when—according to ancient court tradition—not only does the queen give herself to the king but she also brings his mistress to him as a shoal of fish in the days before.

We commonly forget that all bad luck has a hidden element of good fortune in the same way that wheat grows from land that has been spread with compost. The wheat is then milled and baked to make delicious, soft bread. The decomposing element of Yin becomes humble and it turns into the servant to the joy of light.

6. The ripe fruit has still not been eaten. The True Man receives a cart— the common man's hut collapses.
Folktales commonly end with the good one winning a reward and the bad one getting a just punishment. This is not about moral labeling. A person is good who woke up in the trouble, found their inner god, themself, and now sets off to fulfill the next task of their fate. A person is bad who did not wake up in trouble and did not become more, shinier, freer, but stayed on the treadmill and automatically keeps on rushing

forward and repeats and repeats like a failed student. Such types just lament the problem but cannot change as they have no strength—they stay in the ruins. A carriage arrives for the True Man that takes him up to a higher level. In the cosmic sense, this is the symbol of the Final Judgment. But this happens in all decomposition: the spirit frees itself and flies high—the material falls to the deep and disintegrates.

This line wants you to choose life! The seeds of your future life cycle hide within the fruit.

24 ䷗ *Fu*

Return (Rebirth)

Character: Steps return to the path.

The message of Fu, the 24th Oracle Sign is, **Return. Success. It breaks up and penetrates with no obstruction. Companions come. Faultless. Fate turns, you return to your own path. The seventh is the day of return. It is advantageous if you have a planned destination.** This is the winter solstice: light is born in the deepest darkness. In reality, it returns because everything goes around and around like the planets around the sun; everything returns but not to the same place. The spring returns but it is not the same spring and you are not the same either, and not one single blade of grass or experience is the same.

What is it that can return? The joyful experience of "I am!" Everyone has had an experience like this if only for a moment—if at no other time, then as a child. This is inspiration. Inspiration that there is no death! Inspiration that I am an eternal spirit. Even a person who does not become aware of this also experiences a glint of light in a difficult time in their life. The problem starts to pass. They begin to recover and their faith comes back bit by bit, their will to live, and sooner or later, their strength.

The air slowly fills with the encouraging scent of the Future. New plans, new companions, and new opportunities arrive. You feel a strong urge to do something, *but wait*! Enthusiasm is not Power—only the "seventh day" or the "seventh phase" will be the moment of action. The situation is similar to when a woman becomes blessed with child. She knows that her fate has fundamentally changed and yet she still needs many months of calm, quiet, and peace while she and the baby in her womb become ripe for motherhood.

Gather strength, process the memories of your past, and pay attention because where you have broken away, you will be strong, and where you have lost is where you will be invincible. The True Man does not run away from his past however dark it may have been, because failure provides fuel and defeat leads to triumph—his tragedies grow to greatness.

At the dawn of a new era, you must come to terms with the past and gain strength for the future. This requires calm. It is difficult to remain quiet when you would gladly break out, but that is what you still need: your sprouting faith needs to strengthen.

THOUGHTS

What can happen in the energy field of the Return sign? I will list a few things: an encouraging promise, an unnoticed inspiration or idea that later transforms your fate; the beginning of new relationships; old relationships that have gone bad are now reborn; you receive help; you relive your old plan; you regain health; you recover . . . but it is also possible that something will happen to you that you won't even notice.

You are not conscious of the fact that *something fate-like is beginning* inside you. The important thing is to stay calm. It is hard to do this when our spirit gets a springlike impulse but that is what must be done. In martial arts, this is the point when we swing through the dead point. This is when we switch from tiredness, trouble, and loss into the exact opposite, and the spark of hope appears and powerlessness ceases. You should not strike out at once. We have passed through the dead point but still have to wait until we have reached the peak; strength needs to be gained until then.

You should not sacrifice the Great Opportunity for the promise of a little opportunity. This is the everyday advice of this Oracle Sign. Its spiritual teaching is that faith has to be nurtured. The spark is not a burning flame but it has the potential to be so.

LINES

1. He returns before he goes too far. He has little to regret. Great fortune.
If you nip a negative thought in the bud, the second that it appears, it cannot lay down roots. It evaporates, does not take root in you, and does not become "real." This is the key to self-awareness and self-control: I see it, I recognize its cause, I put an end to it. I do not let the weeds flourish and grow in my spirit and in my life. (One moment that starts well can avoid a long-term problem.)

2. Return—calmly. Blessings!
"Calmly" means to accept the will of God. Let it be, this is as it should be. (Accepting something is not the same as putting up with something. We do not "put up with" but we "merge" into the Great Will because this is the Good Will. The Chinese character, *hsiu* depicts a person who comfortably leans against a strong tree. This is the sign of Calm.) You also see people in a different light at such times. We understand them better and recognize their fate-like roles in our lives even if they place difficult challenges in our path.

3. Return, often. Trouble—but not mistake!
It is a well-known state to swing between good and bad, belief and doubt, hope and despair. It is not pleasant and yet it protects us from taking irresponsible steps. However, it would be good if you could eventually decide. You can't go in two directions at once.

4. Return—alone. He follows his own path.

There is no greater thing than obeying the word of your inner leader; listening to your heart; listening to your center point (*fu*), as the Chinese say. It is possible that your path will follow a different path than the one so far and that you step out of your old surroundings. When "our fate" shouts out and we follow its call, we sometimes have to leave behind those who surrounded us for different reasons.

5. Return—honestly. No regret.

The character for *tun* ("honestly") depicts a warrior who grandly attacks and defends himself. You finally confront your own mistakes and you delicately deal with them. You stand before a new life and you eventually have courage and strength to set off on the path. I bravely set off with no self-deceit or lies. I conquer myself and create my fate; now is the time! I am the master of life.

6. Return—with self-deceit. Trouble. Inner-outer misfortune.

If this is how you go into battle, your troops will suffer great defeat and you will bring trouble to the ruler of your land. If this is how you carry on, you will not be able to start anything new for ten years. The illusion of "self-deceit" (*mi*) means blindness. Such a one sees the illusion of the common man, who sees good as bad, bad as good, and harmful as useful. He senses the urge and the opportunity, but from the wrong direction: he is motivated by his desires, urges, and blind ambitions.

Do not act! You cannot see the consequences. Do not deceive yourself. You can ruin a whole phase of your life if you listen to "yourself." Do not reach for the apple however shiny it may appear to be.

25 ▦ *Wu Wang*

Spontaneous Action

Character: Wang *means "false," "self-involved," "stubborn,"*
"mean," "deceiving," "agitated." The Wang *character depicts a*
woman who has set off after some kind of temptation.
Wu, *on the other hand, means "without" all of these.*

Only follow your true, inner voice. In order to do this, you need to free yourself of everything that is the work of your anxious ego: your fears, prejudices, the bad habits of your past, and the continual yearning about what the future will bring. Do not look into the future. Live here and now!

The Oracle Sign marks a dynamic situation when we have to follow our spirit. The Thunder trigram is below and the Will of Heaven trigram is above. The command of the Oracle Sign is to free yourself from the tyrannical rule of your ego. Act freely and spontaneously. We refer to such action as being "spontaneous," but unfortunately, this is open to misunderstanding. If a person frees themself from the control of the ego, their act may just as easily be as animal and instinctive as it is free and spiritual. The inspired artist and brave samurai act without ego as a person who has forgotten himself, who commits an act of animal aggression or who "loses his head" and runs away. Freedom is only halfway there.

This Oracle Sign tells you to follow your spirit. In order to do this, you need to regain your natural childhood state that is free of prejudice and inhibition, the openness that you have lost. Live in the present, here and now. Do not wait for the future and don't be oppressed by the past; trust in the will of God. For Christians, this is the moment when you should not be surprised because the Holy Spirit says what you should say and what you should do. You don't have to formulate, plan, and especially not worry. Let yourself go and you will realize you should not continually stir, push, bustle, and strive; the current of fate propels and the good wind makes you fly.

If you are able to keep yourself in this state, you will have "exalted success," but only if you do not wait for it. If you continue turning the anxious prayer wheel of your mind, you will be unlucky! A person does the most for their future if they don't think about it, if they live the present moment as if this is the Whole.

Your future will come together from these present moments that have been solved with such devotion. If you peer forward, you will steal your attention and strength from the present: you sow carelessly and that is why your harvest will be pitiful. A person who selfishly looks back and forth is anxious and hopes. A person who follows his ego—Confucius says—"lacks the will and blessings of the Sky in his deeds."

You have to free yourself of everything that is not your real spiritual goal. You have to free yourself of bad habits, ambition, and anxiety—you have to discover the voice of your true being.

THOUGHTS

Let everything take shape on its own. Don't interfere because you will ruin it. This is the advice of the Wu Wang Oracle Sign. This does not mean that you should be completely passive but that you should act on inspiration. Poets write their best poems when inspired. Works like these virtually write themselves. If they interfere with sense, ambition, and calculation, the work becomes distorted and the quality plummets. And something else, every poet finds their own voice when they write out of inspiration and don't follow various memories or tortuously give birth to the poems. **You can only catch a glimpse of your own, true self, if you act spontaneously.** It is at such times that you are your real self. Otherwise—under the eye of your ego—you dare not be yourself.

In response to the question of how I can get inspired, Wu Wang gives a negative response: you have to free yourself from your deceitful, calculating, and miserly self and the inspiration will free itself from within you. If you want to fly high, then you have to throw some sandbags overboard. You would be amazed if you found out how many promising things you have ruined in your life simply because you listened to your impatient, greedy, and calculating self. You have spoiled the work of angels because you followed your obstinate head.

If you follow the advice given by the Oracle Sign, many *unexpected* events will occur in your life. This is partly because if a person is spontaneous, they don't expect anything—they live in the present. You also really do come across unknown things, new matters, unexpected events, and chance turns. You do not have to prepare for the unexpected. If it is good, you will be pleased about it. If it is bad, you will move past it and solve it. A person who is spontaneous has a virtually limitless ability to deal with their own fate. Things that they would spend years fussing over or completely mess up, they can now solve in a few movements.

LINES

1. Spontaneous action is beneficent. Keep on going.
The first vibrations of the heart say good things. This might be a new plan, a new goal, or a new acquaintance. What starts is promising. We sometimes have first "feelings" in which we not only see the beginning of a journey, but also its end.

2. If you do not think of the harvest while plowing, if you do not think about the use of the land while clearing, then it is worth taking something on.
Do not peer at the future, to rewards or results. Lose yourself in what you do and do not try to get rich quick!

3. Undeserved bad luck. It is possible that an untied cow is gain for the wanderer and loss for the town dweller.
A person who lives spontaneously also takes bad luck in stride and soon dispels it. They do not panic and may even think, "Well, this could be good for something!" But if you are a "town dweller," you get stuck in the problem and you bemoan the loss.

4. A person who is steadfast remains faultless.
Your real self is irremovable and indestructible—no one can take it away from you. If your inner sun shines all the time, you have no need to worry. Don't listen to anyone except your own power source. "Man's true nature is divine and strong," said Swami Vivekananda. Stay true to yourself!

5. If you are burdened by an illness in which you are blameless, do not use medicine, heal yourself.
In ancient China, *healing* also meant "joy." The artificial should not be allowed to spoil the natural. The human should not spoil the divine. Only repair what you have spoilt (a lot of "illnesses" are like this). Examine whether or not you are to blame. If you are, then put it right. If not, let the matter solve itself. If you fail to do this, you will continue to make things worse.

6. Spontaneous action. Each step is a mistake. Nothing is immovable.
Stay calm. If you listen to your inspiration, then you will do nothing now. Wait!

The reason I have not written here about tactics used in martial arts is because this Oracle Sign describes the fundamental spiritual conduct that warriors always possess. It is difficult to achieve and requires a great deal of work. It is quite possible that the secret of "spontaneous action" also occurs in simple people such as ourselves—like a flash, like a prompt, like a moment that we describe as "presence of mind." We all have intuitive experiences. We are not able to make them last for any amount of time—they appear in a flash and we experience how effectively everything works "by itself."

26 ䷙ *Ta Ch'u*

The Collection of the Great

Character: An enormous Man with arms outspread—the sign of "Great"— and fertile, black earth that formed from accumulated river mud.

The creative energies slowly gather—it is only possible to make the most of these great forces if the conditions for use are ripe. Early action leads to panic and the wasting of powers. The untamed powers burn. The deed needs to be ripened. The energies that create your future stretch you in the same way that a woman is stretched by the new life she carries. Patience. Persistence. Waiting and ripening. Ripe fruit falls on its own. The way is wide open for you. It is a beneficent period. If you have ripened, you can be on your way!

Gathering energy also means not wasting it unnecessarily. You need to concentrate on the real task. As Hamlet exclaims when he is told by his father's spirit the task of his fate:

> *"I'll wipe away all trivial fond records,*
> *All saws of books, all forms, all pressures past,*
> *That youth and observation copied there;*
> *And thy commandment all alone shall live*
> *Within the book and volume of my brain."*

It would be a good idea for you to step out of your accustomed environment into a wider circle—beyond your usual boundaries. The True Man researches the secret of ancient traditions and translates them into the language of his own age. It is from here that he knows what beneficent action is.

Heavenly Powers hide in the Mountains—these two Kua form the 26th Oracle Sign. This is the phase of being before the great action: a time to gather, pile up, concentrate, ripen, and tame held back power, and it will eventually bubble up like a spring.

THOUGHTS

Modern science was confronted with this question when it looked for peaceful uses of atomic energy. In this sign, the heavenly powers are sleeping deep in the mountains. The situation is tense but it is not good if they break out. According to Taoist myth, this is the age in which the "spiritual embryo" ripens.

It is difficult to wait for things to ripen. We already suspect who we are on the inside, but we are not yet able to realize it on the outside. Inside, we already know what we want but nothing is happening on the outside. We ripen during this waiting period as do our beneficent plans. The greatest danger is impatience. A person "who has not yet fully grown" sees limits as a prison. The True Man knows that all spiritual values and beneficent events are ripened within limitations. If something doesn't happen, then don't force it again and again because *its time has not yet come*—neither it nor the circumstances are sufficiently ripe.

We often experience that we keep on pushing something and still it doesn't work. Then—when we don't even want it to happen—it does it all by itself. A person knows this if they unravel the secret of the Ta Ch'u sign.

Don't be disturbed that those around you don't understand,

and they place obstacles in your path. Neither should you hate anyone who obstructs you. It is possible that they are inadvertently doing something for you. See the hand of fate in everyone and everything.

Happy are the meek for they shall inherit the earth. The "Great Man"—the *Ta*—is a meek man. Man's fundamental mission is to tame himself and his surroundings—in other words, to cultivate. Atomic power, solar energy, the earth, and wild animals must be "tamed." Wildness is inhuman and we don't know any Great Man who was not meek: Jesus, Buddha, Lao Tse, all sages, saints, and great artists were meek. You should know that **meekness is the greatest strength**. The rabbit is not meek, only cowardly. This is because it is weak. Only the lion can be meek. A pupil can only become a master in martial arts by becoming meek. Meekness is invincible.

Modern man, who sees that robbers and wolves rule the land, denies his own nature and frantically tries to become wild himself. He knows little about meekness because he confuses it with helplessness. Meekness appears where man has cultivated and calmed his ancient, wild energy and melted it into his dignity. When I meditated on the Ta Ch'u Oracle Sign, I was told by Imre Polyák, the Hungarian Olympic wrestling champion, who was a visibly meek man, that an aggressive opponent never stood a chance against him. His greatest opponents were always meek, just like him.

We not only learn the strength of meekness in the Ta Ch'u Oracle Sign, but also how we should wait while our slumbering energies reach the state of critical mass. *Ch'u* not only means "slowing down," it also means "piling up." You have to wait until the conditions are ripe. Sometimes we have to wait for others, sometimes for ourselves. It is quite possible that we are already ready while our outside world is still not. The opposite is also possible: the world is waiting but we still have some ripening to do.

One thing is for certain, time is working for us.

LINES

1. Danger. Favorable to say no.
Do not move! You are being urged into action by forces the fruit of
which is not good.

2. The carriage wheel comes loose.
You cannot continue. The surroundings have still not ripened: wait.

3. Good horses follow one another. This is the middle of the difficulties,
hang on! Follow the covered carriage. It is beneficent if you preserve
your goal.
The "horse" (*ma*) is the symbol of spiritual energy. It is its meaning.
The goal that you are following is rolling along in a "covered carriage"
in front of you. It is not yet yours; it is still a secret; it still conceals
the future. But you should keep on following it. You already suspect
where the road will take you. Although your goal is still far away, it
floats before your eyes. The difficulties are challenges of character. The
repeated defeat of obstacles raises you and makes you really forceful.
At first, we begin to "understand" something and then we come to
know it. A "good horse" is sensible; it knows that it just understands
something, but it doesn't know it. This is why it faithfully follows a
suspected goal that it still does not know. Obstacles come in the form
of challenges that make the clever wise and those who understand into
those who know.

4. Young bull in the enclosure. Great blessings!
Your strength has come together and the road is open before you—you
still have to wait before setting off. Now you know that you will tri-
umph and this feeling fills you with joy. Trust is the key to success.
Trust in God's help and trust in your own abilities. Now you learn the
Art of Waiting with faith.

5. Tusk of a castrated pig. Blessings.

You are only ready for the gifts from heaven if you have removed all traces of selfishness from yourself. The "pig" (*shi*) is the symbol of luck and wealth. The sage knows that whatever he receives from fate, it is not his own.

6. Where does the path of the sky lead? Tao: eternal advancement. Blessings.

Fulfillment. The spirit is ripe. The forces have been tamed and the inner and outer obstacles removed. You have arrived but you know this as you have experienced it—the road is endless. True wonder is not in divine gifts but in fulfillment. A person is wise whose heart is always full of gratitude. Gratitude for everything.

27  I

Nourishment

頤

Character: Open mouth, and next to it, the ancient sign
meaning the "I" sound: a man's head.

Pay attention to your **nourishment** and that of others. Here, nourishment is to be interpreted in the widest possible sense: you can nourish the body, the spirit, the mind, friendship, a plan, a business, or even the community in which you live. According to the Oracle Sign, it not only maintains and nurtures us but also decides our quality of life.

By nourishing our bodies, we can make them either sick or healthy—you are what you eat. Beyond this, good and bad feelings and thoughts also nourish—you are what you think. But the main **things that nourish are belief and false belief**; you are what you believe yourself to be, based on your magical faith—imagination. The I Oracle Sign speaks about the magical metabolism with which we form and maintain ourselves and our surroundings.

Today, we only consider the material part of this important, but traditionally the first and foremost form of nourishment was spiritual nourishment and the blessing of food. In Christian symbolism this is the "daily bread" about which Jesus said, "I am the bread of life."

A person who wants to make their life nobler and more beautiful thinks noble and beautiful things and processes them in their spirit. A person who wants to get closer to God lives in the ministry of the Last Supper in which Jesus gives his own flesh and blood to his disciples: eat and drink! Only what you *eat and digest* will become yours. This is not only about fleeting thoughts but about imagination. What you imagine with faith will become real! The message attached to the Oracle Sign is **Watch your mouth! Look at the origin of everything that goes into your mouth and that comes out of it.**

Pay attention to who does magic within you and with what. If the "Frightened One" does magic, then you will be afraid and sooner or later you will have reason to be afraid. If the True Man does magic and fills you with strength, freedom, and confidence, sooner or later you will become strong, free, and have cause for confidence. Words are very powerful! This is true of those that you say silently to yourself and those that you say out loud to others. That is why the True Man is *careful with his words*—because he knows that he creates with them!

"With what do you nourish yourself and others?" is the current fate-creating question. If things aren't going as you would like, you have to change the pattern of your thoughts. You have to dig right down to the root. You have to pay attention to what you imagine and why. There are many types of ancient law systems with which it is possible to change the creative "image"—and the essence is the same as with nourishment, that it should be regularly repeated!

The method of "conversion" or "awakening" or simply achieving a more noble life commonly resembled nourishment in the ancient world because they were continual processes that happened every day. You have to nourish your spirit and your faith several times a day in the same way that you eat several times a day; invisible things grow or decay due to nourishment from energies in the same way as your physical body; **a person who "eats" unhappy thoughts every day will become unhappy.**

The lines of the Oracle Sign speak about the importance of the substance with which you nourish yourself and others now. It also applies to how you nourish the world and how the world nourishes you. A person is responsible for how they nourish the spirits of others with words, feelings, and thoughts.

In the wider sense, the I Oracle Sign is also concerned with the satisfaction of needs, material wealth, and money, but just as with everything else, *this is also determined by our spiritual approach.* It is important to decide whether the money belongs to us or we belong to the money and whether we are master or slave of material things. (Your heart is where your treasure is.)

Beyond this, whatever happens to us has a spiritual precursor. If you swallow a poisoned, false belief, you can ruin your life. Everything is decided from within. A person who does not know this becomes a prisoner of their circumstances.

THOUGHTS

Our era is plummeting and we nourish ourselves badly in every sense of the word. We live on chemical cuisine, eat plastic animals raised on artificial foodstuffs, and we consume a daily ration of fears, anxiety, aimlessness, agitation, anger, hate, revenge, and depression in indigestible amounts. Today's message of the 27th Oracle Sign is to live against your age. Don't eat what you are fed. Eat strength and encouragement. Drink immortality.

"Give us this day, our daily bread" doesn't simply mean that we want something to eat; it primarily means "I am!" He is in us and we are in Him. We pray to experience God and for the everyday experience of not forgetting who we are and where we belong.

You can understand the best advice in battle tactics if you look at the structure of the Oracle Sign: Thunder below and the calm of the Mountains above. One is the elemental urge to break out and the other is the calm of motionlessness. The tactic is that calm constantly nourishes your movement. Forceful movement on the outside and calm on the inside. Always look after it and if you lose it for a second, always find your way back to your calm state.

To translate this to your everyday situation, whatever moving, tense, or dramatic situation you find yourself in, always preserve your inner calm. If you feel the urge to overdo things, it is better that you don't speak or only a little. Every word that you utter creates. The considered word creates success. Nourish yourself and others with Calm.

LINES

*1. You have forgotten about the holy tortoise (*ling kui*) and now you stare at me with your mouth wide open. Trouble!*
The ling kui is a magical tortoise who lives from air happily and for an unfathomably long time. You have forgotten that you are creative; you are the magician of your fate. At the moment, you think that you live under the control of your surroundings. You envy the good fate of others and you feel sorry for yourself, you are helpless. You think that you are one of life's victims. Wake up! Instead of sinking into the marsh of self-pity, look for the ling kui in yourself and magically transform your fate. The line may mean a lack of energy and it warns that it is possible to live more happily on air than it is on millions of dollars—if you know that you are immortal.

2. He seeks nourishment above and then, denying the spirit of tradition, down on the side of the mountain. If he continues, he will end up in trouble.
You see yourself as being weak and that is why you are not able to look after yourself. You depend on others, either those around you or the goodwill of those above you. The spirit of tradition says our true spirit is divine and strong. Do not deny it because then you will be forced onto your wits. The line encourages independence—but carefully.

3. You don't live on real nourishment. Carrying on: trouble. Do not act like this for ten years.
Not "real nourishment" means to be dependent on success, the recognition of others, unworthy thoughts, company, passions, external

expectations, fashions, momentary interest, pleasures—when you forget about the Tao and you say, I only live once. You are looking in the wrong direction for your happiness. Stop now because if it becomes a habit, the change will symbolically take "ten years" of hard work.

4. He looks for nourishment above. Blessings! He looks and watches with his eyes like a tiger hungry for its prey. Faultless.
You still lack the necessary power but your intention is selfless and you receive help. Listen to your inner self. The precondition to inspiration is concentrated attention. (The tiger's prey is truth. It is hungry for truth and waits for it with piercing eyes.)

5. Detour from the path. Remaining is beneficent. Do not cross the Great Water!
You are powerless to take an independent step or undertaking, and the time is not right, either. Remain in the service of the good. You can depend on the help of others. Do not nourish yourself with false ambitions.

6. The source of nourishment. Knowledge of danger is beneficent. Cross the Great Water!
The danger comes from the past (memory, habit, or karmic connection). The sage is "lord of the stars." The task is not easy but fateful. This is exactly why sight and caution are required. The Oracle Sign encourages, it may bring blessings if you can carry out your plan. This is not about a selfish plan—it also nourishes others.

28 ䷛ *Ta Kuo*

The Preponderance of the Great

Character: "Great Man" with outstretched arms—
and a house that is too heavy for its supporting beams.

Great crises come before the birth of all great things. A crisis of our fate is that moment at which the old is no longer sustainable—but the new has still not been created. It depends on you as to whether you fall back into the outlived and unsupportable state or whether you tip in favor of the new. You have to solve the crisis like a challenge in a fairy tale. No one helps you now as you have to pull yourself into harmony. The Oracle Sign shows an energy structure in which the creative energies have no support—they will not last for long. Either the pressure of the outside world is too great or you have to win back your faith and strength within—you have to take account of yourself.

The message is, the inner and outer events are filled with a promising future, although the danger of giving up and falling back still threatens. Either up, or down—you cannot stay where you are. In modern terms, you are under great stress. Your old beliefs no longer work and your new faith is just being born. Don't look back—go toward your future. Courage. You have to follow your path on your own; follow it with joy and not sadness.

The sages say **a person does not come out of a tight situation**

well by simply fleeing, but only with a planned destination. Follow your goal.

THOUGHTS

The disharmony is caused by too much anger. You can experience this disharmony as doubt, fear, anxiety, uncertainty, disappointment, the agitating pressure of the outside world, or the challenge of a fate situation. The overpowering Yang forces do not give out good impulses, and it is not possible to solve the situation aggressively, obstinately, and hurriedly. It is not attack you need, but careful retreat, submission, steadfastness, and patience. It requires calm and not panic. You will get nowhere with aggression and especially not with aggression toward yourself.

You now need spirit presence. Spiritual presence is the state when a person fetches their most important valuables from a house that is falling down. Have faith in yourself! The crisis means an extraordinary time. What is the crisis? Is it inside? Is it in relationships with others? Your question decides.

One thing is certain, extraordinary times require "great men." They need heroics. The True Man does not fear being alone, and he is not sad if he gives up the world. This is the spiritual basis of bravery. It means that God is with us even if we are left with no companions and our earthly ambitions are not fulfilled. It is only with this faith that a person is not anxious or depressed.

LINES

1. Laying clean white sedge underneath. Faultless.
The heroic act is self-sacrificing but not reckless. Be careful and cautious. The situation cannot be solved suddenly, rather one step at a time. This is how a surgeon works in the operating room: cleanly, carefully, and not hurried.

2. The dried-out tree produces a new branch. An old man gets a young wife.
Everything is desirable!

Renewal. Its secret is that there is still life in what appears to be an outlived situation. This might be recovery or the reawakening of a relationship—but it might also be the rejuvenation of our inner being. The situation is extraordinary and it tells us that even extreme things may be fertile if there is harmony between them. Modestly accept fate's gift.

3. The main beam is overstretched. Trouble!

The situation is not sustainable and not repairable. Everything that suggests something else is illusion. You have to get out of this state of being.

4. The main beam is strengthened. Blessing! If he wants more: shame.

We are only humble as long as we need help. If we get the help we require, we easily become cheeky. The ego is immortal. Do not forget about help from either the visible or the invisible world. If it wavers, it is modest but if it gains strength, it wins back its arrogance. This is not only about death but maintaining vigilance. Religious people say that all things happen for the greater glory of God. A samurai would say that if you get out of trouble, you should not become careless.

5. A dried-out willow tree blossoms. An elderly woman gets herself a young
husband. Not a mistake but not praiseworthy.

Fleeting joy in an outlived situation. We call it illusion, a superficial solution. It does not make any difference to the crisis. The roots of the tree are barely alive—the elder woman is infertile—man weaves colorful dreams instead of living through his catharsis.

6. If you cross the water, it will cover your head. Dangerous but no mistake.

This is just as likely to be catharsis as inadvertently getting into trouble. The sign suggests that you do not know how deep the water is. Like all unknowns, it is dangerous and yet still experiencing the unsustainability of a situation and living through something to its absolute depths could mean the opportunity of complete transformation. This is historically the moment of heroic deeds. In your personal life, it is the realization that the state of crisis can no longer continue. Something has to be done. Be brave—but not reckless.

29  K'an

Conquering Difficulty

坎

Character: Earth—and a deep gorge with water running through it.

The situation is difficult. It has to be overcome. The difficulty—or "danger" as it is referred to in Chinese texts—is that Yang has become imprisoned by two Yins. This is the Water (Danger) trigram that is repeated twice in this Oracle Sign.

Here, "danger" means that **the spirit has been captured by material.** The situation can be neither accepted nor overcome with rebellious impatience, only with the wise tactics of Water, which are essentially the following: flowing continually, and just as it adapts to everything, it avoids all hard things, it flows over it, and dissolves it; it does not change in itself. Water has no form, only essence. That is why it overcomes everything and gushes unstoppably into the endless sea. This is how to overcome difficulties.

What could the difficulty be? It could be the inner loss of faith; that you are not the master of your fate; that you have become helpless; that nothing succeeds; that you are overcome with certain desires, passions, or dark thoughts that you are incapable of subduing. You would like to live a different kind of life but you cannot change it because your magical power does not work. Your fears and anxieties are strong—you don't even know where they come from because their sources lie deep in the subconscious.

The difficulty could be a life situation that is karmic and recurrent that you could not solve internally. It stands on the outside in front of you, it frightens you and upsets you and silently whispers, "I am stronger than you, I will defeat you." Pessimism and the abuse of negative energies really are dangerous because when the divine experience of "I am" dies in a person, they become prisoner to their own instincts. (*K'an* can mean "gorge" or "pit," but can also mean "grave.")

K'an is still an encouraging Oracle Sign. Its message is, **Recurrent difficulty. If you are true and blessings are hidden in your heart, then whatever you do, you will be successful.** The True Man sees difficulties as tasks of fate that are to be defeated. The person "who has not yet fully grown" takes fright and gives up the battle or—even worse—tries to battle with bad tactics.

A good tactic is the following:

1. You should never lose your inner confidence in the final victory. The river continually thinks about the sea.
2. You don't have to defeat the obstacle but overcome it. You have to keep on going. The river does not stop to argue with a rock in its path but flows over it and joyfully rushes toward the sea.

The ego is stiff. It snaps and gets stuck. It is cramped and obstinate. But a person directed by their inner being is flexible, adaptable, relaxed, and does not take up the gauntlet. This is not a character fault, but wisdom. Do not look for your self-respect in the triumph of minor battles but in winning the whole war. You should know what is important—within you and in life—and continually protect that. You can give the rest up at any time. This is the invincible strategy of the Water.

It is not only about the fact that the difficulty recurs but that it can only be defeated with training that is continually repeated. A life problem needs to be regularly worked on. It needs to be defeated little by little, every day—a virtually unnoticeable amount. It took time for the problem to appear and it can only be defeated with time. This persistence is decisive—this may also include you falling back time and time again, or that you don't succeed and you sometimes feel that you have to start all over again from the beginning. No problem.

That which is valuable in me became mine through the defeat of difficulties. I have all my problems to thank.

THOUGHTS

The divine spirit inside me is invincible. The danger of which this Oracle Sign speaks is that I have forgotten about it! I have identified with my body's problems, with my fears, my failures, with my emotional whirlwind, with my pessimism, with my weakness, my desires, and my obstinate theories—I am a prisoner of "Nothing ever goes right for me. Everything is hopeless." I could go on. The plummeting of the spirit into material means that it identifies with material. It forgets its immortality and it thinks it is mortal. It identifies with fear, trouble, pain—it thinks that the body "is me" and that transience is its life.

The Chinese consider the movement into material as being a universal law. Water is one of the ancient signs of creation. The danger does not lie in the fact that you live a material fate on Earth, but in you becoming "stuck" in it . . . if you forget about the Tao or, as we would say, about God in ourselves.

If you look at a dry riverbed, it is a surprise to see all the rocks, stones, carcasses, bent pieces of metal, tree trunks, and gnarled branches that the river flowed through and over without having been obstructed or "depressed"—without having identified with anything. *This is how you should deal with all problems in your life.* Do not stop. Do not build any external or internal obstacles into your spirit. Don't be ruled by the belief that anything here is yours—the pain, the problem, the fear, and the deceiving hope and anxious expectation is not yours either.

"I am free on the inside!" is the secret of the Water. No road exists down which it would not be able to freely flow. Difficulties teach you that there is someone inside you for whom this is not difficult. Someone who is in life and yet not and who solves everything with Time because they are free and divine.

Water is the greatest blessing—ancient creation itself. That is why we like to splash about, bathe, and relax in water—water is good and it caresses the spirit. But water is an invincible opponent. It is even a struggle to redirect a stream and it is impossible to defeat a flood. Be Water! Be full of love and softness—and invincible.

Psychologically, this Oracle Sign means the subconscious reserves of the instinctual world.

LINES

1. Recurring difficulties. Pit within a pit. Bad luck.
Don't get used to difficulties, solve them. If you see that it is a cul-de-sac, don't carry on. Small doubt will lead to Doubt and small weakness will lead to Weakness—if we repeat our misguided deeds and thoughts, they will become habit and habit will become fate. Stop!

2. Dangerous (risky) difficulty. Only move forward by achieving little things.
The situation is still unripe to defeat difficulties. It is possible that you feel the strength to do it but acting too early will only lead to failure. Be careful and be satisfied with your modest goal. You can only validate your will with the patient Water tactic—and only in small things. The big things can wait.

3. Difficulty followed by difficulty. Stop and take no risks; otherwise you will fall into the pit of pits.
Even though you feel an urge to step beyond the problem and to solve the situation as soon as possible, don't do it. Wait. Relax. You cannot

see clearly enough to act effectively and so the only thing you can do is to wait for the time—however difficult the situation may be. You have to move away from the problem internally at the same time as living it on the outside—you have to see it and recognize it for what it *really* is— because you have not seen well until now. You also have to give others time for their various false beliefs and illusions to disperse. You cannot solve any problem without the appropriate perspective because all you can do is operate the old forces that created the problem in the first place. Wait. Relax in the "pit."

4. A glass, sacrificial tray, and a flagon of wine passed in through the window. Faultless result.
The sage rushed to help his pupil in trouble. Here—like light coming in through a window—the help comes from above. If you pay attention, you will even see it. Two thoughts: sacrifice is the path to solving problems, and take some good advice. Such advice is simple and practical. A single word is worth much more than reams and reams of clever theory. You have arrived at the boundary of new events.

5. The pit cannot be filled to overflowing. It can only be filled to the brim. No mistake.
Things can only happen if the time comes. If you are impatient and want it sooner, you will just be tense and agitated. Let everything happen on its own in the natural way (path of least resistance). This is a time for patience, not for great deeds.

6. Tied with rope, the court sends him to a place surrounded by walls that are topped with thorny branches. Nothing happens to him for three years.
This is what happens to a person who has lost their way. Return at once because if you don't realize this yourself, fate will wake you to your sins. The difficulty that we do not solve on the inside, we now live on the outside as fate. "Three years" is the symbol of a long period of time.

30 ䷝ *Li*

Enlightenment

Character: A yellow, magical firebird.

You realize and awaken to self-awareness. Your eyes open; you become a seer. What you have done subconsciously up to now, you now see through and understand more and more—and get to know. "I see!" There is a decisive difference between intellect and sense. Intellect is short-sighted; the person "who has not yet fully grown" is, at best, clever. Sense sees; the True Man is wise.

All the problems of a sage are solved because, without exception, **all problems come from a lack of recognition.** Your spirit is illuminated by your inner light and the truth makes you free. Things only depress us until we understand them. Fear ceases in light, suffering gains sense, and the demons of the past follow us no longer. (The forest is only frightening while it's dark.) Now you wake up. Now you understand and solve.

Li means "fire" and "radiance." In Li, you shine, give warmth and light. Not only to yourself but for others as well. Now you can understand your fate, the meaning of your life, your relationships; it is just like sunrise when the mist clears and everything comes into light and gains a meaningful outline. (It puts an end to the chaotic din of emotion.)

The greatest failing of Li is vanity. The light is never self-light! The candle flame is fueled by dense tallow and is given life by the invisible air. The True Man lives "with the humility and devotion of a cow," faithful to the gifts of the earth and attentive to the high spirit world. One cannot take anything that was not given from heaven. The person who believes that their knowledge is their own knows nothing.

Li also means "differentiation" and "separation." According to ancient tradition, the cause for our suffering is that our spirit identified with things. It confused itself with them. It identified with its ego, its transient body, its past, its emotions, and many other things. It got lost in life's drama like the actor who becomes so involved in their character that they no longer realize they are acting; the mask has stuck to their face and they think they will die along with it at the end of the performance.

This identification ends in the light of Li. A person who acts in it shines and will become master of many roles. Differentiation is the path of self-knowledge. Our immortal spirit takes on mortal roles on the world stage. In the sign of Li, the performer becomes aware of themself and becomes master of the performance.

THOUGHTS

Sky, Earth, Water, Fire: timeless ancient signs. They are fundamental characteristics that hide in all Oracle Signs. Fire is the sign of creative light. We create with our thoughts. The Chinese say, "A person who knows others is clever; a person who knows himself is wise." Genuine knowledge is self-knowledge.

The message of the Oracle Sign is, **Light up in yourself and from yourself. Remain humble. The way stands open before you. In the light it is obvious what belongs together and what doesn't.** Whatever you ask, the I Ching warns that you have created your doubts and problems and only you can solve them. Self-knowledge does not mean passive knowledge but *magical creative ability.*

Knowing someone means that they come under your control. This is why humility is the most important thing in this Oracle Sign. The world can be ruined with selfish knowledge. We can see it today. The world can be saved with selfless knowledge. We call selfless knowledge love. The humble knowledge of the sage radiates heat and it is so enduring that it continues to give off warmth after his death. It even comes out of his abandoned shoes.

If you live in your own light, you will soon go out and you will burn your switches. You have grown mature enough to hear the whisper of truth. You burn brightly but you should know, just like everyone, you were only given the light. If you believe this is yours, it will burn you. A person born in the sign of Li was given the defeat of knowledge and vanity as a fate task. Today, these "firebirds" are often tame, lonely people because our age of darkness does not like light.

The lines of the Oracle Sign describe the stages of enlightenment.

LINES

1. Departure, purification, and respect. No mistake.
Everything depends on a good start. When a beginner fighter enters the training room, they gather their thoughts and bow not only to their future master but also to the room. What begins as a tiny interference can later grow into chaos. The first step is decisive. It is the sprout of plans. It is spiritual togetherness. *Ching* not only means "respect" but also "wonderment." Respect is the forerunner of knowledge. The pupil still doesn't know the master, but only respects them, and this preliminary respect is the guarantee that the pupil will go on to know him and also become a master. It will become what you begin and how you begin it. The common man begins with a confused spirit and he doesn't respect anyone. You are not like that.

2. Yellow light. Exalted blessings.
Yellow is the color of the center. Your center spirit is the place of the creative center and clear vision. What starts from here is blessed and will succeed. This is partly because you are strong enough and also because you see through your fate. The inspired step is the wisest step.

Now you not only know what you do but also who you are. Your mid-day sun shines brightly.

3. At sunset, instead of drumming and singing, you lament your old age. Trouble.

This is the trap of transience. The mortal part of your being has taken fright and become stuck in the mud. You have forgotten that you are immortal. If you believed it, you would drum and sing. If you believed it, you would know that the sun not only sets but also rises again the following day. It is difficult to defeat our bad mood because our ego insists on it. It says, "I will live as long as I feel sorry for myself." Infertile sadness. This is false catharsis—do not give yourself over to it!

4. He rushes, collides, burns out, turns to ash, and is discarded.

Flash in the pan. A person who contains no humility wants to hurry their fate. This is impossible. A person who glows in their own light and breaks away from the divine power source soon burns out. This sign is a warning: do not be awed by your talent, your ability, your flaming mind—because nothing is yours. The one who says inside you, "I have to hurry," is lying. Patience.

5. His tears run in streams and he sadly mourns—and Blessings. Luck.

The 3rd line is false catharsis. This is true catharsis. Here, we purify and change heart. The rule of the ego breaks—this is painful. Our real self wakes within us—this is cheering. We see that all failures had deep and beneficent causes. We were the obstacles to the fulfillment of our fate. The experience is similar to waking. Not only has the oppressive dream passed but also the dreamer—you have become a different person.

6. The ruler punishes the rebels. He only kills the head and he leaves the demons to run. Faultless.

The master of our spirit solves the problem. He sees that everything has *one root*. He now determinedly destroys this—and everything gets better. A person who sees clearly often experiences that the most complex problems have only one cause. This can often be named with one simple word—for example, *vanity*. And this, like an inflamed tooth, poisons the body and the whole life. The master of our spirit knows what the problem is and acts precisely. He does not fall into the sin of exaggeration and does not cause unnecessary suffering.

Chou means "demon," "bad spirit," "bad temptation." Lead us not into temptation but deliver us from evil is the secret of this line. If you put an end to the "evil," then you can no longer be tempted. The master of our spirit knows that any kind of evil within us attracts all similar evils from the invisible world. Ghosts of vague aggression hang in bunches around the aggressive person. The vain person becomes the medium for all the vanities of the world. A person who has the suppressed fire of ambition burning deep in their spirit can easily become the pitiful instrument of the semidivine ambitions of mercenary politicians. The secret of liberation is stopping the cause of the problem with determined strength—and then releasing and forgiving—putting down the sword and making peace.

31  *Hsien*

Harmonizing

*Character: Two pieces of a broken plate fit together—
because they were once one.*

Meeting; fate is not solitary but a shared undertaking. It requires companions. The true companion is a spouse but it could also be friends, colleagues, comrades, similar people, like-minded people, or those with whom you share a plan or a dream. This is a beneficent divination. This is the time to meet people. It encourages persistence. The True Man's secret is openness. He accepts others while his own heart is empty (hsü). It contains no prejudice, hostility, obstruction, self-defense, or any kind of thought or feeling that would shut out or condemn the being of another.

Joy is above and the solidity of the Mountain is below in the trigrams of the Hsien sign. Joy on the outside and strength and calm on the inside.

THOUGHTS

Hsien means "unity" and "togetherness." We were never and never will be solitary. Life only has meaning with others. Modern, alienated man suffers not only from a lack of himself but also the lack of others. The two are related: a person who is not in "unison" with themself cannot stand others either; they do not "fit in" with anyone.

The secret of this Oracle Sign is described by Jesus: "What God brings together, let no man put asunder." This is not only true of marriage. Hsien says that the preconditions for true meetings have already been created in the "Sky" and in the supernatural world. We brought the broken pieces of the whole to earth with us and, having lost our memory, we blindly try to put the broken pieces together based on smell, suspicion, and feelings. Hsien means the flashes of love, the experience of belonging together, and the enthusiastic joy that says, "Hey, this belongs here!"

We are artists of division and scattering, but stupid and unlucky when it comes to collection and bringing together. This is why relationships, marriage, and friendships are so perishable in the modern world and why striving for a shared goal will be destroyed by selfishness sooner or later.

The I Ching says that **all relationships are spiritual relationships.** Modern man, set for work mode, is greatly mistaken in believing that his spiritual relationship is only with his lover and not with the shop assistant sitting behind the counter in a department store. Of course, various relationships have various degrees of depth, but whoever looks at a single person as an object or tool will soon look upon their spouse in the same way. Their love will be love of themselves, their embrace will be self-gratification, and their friendship will be selfishness.

Alienated man needs to learn to love. We need to learn the art of harmonization. This is difficult. Not one of the six lines is totally cheering. Harmonization has three secrets: the first, what I give of myself; the second, what I accept of others; the third, persistence or the assertion that **I will not allow either myself or the demons of the outside world to destroy the hard-won state of love!**

We need to know that our spirit is continually transmitting. This is called "the butterfly effect" in modern language and has been known in China for thousands of years: you can influence the whole universe with your pure thoughts and feelings. We constantly transmit signals whether we want to or not. These can be attracting or repulsing signals. All our harmonies and all our problems are transmitted outward. A relationship is not born when we see one another for the very first time and it doesn't go wrong when it has become impossible on the "outside." Everything happens beforehand in the invisible world of the spirit. That is why we need to know ourselves! We need to hear our inner subconscious voice—because this is the "calling Sign."

Harmonization primarily means the harmony with ourselves. We need to be harmonized to the more beautiful and unselfish melody within ourselves. This is what should be transmitted—but you should know that the outside world picks everything up: uncertainty, arrogance, hate, condescension, temper, as well as secret contempt and disgust. Most actions are reactions. Take a look at what really radiates from you.

It is even harder to accept others because our self-defense is continually on the offensive. You can only accept someone if your ego moves over or isn't at home. This is hsü. It means "I am empty." I am empty but I can be impregnated. I have no prejudice, opinion, or picture of you that I have created—I see you and accept you as you are. I allow you to affect me—without coming under your influence. The true mirror image of your being appears in my heart—without you effecting any influence on me. I give myself; you can come into me—but you cannot rule me because I have allowed you to live inside me not out of weakness but out of strength.

This is a great mystery and it is difficult to believe that not only lovers work like this but so do the samurai in a battle for life or death. They perfectly sense the intention of the other—but this is objective knowledge—and they do not become its slave. If the harmonization is perfect, this is how we live whether there are two, three, ten, or one hundred of us. This is how a married couple lives in unity, but the same is true of a family, an orchestra, a group of friends, and even a whole nation in a moment of clemency. At times like this, we are together and still separate—like the planets in the solar system and all the stars of the cosmos.

The various stages of preparation for harmonization appear in the lines of this Oracle Sign.

LINES

1. Urge in the "big toes."
Involuntary urge. Just as likely to mean a real promise as it is to be an illusion. Wait until you know better. It is still hard to know whether this is your Fate or you are being tempted onto the path of your life. Pay attention!

2. Urge in the "leg." If you take a step, you will enter shame.
Do not try to influence others and don't let others influence you. A lot of selfish force is at work here: desire, temper, false promise, and self-deceit. You should wait until the air clears. Genuine harmonization can only give birth to unselfishness and honesty. Wait—and look into yourself. And also into others.

3. Urge in the "thighs." Stay and don't go after it!
The urge is strong but do not run after it. It is probably empty enthusiasm and false attraction. The difference between instinctive and spontaneous action is that instinctive is blind while the spontaneous sees. It is not enough that you feel the urge. Think what you want from others and what others want from you. It is one thing to listen to our emotions and our desires and another thing to follow the path of our fate. It is still early to set off.

4. The regret comes to an end. The urge starts from the "heart"—but the heart still sways. Beneficent divination.
You are now on a good path. But despite all of the good signs, you are still in two minds. According to Chinese tradition, the "heart" is

the home of thoughts. You are not lacking anything other than your certainty. But because of this, you want to influence your relationship with your companion(s) by applying conscious intention. It is possible that others are doing the same with you. Like someone who still doesn't trust the music—you count your steps while dancing. You still don't trust God with the matter. You also interfere—especially mentally. Everyone senses the thoughts of others and automatically responds accordingly. No one likes to be influenced. You don't like it either. Real harmonization only occurs when everyone is free.

5. Urge in the neck. There is no cause for regret.
There is some kind of cramp in the urge, some kind of obstinacy. Others really don't affect us at such times and we don't affect them either. It is unavoidable that there should be such dry and selfish periods in harmonization.

6. Urge with the "mouth," "face," "chin."
Harmonization is impossible with just words—because words are empty. A person who wants to create harmony with nothing more than reasoning, logic, and speech is spouting hot air. You can only analyze with rationality, not synthesize. The intellect does not substitute for wholeness of spirit. The sage does not say a great deal because he knows that he influences with his spirit; he does not believe in words. No one has ever been convinced with words—only with the being and deeds of the other. A person who loves does not explain; a person who talks a lot is commonly a slave to self-love. They speak instead of loving, chattering away instead of giving themselves and accepting others. You should know that words are only to give signs—they are no substitute for the essence. It is a sure sign of alienation when a person wants to fill the void with speech and the void is due to a lack of love. Infertile experiment.

32      *Hêng*

Persistence (Permanence)

恒

Character: A heart and a rowing boat between two riverbanks. Life path.

"Good and bad can come if we row with one heart in one boat." This Chinese proverb probably originates from the Hêng sign. Whatever happens, hold your direction! Do not, under any circumstances, leave your path. Not tomorrow or the day after—hold on for a very long time. This is the path of your fate.

The Book of Changes teaches that everything changes and that there is nothing other than eternal Change—this sign is about **permanence and endurance**; it is about the fact that **the Heart—the center point— must not change**. The secret of permanence is that, while everything dies, it is constantly being reborn. If faithfulness does not change and the heart remains, then the alternating between "passing" and "birth" is given meaning and direction. The center point does not change.

Hêng is the sign of ideal marriage. I have been living in this for nearly half a century. In it, I have been a lovesick kid, a preoccupied man, father, and now grandfather—my every cell, brain cell, circumstance, friend, home, house, and the history of humanity and even the climate has changed. My wife and I have also changed but our marriage has not changed because it was made in the "Sky."

The message of the Oracle Sign is, **You are following a good path,**

stay on it and keep the direction. The sages say, "Success. Steadfastness is desirable. It is desirable to know where a person is going."

In this sign, the True Man does not allow temptations that accompany change to affect him. He is just like a good boat captain: the storm doesn't affect him, neither do stormy seas and neither does he lose vigilance in quiet waters, and the shores he passes do not attract him—only the Destination. He can only do this if he is in unison with himself and if he is convinced that the Path that he is following is taking him in a good direction.

THOUGHTS

This is not about immobility but about constant movement that renews us. Persistence is difficult because we are different every minute. Everything changes, just not our essence. Feelings, desires, and passions come and go in our being—and yet still we somehow remain the same. I experienced "I am" when I was a child. A lot has attached itself since then and yet still "I am," and that is how I will stay.

What are people loyal to? They are loyal to what it is worth being loyal to, but what is that? It is hard to tell. What they like? What they have undertaken? For what is life worth living? The drama of loyalty is hidden in your question. If you have received an Oracle Sign with no changing lines, then persistence is beneficial. More precisely, it is beneficial to learn how you should persist for a very long time. If you have received changing lines, then these lines are about the diverting temptations or about the fact that it is not worth persisting in certain life situations.

The confused ego thinks that permanence is boring when, in fact, it is the greatest adventure. The ego needs constant sensation; it chases constant turns, the different, the new, fashions. The thing that is permanent in the ego is bad health and its eternal confusion. On the other hand, a person who lives from the heart has no need for sensation and does not pursue change because what is permanent within them is good health and inner calm. (This spiritual state shows if someone lives their fate—even if that fate is difficult.)

"A happy family has no history." It is possible that you are standing before something new. If your heart wishes for this new thing, and not simply your greed, then go for it as you have been preparing for this for a long time; the secret of permanence is constant renewal. The only thing that needs to be preserved is the goal. Permanence represents a hint of Eternity in transience.

LINES

1. Jumping headfirst into permanence: trouble! Do not set a goal. It is not timely now.
The other meaning of *chun* ("jumping headfirst") is when a root suddenly wants to plunge deep down. You are running long-distance—you don't want to win in the first one hundred meters. An enduring result can only be achieved with long work. Think through what you have taken on.

2. Regret stops.
Carry on just like this. The outer circumstances still don't confirm your inner strength. The time will come. Stay on the middle path.

3. He cannot persist on the path of his fate (his Tao). If he receives something, he will feel guilty. Divination: shame.
If the fear, anxiety, ambition, and panic of your ego direct you, if you come under the influence of the outside world and you lose your inner path, you will find yourself drifting. You will be the victim and not the master of events. Listen to your most inner voice that quietly speaks behind the clamor: "Not over there—over here!"

4. No wild bird in the field.
As they say, "This isn't your game." Being persistent here is pointless, you win nothing. The path of your fate does not go in this direction. Perhaps your desire is unrealistic. Carry on.

5. Persist on the path of your fate (your Tao, your strength, your religion). If you follow it like a "woman" (Yin), the road is open. If you follow it like a "man" (Yang), the road is closed.

Here you have to select the method of your persistence. It is possible to follow a good path badly. Here the danger is stubbornness, pigheadedness, hardness, aggressiveness, unscrupulousness, ambition, and "I can do everything better than you!" "Let yourself be led," says the sage. "Give yourself over to me and follow me." Listen to others and be adaptable. You already have your persistence. All that is missing now is your humility.

6. Problem is the agitation becomes permanent.

Here *chen* means "agitation," "trembling," "nervousness," or "a disturbed state." The character depicts a trembling hand. I have a tendency to always be nervous about something. This has its roots in a lack of faith. It is an ever-present fear of mine that I will not receive what is mine and that there will be a problem or that it won't succeed. "Do not worry about tomorrow," says Jesus. This line says, "There is trouble if this quality of the ego becomes an enjoyable habit." The ego not only suffers from anxiety but also enjoys it, as this is "all about it." If someone worries a lot, they become a worrier and it is hard to give that up.

33  *Tun*

Retreat

Character: Halted foot, a pig, and a knife: someone sacrifices a pig while retreating.

We find the character rather amusing and what it says is this: **Do not move one single step further! Retreat and sacrifice your various earthly ambitions; this will be the key to your success.** The message of Tun is, **Retreat. Success. Advantageous divination for the Little.** Whatever you have asked, the answer is that you should retreat and prepare for times when your situation becomes more favorable. Retreat does not mean giving up, but rather the wise recognition of the character of the times.

The Russian general Kutuzov applied the Tun Oracle Sign with such genius that he was able to break the invincible Napoleon. It is a difficult tactic and very few are able to carry it out. The first thing you have to do is recognize that you now have no chance of victory. Time is not working for you: if you sow seed, it will not grow; you cannot sail your boat out because of the low tide; the enemy is stronger and more active—it is not enough to stop, you also have to retreat.

You have to make a conscious and considered retreat. The psychological secret of this is that you have to clamber out of what you are wrapped up in and break away from it. Is there something that you really wanted? Don't! Is there something you desired? Is there something you were frightened of? Was there something that you really needed? Tear these feelings from yourself as if they didn't belong to you. Be indifferent. Do not identify with your mental state. It is as if you were looking at yourself from the outside and from above—as if the whole thing wasn't happening to you.

Conflict needs two people and if you don't "stand there"—there is no conflict. This is a trick employed in martial arts. It can be very effective. This was demonstrated when new rules had to be formulated for wrestling because it became clear that a weak competitor could obstruct the victory of a world champion if he stayed passive and continually withdrew from all maneuvers. You cannot start anything with someone who doesn't want to.

It is not enough for you not to argue and not to try to convince anyone, and it is not enough for you to avoid conflict—you also have to retreat within. Shed your concerns and take your energy from them. Save yourself from tensions by not getting involved in fights with evil . . . by avoiding them. Do not fight against high tide but step back if it comes. Don't even be there when it reaches that point.

The task is not to panic in this situation that appears to be temporarily lost. The more "efficiently" you back away—the more strength you will gather for the advance.

THOUGHTS

Tun also means "to hide away," "remain unclear," "disappear," "become invisible." Today we would say something like, "I am taking myself out of circulation." I am retreating to my home territory. *I am turning inward.* I retreat from the world and having quieted the noise of my internal and external struggles, I step out of the whirlwind and try to become not a participant but—for a short time—a witness to my fate. This is called meditation. This is the kind of thing that happens in a Zen monastery just as it does in any kind of genuine religious order: people retreat from time to time, to put their lives back in order.

While man still knew the mental and spiritual secrets of life, *he would not set about any significant action without having first set time aside to pray, look within, or meditate.* A matador, a champion athlete, or a genuine artist still retreats before a dramatic moment in their life in the same way as great military generals and kings did in ancient times. They do not simply ask for God's help but step out of the external and internal complexities and take a long, calm look at where they stand both internally and externally and, in light of that, they consider the most beneficial route to take. This is just like when a painter "steps back" from their painting and takes an objective look at where corrections need to be made. While the painter is "still in the picture," they don't see it.

If you have a conflict with someone, you can't tell whether it is because that person behaves in a particular way or because you have caused them to behave in such a way. If you retreated, you could partly see yourself more clearly and partly leave the other party to deal with their own whirlwind. Of course, external and internal is not enough for this as it also requires retreat. This has to be genuine and not hypocritical. In a business negotiation, it is not only important that you do not show how important a victory is to you—but you have to convince yourself that it *really isn't all that important*—and you have already stepped closer to a good solution.

If the Retreat Oracle Sign changes to its opposite, it becomes the "Great Power" sign. This phase of being does not mean ultimate surrender, rather the preparation for victory. You do not need to meditate to escape but to become useful to the world. When you retreat, it is recommended—as the sage would say—"to keep common people at a distance. Do this not with anger and condemnation but with fear inducing severity." Your retreat does not happen out of weakness but out of strength and it is advisable to sometimes make this known to those around you. The *how* and *when* are extremely important to consider when planning to retreat as we see in the lines.

I usually received the Tun Oracle Sign when I didn't notice that I was getting wrapped up in something externally and internally that I had falsely valued. I was almost ready to take the next step when I was warned, "Stop! You can't see what you are doing. Step back and take another look. Take a clear and calm look."

And one more important piece of advice. If you get this Oracle Sign, you should not be frightened by any form of external aggression, even if it is threatening or appears to be so. You can only solve things with retreat and calm avoidance of open conflict—without fear. You don't even have to be afraid of a "Napoleon."

LINES

1. Retreat as a straggler. Dangerous. Do not move in any direction at all.
You are late with your retreat and you should have made it earlier. Now you are in the situation and it is better if you stay calm and don't move.

2. Held tightly by yellow ox skin. Nothing can break it off.
Don't give yourself over to outer or inner situations. Stay passive, empty, and neutral as if this wasn't about you. To put it in a humorous way, play dead and trouble will pass right over your head. A person who retreats into their neutral, wise center is under protection.

3. Confused retreat. Trouble and danger. Servants and mistresses can help the situation.
The "trouble" (chi) may be hatred, illness, insult, or injury—while "danger" (li) may be threatening, hostile, and ill willed. This is the kind of tangled situation when someone was unable to make a genuine retreat in a timely fashion. They insisted on a lot of things and were late. They now find themself in a hostile situation that may only be lessened by making a certain amount of compromise. (Kutuzov's retreat was full of such moments when they did not retreat out of strength but out of weakness, they fled in panic and were regularly late. It was

at such times that they were forced to make friends with the French soldiers.) Chinese thinking does not disapprove of compromise if it means that the Essence can be saved. Compromise is better than nothing. It is inappropriate for attaining great goals, but it is possible to solve small, temporary problems with it. That is what is happening here.

4. Unselfish (loving) retreat. Beneficent for the True Man, trouble for the common man.
Common man is incapable of withdrawing. It isn't possible. He is stuck to his desires, his possessions, and his routine existence. The True Man is free. He happily leaves his old world and easily finds a home in the new one. "The Well Frog is held prisoner in its own pit" is what Chuang Tse says about the common man. The True Man wanders in infinity—his home is where God is; He is everywhere. The Oracle Sign advises you to dissolve away from your situation in a light and friendly manner—you don't have to prove and defend what you do is right and natural. Step out of the situation without argument—but with commitment. (You can be soft moving outward but not inward. Be careful!)

5. Excellent retreat. Persistence is beneficent.
In a good psychological moment, everything is easily solvable and virtually solves itself. You have the strength and tact to do it; it is also possible that your goals change. It is possible that you do not leave entirely but just remove your spirit. You retreat within. You no longer depend on the outer surroundings. Be committed and steadfast in your intention. What you do is good.

6. Happy (glorious) retreat. Everything is advantageous.
You are free! And when a person is free inside and out, anything is possible and, sooner or later, everything turns to their advantage. This is where the retreat really comes to an end. Nothing ties any longer. When the doubts evaporate, certainty appears.

34 ䷡ *Ta Chuang*
The Influence of the Great

Character: Great Man—and a weapon and a strong servant.
This later became the sign of the intellectual caste.

Strength is gathering. This could be life strength, mental strength, or spiritual strength . . . but it is most definitely an **inner strength that influences and inspires**. The Influence of the Great is a promising Oracle Sign. "Man's true nature," says the sage, "is divine and strong. The weakness in him is false desire and false thought."

Either consciously or not, your strengths are coming together swiftly and you radiate this. Those around you also sense this. Be careful because you influence others as well and if you are not conscious of this, you will not recognize that **what you experience is what you brought out of people**. If you are cheerful, then they will be cheerful; if you are anxious, they will be anxious; if you are nervous, everyone around you will be agitated and confused—because your influence is strong.

Your creative powers are gathering and aiming for manifestation—the deed is ripening. The only problem is that the *enriching energies are not in balance*. There is a lot of Yang and little Yin—and that is why danger threatens that you exploit your power. Several lines, with the symbol of the eruptive billy goat, warn that the gathering strengths, if they are not directed by consideration, calm, and humility, may cause serious damage. We all exploit our power; this is our ancient sin. One of the most common human sins is when we suppress and exploit others, when we are not strong, but just aggressive. An aggressive person not only ruins the lives of others but ultimately ruins their own life as well; they rule by pushing others down and that finishes them both. There is no such thing as a "victorious" suppressor.

The other common but hidden sin is when we fail to recognize our own strength. A person who does not know that they create with every thought and deceives themself that they are weak and helpless sins against themself by forgetting their divine origin.

Your plans reach fruition. You are helped by internal and external forces. For this you need to know that the True Man does not step on a path that does not abide by tradition. The tradition says that *power is service.* The stronger you are, the greater power you have, the more you are responsible for others. The person at the very top has no "self"— they serve with every thought and every deed—and even draw breath for others. (Think of the power of Jesus.) A person is aggressive who serves themself—and that is the greatest source of failure. The sign is encouraging and also provides a warning: the driver of a powerful race car has increased responsibility.

THOUGHTS

Every deed has its own timing. It is possible to act with greatest effectiveness when your strengths are at their actual peak. This is the explosion point in physics. They build up until that point and then lose energy; the peak is when the gathered energies explode into an act. This is also the message of this Oracle Sign for the martial arts: the exploding act that takes place at the peak is typically precise and calm. A person who does not experience this may easily be cramped, aggressive, hysterical, impatient, and reckless.

This very promising Oracle Sign continually warns of the dangers of longing, impatience, and irresponsible aggression toward others (dominance). A truly strong person hardly does anything, and yet everything still happens around them. A person who is not clear about their strengths is constantly whining, wanting, doing, interfering, and hardly achieves anything. What they succeed in battling to gain is worthless and muddled and, in many cases, hazardous.

This is the Influence of the Great. Concentrate your strength and realize your goal calmly and patiently. The hidden message of the Oracle Sign speaks to the Magician within us: **you can realize your creation, but you are responsible for it.** You can take advantage of it in both the positive and negative sense. Let the will of God be done by you.

True Power works in such a way that it isn't even noticed. It is just there and no one knows who did it and how. The sign of divine magic is that it is unnoticeable, because the one who does it is invisible. It is done from another dimension and no one appears to take a bow.

LINES

1. Strength (power) in the feet. To continue is bad luck. Preserve your honesty (yu fu).
The situation is too early for action. Collect more strength. Originally, the word *cheng* did not mean marching on or action but rather commencing a "punishing expedition." And *yu fu* did not mean honesty but rather the "support of good spirits." This was accompanied by harmony between loyalty, the ego, and the Self. In other words, the good spirits are with you but wait for the time to act. If you set off early, you will soon grow tired because you will run out of strength.

2. The road is open before you.
You can set off. The signs are encouraging. But be steadfast and continually preserve your center point—the calm of your heart. The secret of an effective act is that a person should not get lost in it; they keep a cool head while acting with balance and clear vision. Difficulty does not worry them and success doesn't enthuse them.

3. The common man exploits his power. The True Man uses a net (emptiness). To continue on: trouble. A billy goat charges into the hedge and its horns are damaged.

The ego not only creates trouble when it has reached power but it also creates ugly and difficult karma on the road that leads to power. The True Man is triumphant by not acting. "God's net," says the sage, "has large holes and yet still everything becomes caught in it." Don't do anything now. Be empty. Nothing is yours, least of all power. If you do receive it, you do not receive it for yourself. The most beautiful statue of Buddha depicts a throne on which no one sits. The more powerful an individual is, the less they use their power. It is the common man who struggles inside you—he only brings trouble and creates enemies.

4. The troubles and strife come to an end. Steadfastness is beneficent. The hedge opens up, there is no obstruction. The power rests on the axle of a large carriage.

The divination is encouraging. Your inner being is now leading and not your ego. The axle of the carriage is invisible and yet it still bears great loads. Power never shows in a person who deserves it. The obstacles slowly fall away. You can begin. We receive when we eventually realize that nothing is ours.

5. He abandons his goatlike nature and easily changes. No regret.

You are no longer obstinate and aggressive. You should use the tactic of water: you defeat opposition by adapting patiently and softly; you easily turn your sails. Follow the flow.

6. The goat butts the hedge. Nothing can be moved either forward or backward. You can continue with hard work. The mistake is not long-lived.

You want and want and want over and over again—and in the end, you can neither move forward nor back. You have become a slave to your own obstinacy. You cannot continue; all tension, longing, desire, or ambition only tightens the knot. Here, "work" means reduction. You need to stop the magic of false thought, longing, or even the hustle and bustle of everyday life. Stop and free yourself of your obsessions.

35 ䷢ *Chin*

Progress (Emergence)

Character: Birds take to the wing in the light of the rising sun.

Your sun is rising and everything is enlightened. Chin is the time of progress, emergence, blossoming, and growth when things shine. You step into light and everything "comes to light." This is the time of prosperity. You get strength in the sparkling sunshine and you also become stronger in yourself. Welcome the spiritual forces into yourself—and give of yourself to others. What you experience with closed eyes if the sun shines on your face: this is the experience of Chin. Desires, obsessions, everyday goals are no longer important at times like these; you feel that it is good to be alive, the earth is good, and the sky is good. Everything is good. This is the inspired state. You feel that you are more. What has been difficult becomes easy, and what was cloudy becomes clear.

"Let there be light" is our greatest wish. Of course, everything becomes visible at such times, not only the beautiful but also the ugly. Your faults come to the fore along with your weaknesses and hidden sins . . . but this is not a problem because at least it means that you can see and know that **Light is stronger than Darkness** and you can work on yourself with enthusiasm. The sun that shines so brightly is inside you.

Everything was shrouded in external darkness: the opinions of others, their stupidity, their ill will, the blindness and evilness of our age. Ever since you were born, this world has been trying to make you forget that God lives within you. Now it shines. The light shines from within you. I could say that it shines through you because at times like this the help of the spirit world shines through your life. You not only see, you also illuminate. This is why others see you better than they did before. They respect you more and value you.

The message of the Chin Oracle Sign is **Progress. The prince who has faith in his own strength (*kang*) receives the gift of a large number of horses. This happens three times (many times) in one day.** *Kang* also means "calm, solid, peaceful, joyful." All these things together. A person trusts in their strength who is *at one with it all*—at one with God, with the Tao, and with the invisible world. Such a person is invincible.

THOUGHTS

The first secret of this promising sign is that man's ego steps aside and does not bring about the good spiritual effect but accepts it. The sun rises on its own, it doesn't need to be dragged into the sky and you do not have to create the light from within yourself. All you have to do is to accept it. Open your eyes! A person is talented if they begin to listen, to see, if they are selfless and accepting.

Darkness is nothing more than the false belief that you illuminate. Light can only occur if you let the light in—"people of light" always looked up and if they were already high up, they would look even further—no one was at the highest point, not even Jesus Christ because, in heaven, the smallest is the greatest. If someone does not obstruct themself from shining, they will become enlightened. Allow good to happen.

The second secret is that your true nature appears in this sign. This is why you can be successful. You say that you do what is yours to do and what genuinely comes from you has a magical power. Everyone is the most effective if they live according to their own nature.

The third secret is that everyone can be the most successful in an area where life presents the most obstacles. Light is born out of triumph over darkness. Success is born out of triumph over adversity.

The fourth secret—accept this divination with care—is that the outside world can also help in the phase of fate. If you do not receive changing lines, that makes the Progress sign very difficult; the Oracle Sign describes extremely favorable coincidences and a state when the world has a "wise leader" who values your efforts. But where are such things today? It is sure to exist even in total darkness.

LINES

1. Progress—but restricted. Divination: the road still stands open. Be "empty." Gaining wealth will not be a mistake. (He makes lonely progress; he has still not received a commission.)
The message of the Oracle Sign contains the word *empty*, which originally referred to a net. This means that the darkness is still dense, your little light is tiny, and you stumble about all alone. You still do not hear the voice of your spirit, but you are progressing in the right direction even on your own. Try to be open and empty to accept the will of your spirit in the same way that an open and empty net accepts a fish. You are living your fate—unconsciously but correctly. Carry on like this.

2. You are progressing but you are frightened and sad. The road is open. Armor of dense chains is a blessing from the queen Mother.
You are stuck. Nothing works. You are worried about the future. See the obstacles as protection and lack of success as preservation; the great Yin force looks after you and promises happiness. It is sometimes better to travel in fear and sadness than to travel with others on a road that is not our own and is unworthy of you. The Oracle Sign also says that we are attracted to something Higher—but we have been unable to get closer to it. Loyalty and persistence bring the solution. (The attraction—although you didn't feel it and it filled you with pain—is not one-sided. The Christian cult of Mary is hidden in this line.)

3. Shared trust (agreement). The end of regret.

Fate is not a solitary undertaking. You do not have to do battle with everything on your own. You would not have the strength to do it but don't be sorry about this. You will be much stronger than this. This is a task that you can only do together. Join others and accept others.

4. Progress like the rat. Trouble.

The uninhibited greed of the ego causes trouble. Stop! There is nothing more to say about this line. This is the progress of our dark world and selfish rat morals—everything for me, whatever the price! "Trouble" means that the rat and the world will both be destroyed in this struggle.

5. The end of regret. Winning or losing no longer affects you. Carry on, the road is open. Everything becomes a blessing on you.

You are only free if your desires no longer bind you and you do not depend on external things. "Does not affect" (*wu hsü* in Chinese) shows a picture where the heart does not beat faster. Whatever happens, it beats in time to the pulse of divine life. A person who achieves this state is able to succeed in everything on the outside, although that is not important to them. The important thing is that the Self has become transparent and that they are at one with themself and with the spirit world. It doesn't matter to a true warrior whether he wins or loses. That is why he is invincible. His opponent is prisoner to a thirst to win and fear of losing, while he is free. This is a great advantage.

6. Progress with your horns. You can only discipline your own city (yourself). You should know that this is dangerous but not a mistake. Regret.

Aggression is never beneficial. This is, however, a situation where "increased pressure" is forgivable, especially if you have to slow down your own ego, ambition, or selfishness. But do not continue because the road goes down from here.

36 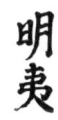 *Ming I*

Darkening of the Light

明
夷

Character: A barbarian warrior shoots at the sun/moon with his arrow.

Difficult and dark times. Don't lose your faith. Here darkness refers to the darkness of the spirit and the state that is referred to as "evil" by Christian tradition. Béla Hamvas calls this "ruination." It is a force that fights against the spirit, clear vision, and humanity. God said, "Let there be light." The barbarian warrior of Ming I shoots at the sun: let there be darkness! We should know a lot about this world because we have been in it for as long as we have lived. According to tradition, the Book of Changes was born in a time of such darkness and this is precisely because its authors abided by the advice of the Ming I Oracle Sign.

The advice of this Oracle Sign is, **Do not enter into conflict with the world because you cannot defeat the power of darkness now. It is better to preserve your faith and your wisdom and hide your spiritual values from people so that they will not trample on them.** The term *hiding sage* originates from this sign.

A spiritual person should know that the "barbarian who wounds light" is not only ignorant but also evil; he hates everything that is quality, purity, of a higher order, and goodness. He hates everything that is noble, spiritual, and divine. You don't even have to say a word, the simple fact that he thinks you are better than him makes him envy and even despise you. The exact translation of the Oracle Sign is "the wounding of the light." *Light is wounded. Persistence is beneficent amidst great difficulty.*

The whole history of our age takes place in the energy field of Ming I: this is the Iron Age. Hinduism refers to this as Kali Yuga. In such times, everyone is exposed to the danger that they will lose themselves. They will go crazy, become evil and become stupid and base in the world. This is partly because this is the only way to survive. The other reason is to make their treacherous otherness disappear so as not to antagonize the ill will of the "barbarians." It is important to know that darkness does not despise light because it has a different worldview, but because **light illuminates it and uncovers its lies with pure being.**

You can measure the genuineness of your spirituality by the ill will of others. If they only look down on you, reject you, and see you as nothing, you are on a low level. If you bring passion out in them, then you have moved to a higher level. If they persecute you, then you can be really proud of yourself. Then you really are somebody!

The Oracle Sign says that you should prepare for a difficult time. What you ripen and preserve within yourself will become your bright future. Work is hard, it is hard and thankless and requires persistence. Do not count on help from the outside. Darkness tends to come from the outside: bad air, deceit, and poisonous spiritual influences. Do not give yourself over to negative thoughts. It is not negative to think that the situation is difficult—because it is—but it is negative to think that everything has always been this way and everything will remain like this. That isn't true. Chinese tradition does not believe in a deed that lacks wisdom. It does not believe in martyred fate. To set about a world that cannot be changed is senseless.

Do not lose your faith. Preserve your hope. And retain your relationship with your real self and with your guardian angel—because you have one—hold tight to their robe with both hands, but in a way that nothing can be seen on the outside.

The Zen master Taishin Deshimaru was asked, "What do you advise a wise samurai who is confronted with invincible power?" The answer: "Run as fast as his legs will carry him!" You have to hide rather than run. All tricks are allowed, as in the animal world where creatures change color (merge into stones, become white in snow, become yellow in the desert, and green in the forest) and *yet they change nothing about their real being*. The character for *Change* and *I* depicts a chameleon. What you hold in your hand is the Holy Book of the Chameleon! And it can thank the chameleon tactic of being for its existence.

Prince Chi made himself appear mad, and it is said that King Wen did the same in the prison of Shin the Tyrant. He hid, smiled, and played a part while working with unshakable spirit and dedication to create the spiritual basis of a period in the future that would be truly great. The Darkening of Light is the Oracle Sign of King Wen. Its essence is the Chinese proverb *Tao kuang Yang hui*, "Hide your light and wait for your time."

THOUGHTS

Take care and do not plummet with the fall. You will get nothing from the outside world now because it is dark, rotten, ill-willed, and ignorant. Do not be afraid to see, feel, and know things differently from the way those around you see, feel, and know. Your truth is in your otherness. This is also your strength. Stay in the background, behind the scenes so that no one notices you; stay superfluous. The advice of the Oracle Sign is, **Be cunning like the snake and tame as the dove.** Be both at once, cunning and pure. The Art of Holy War allows all tricks!

A sage is not "moral" in the sense that he runs onto the sword of his dark opponent with open arms but in the sense that he claims victory over him. Sun Tsu's book of strategy, *The Art of War*, is a collection of cunning tricks. You can show yourself to be weak, harmless, stupid, and meek. You can wear any kind of cocoon over your real feelings. (The East realized this advice, especially Japan. Thousands of years of spiritual self-defense lie behind the "expressionless Japanese smile.") Don't let them know or even suspect who you really are. Darkness should feel that you have come to terms with it. It should feel as if it doesn't have to fear you; it should feel that you are not going to take its bread. Do not argue with its stupidity, just nod; don't enter into conflict with it, tell it that it is right.

You are never going to convince the darkness because this is not about principles and theories but about barbarian and merciless values, with no exceptions. Do not give in to one single "ism." Unfortunately, a raw battle for power is also taking place between religions in the dark age as well as between principles and worldviews. This is even while they are trying to convince themselves that "it is a matter of principle"—this is not the case at all!

Let them win. They will only crumble in the end. This is what the last line of the Oracle Sign describes. You do not have to win now—you wouldn't be able to anyway—but you should wait for your time and preserve the light within yourself. No one should be able to get a grip on you; be flexible and adaptable. Bamboo does not snap and break under the weight of the snow because it bends right down to the ground. This is the most important secret of martial arts.

Do not see it as being spineless to mislead the world. (Krishna did the same in the war and he was the embodiment of God. He used every trick, trap, and cunning plan.) But be careful! You have the right to act a part but don't lose yourself in it. Do not give one single iota within. You should know inside yourself who you are and what you want. You should be a gleaming, pure dove inside and a clever and cunning snake on the outside. This is how you should prepare for the future. That is where your victory awaits, not here. You need to get through this period without damaging the Light that you hold within.

It is important to note that psychologically this Oracle Sign means (internally) that you don't see clearly. The result of this is that you are overcome by anxiety. You have to deal with your own darkness!

LINES

1. The bird of light goes dark (is injured) during flight. It drops its wings. The True Man keeps on going and does not eat for three days but he does not abandon his goal. His master reprimands him for this.

There is a historic moment behind this line when a noble-minded prince hides from an evil dictator. "He does not eat for three days" means that you cannot be bought. It is rare now not to be able to buy a person. Modern "barbarians" wound the sun with money, not arrows. The light of the dark world is money; those who don't have it are like the living dead. The answer to your question is *even though the situation is nerve-wracking, do not give up; prepare for a time in the future when the "eclipse of the sun" passes! Do not concern yourself with the fact that others speak out or your boss condemns you because your thinking differs from what the dark world calls "normal." There is genuine light inside you. Retreat and look after it.*

2. The light darkens. He is wounded on his right thigh and yet he still keeps on riding and saves you from trouble. Strength and inspiration: blessings!

A historic example is given by King Wen, who created the Holy Book of Changes while in a dictator's prison and later became the savior of the people. It is important that you keep to the general advice offered by the Oracle Sign: wait for your time to come wisely and in secret but with great inner activity. Serious problems and difficulties should not break your faith; these are timely now.

3. Darkening of the light on the noon hunt. You catch the ringleader. You free yourself from trouble but remember to be determined and persistent.

The historic example here is when King Wen was released from seven years of imprisonment but did not see himself as having won. He taught his son, Prince Wu, the great science of how to rule and how to topple the rule of the dictator and create humane order in the world. The Oracle Sign says you stand before a crucial event but do not forget that the solution depends on your patient work and not on a single moment. The trouble did not come about as the result of a single moment, and habit, even if it is bad, can only be made good slowly and gradually. You have eventually recognized the cause of the problem.

4. It penetrates the left abdominal cavity. And it catches a glimpse of the heart of the damaged light! It leaves the house through the front door.
The cause of darkness is always illusion, "not seeing." Now you can see at last. You can see the true cause of the problem. You know it, you understand it, and you recognize it. You can see into the heart of the problem. You no longer have any illusions, and your sight is not over-shadowed by either hope or fear or cowardly, paralyzed habit. You have to decide whether or not the situation can be saved. If not, then carry on. **Feel free to make change.**

An excellent example is provided by the fate of a great number of Hungarian émigrés. They left their homes through the front door and never came back. Paths do exist that we must leave, even if it causes us pain, because they are not our own. The 36th Oracle Sign means abandoning outlived thought patterns, negative feelings, and prejudices. You have to shed what is no longer timely.

5. Hide your light like Prince Chi. Persistence is beneficent!
Prince Chi was related to the dictator, so he could not leave his court. That is why he made everyone believe that he was a fool and he survived the difficult times living among slaves. The Oracle Sign says that you have to stay. Follow the example of Prince Chi and hide your true thoughts and feelings. For the time being, you are the victim of your circumstances over which you have no control. But preserve your light. The line not only sees your dark situation but also its approaching sunrise. Do not come into conflict through word or deed as you will just make things worse.

6. Not light, darkness! It first climbs up to the sky and then plummets to the depths of the earth.

If this line describes you, stop! All dictators and all uninhibited, selfish passions fail. First it flies up into the sky and then it plummets toward hell. We have seen it time and time again, and yet we still don't learn. The better the cards you hold—the deeper the abyss that threatens you. If you carry on, you will fall to its depths. If the line describes your circumstances, you should know that the situation that is causing your problem is becoming increasingly unbearable and, like a boil, it will burst and the whole thing will be resolved. The satanic principle loses its battle when it reaches the peak of triumph and, as it cannot stop, it goes over the top and falls apart. The Oracle Sign indicates the end of an anxious period.

37  *Chia Jên*
A Man's Family

家
人

*Character: The sign of Man—and the idyllic picture of home:
a pig under the roof of the house.*

The family is the smallest unit—and the foundation of everything. In ancient China, the family was such an engrained pattern of human existence that they believed that it survived death, and the spirit family and the earthly family remained in very close contact. This Oracle Sign—in the symbolic sense—speaks about the creation of an intimate and lasting community: this is the present task of fate. "If you want to repair the world," it is said, "you first have to repair a state; if you want to repair a state, you have to first repair a family; in order to repair a family, you have to *start by repairing yourself.*"

This is the first message given by the Oracle Sign: **family members are the strength of your spirit; live in unity with yourself.** A person who has a poor relationship with themself also has a poor relationship with others. We have to begin everything with ourselves. We have to work from the inside out; this is the only direction in which to change our lives and our surroundings.

This is why the picture says the words of the True Man express the essence and is loyal and steadfast even in the midst of change. That is the role of the "Father" in the family. The reason that the Oracle Sign is not simply known as "family" but called A Man's Family is because it describes a community that is not only held together by instincts and interests or subconscious feelings but also by considerate Sense.

Only human Sense is capable of recognizing that **I share my fate with these.** In other words, in this family that is described, it is not blood and emotional relationships that are so important but primarily "divine order" that only conscious Man is capable of creating. In this pattern, the father and the mother and the children of various ages and genders have the same place and quality as the sun and the moon and the planets in the solar system.

Not only in the character Chia Jên, but also all the lines of all the Oracle Signs, from the one at the bottom to the six at the top, correspond to family members. They appear in ancient commentaries as "oldest brother" and "youngest sister" and so on. The reason that I have not spoken about this is because the modern reader does not sense the various special and spiritual forces of the family members in analogous terms. The modern family has fallen apart to such an extent that it is only an emotional and interest community in the very best cases. In more recent times, it has more commonly turned into the stage for tragedy, scandal, divorce, and suffering rather than the idyllic mirror image of cosmic order that it once meant and that—of course now only in "lesser" form—is also appropriate in Chinese families today.

That is why it is important that the words of the "father" express the essence. The father has to know what is good and what is bad. He did not receive this knowledge from social models on the outside—because these could be rotten, false, or of low rank as they are today—but from his own heart, self-sense, and filtered experiences of life. "The food was sweet from my mother's hand. The truth was beautiful from my father's mouth," says the poet. This is what this sign is about.

As far as persistence is concerned, true childrearing does not depend on the thumping-stroking tactics of strict punishment and loving compliance, but it does rest on this example more than anything else. It depends on the pattern. We primarily influence our children with our own being. We influence them with what we are; what we say is insufficient. We raise them with our whole being. The Father gives order to the family. The Mother gives the cohesive strength. "Womanly strength is beneficent!" says the sage. It is the woman who holds all families together—the whole thing falls apart without them. The family is the basis of all communities.

Our spirit is "family" in itself. If we close our eyes, we feel those forces and those spaces by which we become our own directing "father" and caring "mother." We also feel desires, feelings, and aims in the depths of our soul that we have to raise as "good" or "bad" children of our own. The inner world of a harmonious person is the "ideal family."

But the need to become "family" appears in the office, in the shop, in business, in the workplace, in the workshop, or *anywhere there is life on a human scale* because the pattern was born with man. (We still instinctively see the "Father" in state leadership and this is what dictators mercilessly exploit.) All communities that are not built on the family pattern are inhuman. They are inhuman in the same way that a multinational company is inhuman, and this is what all those feel who work for such an organization, however much money they may earn.

The Chia Jên answers your question with the **pattern of the family**. This may be as much about your inner self as it is about your family, or any other question influencing your fate in which the opportunity for harmony may appear as much as the disintegration of the pattern. This may be the realization of opportunities of an idyllic human relationship or its disruption. It shows the strategy of the path that leads to harmony and it also shows the forces that may threaten that same harmony.

THOUGHTS

If you are wounded in the world, the only place that you can retreat to is home. Your family can protect you. There is safety among your own. There is nowhere else that you can feel this. Just think, however many people you have been involved with in this life, it will be your relatives who stand around your grave—because they belong to you! This is why family disharmony is the greatest challenge. A person who has chaos in their own family has nowhere to hide away—in essence, they are living with strangers in exile.

The secret of a good family is intimacy and order. Intimacy means that you belong with these people for better or for worse. It means that you can share your problems with them. It means that they empathize with you. It means that they are within arm's reach. It means that they are your nearest and dearest. Order means that if anyone steps over the boundaries of intimacy, the situation will become hell!

By the same measure, if someone gets too close to us, whoever that might be—our father, husband, sibling, or even our mother—then it can be unbearable. They push us down; they suffocate us, and they gratuitously interfere in our fate. If you live together with a lot of people in a small place (and by this, I mean that you are too close to one another spiritually or emotionally and things become entangled with other related threads), then that which is only You can become damaged. Attraction can turn into aggression; love can become selfishness and a father can become a tyrant. A mother can become an emotional miser who does not let the child of her womb grow and develop and possesses it forever. A child can turn into a rebel who kicks the mother and father away or who simply forgets to grow up and is dependent into old age. Something that is incurable in society as a whole has already appeared like the early cells of a cancerous growth in the family.

You get the Chia Jên Oracle Sign if you have to put your inner and outer forces in order. You have to do this to be able to achieve harmony with yourself and with others with whom you share fate.

In the martial arts, it refers to that strategic task when you have to put your affairs in order. This is either because you are preparing to act or—and this is more common—because you are responding to an action that has thrown you into disarray. This is the gathering of strength and the creation of togetherness.

"Womanly strength" is beneficent because it works from within and is accepting. There are hardly any harmonious families in the Western world. Roles have become pitifully confused: women are forced to play the male role; men turn into children; and children are thrown virtually instantly into the arms of a sick society for some kind of institution such as a kindergarten or nursery school. The ideal pattern has ceased to exist and that is why if the I Ching advises that "womanly strength is beneficent," it is not certain that it is in the mother, who has long been forced to play the role of the father in the family. It is better if you think about the Yin strategy here, the chief advantage of which is acceptance: *I accept others as they are.*

Only pure Motherly Love is capable of accepting someone's whole being, fate, good and bad qualities, and weaknesses—it does not attach conditions to its love. This is nonaggressive acceptance that is the condition of a good community where many kinds of fate and character live alongside one another in harmony. A good mother who has six children speaks to each of them differently because she knows that they all are all different people—each of them was different when they were still being carried in her arms.

Understanding love is a condition of a good community. It never pulls you so close to itself that you lose your freedom. This is the pattern for a "human" community. It is the basis for the relationship between me and you and us and you. But the first step depends on me and not on others.

LINES

1. Solid tie in the family. Sorrow disappears.
When life together begins—whether you end up in it or you are born into it or you create it yourself, at the beginning you need to know what the Order is here. You need to know what the valid pattern is. This experience grows in us at the beginning and then works on its own as time goes on. If the foundations are confused, then disintegration is unavoidable later on. Clarify everything now and you will have no cause for sorrow.

2. Do not follow distant goals. Stay in the center point, nourish, and take care of yourself. Steadfastness is beneficent and fortunate.
This is now the time of little services rather than large ambitions. This will lead to a fortunate future. Be patient and understanding with others. Do not try to convert them but take care of them and let them feel your security. Recognize the large significance of the small matters that are before you. Stay patient with yourself and with others in your thoughts.

3. There is only discipline and reprimand in the family. Regret—and still beneficent! But if the wife and child laugh irresponsibly, then the family will fall apart.
Too much discipline is better than too much compliance. This is about heated moments, outbreaks, and tempers that the one responsible for order in the family cannot avoid. He also steps over the boundaries; he is too hard and may create order with temper. This is still better than being too easygoing. Community life becomes fetid in an overly easygoing milieu, and everyone in it will become the victim of their own whims, selfishness, and untidiness.

4. The wealth of the family. Great blessings!
This is about the Yin power that creates well-being. Everyone is safe around wise mothers, not only in the spiritual sense but also in the earthly sense.

5. He approaches your family as a king. Don't be afraid. Good luck.
This is about the Yang force. It is about the wise father who sees with his heart and who does not need discipline to gain respect. A community is happy that has such a head. In the ancient sense, this line depicts a man who was able to adjust his community to the cosmic order. Peter was given this role in the "House" of Jesus. A "father" like this not only sees what will benefit his family but also what will appeal to God. In other words, he leads his family so that everyone is able to fulfill the life

plan of the community as well as their own. He does not make things uniform but allows the most diverse of fates to be lived, as everyone is different.

6. Honesty, yu fu, also has an effect on others. The end is blessings and fortune.

This describes a person who is at one with themself. This is a genuine individual who practices what they preach and makes a good leader. People are able to align themselves to a person like this. Such a person— whatever shared problem may arise—examines themself first and only then goes on to examine others. They make changes to themself first and use this to force others to change.

38 ䷥ *K'uei*

Opposite

Character: Eyes looking in opposite directions,
hands turning away from each other.

The meanings of *K'uei* are "opposite," "pulling apart," "alienation," "difference of opinion," "division," "conflict." Only **little steps** can be useful in such a difficult situation. "Those who are with me, gather—those who are against me, scatter," said Jesus, and what you are experiencing right now is scattering. **This is the opposite of love.** It may also be the lack of a shared goal or shared principle. Everyone is looking out for themselves in this energy field. They want to validate their own principles and interests and that is why they don't want to combine efforts with anyone else. Today, we refer to this state of being as the rule of hatred: we do not see polar complementation in opposites—no "other side of the coin"—we see an enemy that has to be destroyed.

Ancient wisdom teaches something completely different: all otherness is important. At times like this you can discover the person that only you are and who is different from everyone else: "I am not just the relative or friend of anyone." And you can catch a glimpse of that otherness in other people and not only who they really are but also what you project upon them. What you hate, despise, and lie about is reflected in the faces of others. The characteristics that irritate us the most in others are those that we have hidden away in ourselves. (The reason that we have hidden them away is because we hate them.)

This Oracle Sign teaches you how to find common ground with forces of being that are opposite to you. K'uei is the school of tolerance. A person who learns this is able to make a situation blossom that is otherwise fruitless and tense because **if a shared goal and common ground is found in diversity, then great things can be born.** Everyone preserves their otherness but they all pull in the same direction. This is the path of development in all fields of life. The question is what do we share? What is it that binds us together despite all foreignness?

If no central force existed that pulls diverging planets onto a shared path, they would fly apart into nothingness. As this opposing force is large, you can only progress carefully, taking little steps. You have to start on yourself. You should not make such allowances that you end up losing yourself. The tension between the two of us does not become harmonious if I weakly abandon myself.

The True Man preserves his own difference in all unity. True unity is created by diversity. Those "satanic" attempts at unity that want to mold people's individuality into a shared mass are alien to tradition. The True Man fights to the bitter end against communism, fascism, and multinational efforts that wash everything in together. He will not allow himself to be robbed of his being if he is rejected by the whole of society, even if he should lose his life.

The True Man always confronted the thinking that characterized the period and knew no tolerance in this regard. Do not look for a compromise but look for a solution. Compromise will not achieve anything here. It is as if you were to try to resolve the tension in a personal relationship by being less of a man or less of a woman— two genderless beings would perhaps understand one another better. Never! *You must respect the otherness of a separate individual.* Count on resistance, opposition, misunderstanding, temper, indifference— but still look for the point behind it where there is no resistance and no obstruction, just a deep-lying community or distant but similar goal. You need to understand the motivations of others. You also need to understand your own.

THOUGHTS

As a playwright, this Oracle Sign is my bread. I am all the interacting characters in my plays. I am in them; I live their lives and I know what their intentions are. Each and every person is a unique and separate universe. I once made the following note for myself: "There is some kind of madness in all stage characters: they revolve around themselves and they think that only their world is valid and are incapable of understanding anyone else's world. They imagine that others work in exactly the same way as they do—just stupidly, stubbornly, and wickedly. They would rather choose death than—even for a single moment—think with the head of the other person."

It is the battle of the turncoats and obsessional people that forms the stories of tragedies and comedies. But this also makes them all the more rich, lifelike, and universal. The best examples of this are found in the works of Shakespeare. His heroes revolve around themselves to such a degree that they even return from death gasping for revenge. (Of course, they see this as "truth.") Samuel Beckett is succinct in his comment, "People are idiots."

The Chinese character symbolizes this: eyes look but they don't see each other. What should be done? The Oracle Sign advises, **don't push matters.** Try to place yourself not in the "truth" of others but in their world, but stay yourself while you do this. Don't lose your inner faith that you are also one of God's unique creations. Understand the difference and seek the shared. There must be something shared, says the I Ching. We rarely experience this today. If there is nothing shared, then let that person leave—don't hesitate. The contradiction can only be dissolved, it cannot be defeated. If someone does not ultimately belong to us, then we have to let that person go.

In martial arts, it is warned not to adopt the battle mode of your opponent. Do not adjust to them. The first thing to do is to familiarize yourself with their mental world; you need to know what they want, what they are thinking, and what they are feeling. Stay out of striking distance. Look for the familiar points in them. Don't allow yourself to be made to jump with either fright or temper.

The I Ching looks for harmony until the very last minute. This is the most fertile state of the development of the spirit. Division eventually reaches a stage where there is no longer any hope of meeting. Avoid conflict even then because you do not know yourself or the other party well enough at this stage to be able to win the battle now.

LINES

1. Sorrow comes to an end. If you lose your horse, don't run after it as it will come back on its own. If you see malicious people, then remain faultless.
You cannot resolve this contradiction, but don't be sorry. What appears to be lost will return. Things that move away have not been lost. It is possible that you cannot come away from unworthy people and the influence of their maliciousness, but do not enter into conflict with anyone. Don't take up the gauntlet. The only thing you have to ensure is that you do not give yourself over to your negative feelings. Nothing from the outside can infect a person, only what comes from the inside. It is a familiar phrase used by Jesus, isn't it? Bad only affects you where you are still bad yourself. Work on yourself.

2. You meet with your master on a narrow road. Faultless.
A person who lives beyond conflict is in an era of opposites. "Master" is your own self, your teacher, or your advisor who translates the message of your being to you. Listen to them because they know the beneficial solution. The line means an unexpected meeting of the kind when fate appears before you wearing the mask of coincidence. Its deeper meaning is the "narrow road" that Jesus describes that leads you to "your master." The conflict is on the wide road, and the great merit of conflicts is that

they force you onto really narrow roads—and this leads to us meeting with ourselves.

3. They pull your carriage back and hold back your oxen. They cut your people's hair and noses off. Bad beginning but the end is good.
One obstacle after another. It would appear that the situation is unsolvable. It is humiliating, as if fate were trying to punish you and yet there is still hope of a harmonious ending. (In stage dramas this is called "intrigue.")

4. Total alienation; he is left alone. And yet he still meets his genuine companion (fu). Shared confidence. Danger but no mistake.
Fu can be "genuine companion," "husband," or "loyal friend"—someone who gives strength. You can solve the difficult situation together. Longing is not sufficient for such meetings. It also needs self-awareness. It needs inner harmony and faith that does not disintegrate in even the most hopeless of situations. Only that which has already been born on the inside can come on the outside.

5. Sorrow disappears. The person you belong with bites his way through flesh. Come home and you will receive your reward.
Catharsis is required to solve opposites. A person to whom this has happened becomes someone else. Forget it if someone has wounded you. Go over and hug them. They truly belong to you now. The picture is partly about forgiveness and partly about bitter struggle leading to harmony. It is like tearing off our own flesh. King Lear could tell a story or two about this.

6. Left alone because of the opposite, he sees his companion as a filthy pig or a band of devils. First, he tenses his bow before putting it to one side. He is not a brigand but a legal suitor. He goes over, it is raining, and blessings follow.
A real happy end. The point is that the person retracts their projections. We see our fellow humans as all kinds of things in times of conflict

and hatred. How often does a murderous thought come up in a hostile debate? The cocoon that we have projected onto the faces of others now falls away and a lovable face appears beneath it. We later realize that this war is a war between brothers. Fulfillment depends on genuine self-awareness (human awareness). It is at times like this that we find something in each other that is shared in otherness.

39  *Chien*

Difficulty

Character: Cripple in a cold house.

This is not the Difficulty at the Beginning of the 3rd Oracle Sign that accompanies all new ventures. This is about the problems and obstacles that appear through fate throughout our lives. It is not caused by initial resistance but by matured karma: a challenge that a person brings about through their acts. The situation is difficult.

Chien teaches you how to wrestle with difficulty. The first piece of advice is: **Dangerous water on rocky mountain: the image of difficulty. The True Man fundamentally reorganizes his inner being in order to renew the power of Tao within himself.**

What does this mean? It initially means that he does not go blundering into the obstacles—he examines himself. There are no external obstacles in our lives that have been moved independently of us into our path by some pigheaded stage manager—everything is our creation. This is called karma.

What a person cannot resolve within, appears on the outside as fate. An illness or life event is nothing other than an inner spiritual problem that has become visible. You can see it, you can hold it, and you can knock against it. Something that was no more than a mental mishap in your mind, an emotional or physical attack against the Whole, leads to trouble. It can create a "real" problem that you do not like.

The way that others react to us is also a reflection. You have played your part in building the boundaries. It is a waste of time throwing yourself against them. This isn't because they are too hard but because, while you still don't recognize that they are of your Work, you will keep building them over and over again. The cause has to be stopped and that is in you. An obstacle is not there to punish you but so that you may become more. *Be free!*

Difficulties and challenges destroy the common man but they strengthen the True Man and make him divine. I am not exaggerating. The word that I translated as "reorganizing" (*fan*) the inner being is exactly the same as Christian "conversion" (*metanoia*). It means to turn back to Tao-God. The first piece of advice is look inside yourself and change yourself.

The second piece of advice is, **if you succeed in finding the source or trouble within yourself, do not take fright at the situation that has already appeared on the outside.** Be persistent and gather strength. The eye of the sage sees that you have a tendency to give up. Don't do it. You will become strongest in the exact area that you claim to be weak. I don't want to hear the word *hopeless*. Everything changes and only the hopelessness stays the same? Who told you that? Is it the bad magician who conjured this whole difficult situation around you and now wants to stop you from waking from it?

The third piece of advice is, **turn to the southwest, the solution is there—and avoid the northwest!** This means don't go rushing on. Do not try to defeat the difficulty at any price. Avoid bitter battle. Do not tighten the knot any further. It is possible that time will solve the problem. It might also be you, but not now because it is not timely. Wait. Retreat. This is how you will find the Center (chung).

All difficulties will hold you in the vice until they squeeze the sweet juice out of you. Old soothsayers see an encouraging view in the difficult situation. The ground is frozen while winter lasts—but the spring is coming. This requires you to think differently. You also need to be a little different. Wake the sleeping Magician within you who creates magic with love.

THOUGHTS

Modern man has no transcendence and that is why if an obstacle stands towering high in his path, he gathers his remaining strength and runs blindly at it—or he gives up the struggle there and then. Our lives are full of obstacles. They are full of unavoidable difficulties—there is hardly any life now without karma-congestion. There is problem after problem. The greatest problem is that the dark age does not offer any solution.

Many seek comfort in religion but this is not what this Oracle Sign is about. It does not tell you to seek shelter under the protective wings of the Mighty Power in times of trouble but that you should become a Mighty Power yourself. Find the unmoving axis in the cyclone. *Find the solid and calm center point* in the chaos of fear, panic, and hopelessness.

At times like this a warrior stops flailing around. He wounds himself with every new attack. He stops and tries to rediscover himself, which he does with a special technique called "hara breathing." He regains his calm. He now sees the reason for the difficulty: he was egocentric. He wanted something too much. His "self" directed his sword. He forced his own idea instead of trusting himself to inspiration. The problem was caused because he fell out of Tao. At times like this, the main thing to do is not to cut and thrust on the outside but to **rediscover Tao** just as quickly as possible. You need to quickly take hold of God's hand and sense his strength. This is the strategy for solving karma.

The answer to your question is, *don't attack and don't give up. Change. Rise to a higher level. Solve.*

LINES

1. Attack is difficulty, retreat is praise.
This is not a time for struggle but a time for consideration. Do not run into the obstacle. Wait and measure yourself and the situation. Be open to all things new. It will have its rewards.

2. Difficulty follows difficulty in service to the king. This is in no way your own personal fault.

The situation is difficult but your karma isn't. The difficulty is a higher affair and probably comes from the service of others. Don't back off and there is no reason for you to turn inward—you are a tool in the hands of fate and not the cause of the obstacle. Act bravely but not excessively. (This is where *wu yu* appears in one of the commentaries—"Not excessively." Good service is sensible and considered and does not fall into the trap of overenthusiasm or heroism. It is unposed; it is practical and does only what it has to. It does not do more even "for the king" because God does not like excess.)

3. Attack is difficulty. Stepping back is turning.

Here is the opportunity for you to find yourself. This may bring about a change in the whole situation. A lot of commentators promise greater inner joy here. This also transmits to those who are close to you. The cause for joy is not victory but the sense of security. Do not struggle, wait.

4. Attack is difficulty and retreat brings allies.

You are weak on your own. You have not measured the situation wisely. Don't struggle but stay in your place and wait. You will change and so will your obstacle. Life may bring companions as well as new solutions. These are solutions that you do not yet know about and they do not appear in your current logic. It is pointless wracking your brain.

5. Companions (friends) come at the time of greatest difficulty.

The deep meaning of the Oracle Sign is that a person suffering from self-cramp and who is stuck on the treadmill finds inspiration—from the deepest point of helplessness they tip over to the high point of Clear Vision. The calm of Tao and its power to solve fate appears in them. Its superficial meaning is that it really does help you to find companions—the sort with whom you can and must discuss your difficulties (the word has power because it can only be uttered by a person who already knows) and overcome the obstacle together.

6. Attack is difficulty. Retreat is maturity. The road is open. It is beneficent to see the great man.

You are ready for the change. The difficulties become solved and the obstacles fall away. Richard Wilhelm sees in this line a "great man" who has already solved his fate and does not abandon the world but returns to help. Others see a figure in whom the tactic of the Oracle Sign is emerging: he starts to rediscover himself; he has reshaped his being and has faith in advice from above—and a road begins to open up where a wall once stood. He is still too weak for open confrontation. His strength is in acceptance. He must become ready for everything and that is what is happening now.

40  Hsieh

Solution

Character: A knife made out of ox horn that is used to untangle knots.

The Hsieh Oracle Sign could be translated as "liberation" or "relief." It represents a situation when the oppressive problem ceases and obstacles gradually fall away. This is the stage of being when a problem is finally solved. The Chinese character warns of a knot that needs to be untangled that tied you down up until now. This knot could be mental, it may be physical, it may be an oppressive burden of fate, or a strangling problem or pressure from the past that restricts the free flow of energy.

A complete life cycle comes to an end and a new one is born. Difficulties, obstacles, misunderstandings, worries, anxieties all pass away—this is partly because their time is up and partly because **you have finally understood how to solve your problems.** You need your wisdom, patience, and dexterity to untangle these knots. You have to realize at long last what it is that caused the knot. You have to work out where it is tight and where it will come undone on its own. You need to know where you need patience and where you can cut straight through.

The Hsieh is a time of relief and release of tensions. The message of the Oracle Sign is, **If you have nowhere to go, then return is benefi-cent, and if you have somewhere to go, then leave immediately!** People turn away from themselves in periods of difficulty. Here, "return" means our center point and our real self. "Come to your senses and calm down and regain your balance." This is the advice given to practitioners of martial arts after a difficult and bitter battle. It is also possible that you need to make the most of the liberated moment and start a new action or a new phase of your life. If you have an image of the future, go for it. If you don't, step back into yourself and find the calm of your heart.

The knot comes from the past. The strangling knots of the past— after we have recognized them and named them—can be solved in one of two ways: by forgiving or by forgetting. In the Oracle Sign of Hsieh a person is shocked to discover that something pressures them because they insist on it. We cling to bad as well as good. You have to let it go!

THOUGHTS

The human spirit loses its freedom when it *identifies* with the body and, from then on, it forgets that it is a spirit and becomes attached to the earthly world. Identifying means that I confuse myself with someone I am not, with my role on Earth and, from then on, I live as if that were me. In Hinduism this is referred to as *adhyasha*. This identifying creates our earthly being, our personality as well as our feelings and our senses.

For as long as I identify with my body, my tooth hurts—but this identifying stops under hypnosis and I no longer feel the pain. "The best way to treat sorrow and an aching wound is not to even think about it," said Goethe. In most cases, untangling the knot means release. It means putting an end to identifying. It means untying the ties. It is that moment when we are eventually ready for freedom. Our real self is free from its origin. The Apostle Paul said, "Freedom frees us." The truth is that we are all immortal, free spirits. What has bound us is false desire, false sense, and false thought.

"The Well Frog is held prisoner in its own pit," says the God of the Sea. This is because the frog insists on its own pit. The time has come to step out. A karma cycle has come to an end. Life's burdens will soon end and problems will be solved—the solution requires you to step out of the unworthy "pit."

There is a mysterious piece of advice for anyone with a greater interest in the secrets of the I Ching: *The southwest is beneficent but the northeast is not.*

This piece of advice is interpreted in many ways by Chinese academics. The only certain thing is that, in King Wen's system, one direction represented Receptive and the other direction represented the Mountain. The situation here is more involved. According to the ancient Chinese approach, the Moon is born in the southwest and dies in the northeast.

There is a neutral moment in transformation that is neither Yang nor Yin. It is just like a pause between notes in a melody, a break between movements or, to put it in other words: the pause between breaths when meditating. It is the mute, motionless, empty, and passive state between breathing in and breathing out. It is the "nothing" phase. *Something has come to an end* and the new has not yet begun. However, this silence and this emptiness are not totally neutral. There can be two types: the first is when the old slowly moves on within us and *we come to terms with our past.* This is an "after-death" phase. That is northeast. The second is *when we prepare to create the new* and this is a "before birth" phase and is southwest. This is described by the Oracle as being a beneficent direction. In other words, prepare for the new!

LINES

1. Faultless.

The knot comes undone. You are on the right path to the solution. You can see the light at the end of the tunnel.

2. He strikes three foxes in the field. He receives a yellow arrow. Persistence. Blessings!

The fox symbolizes lies, falseness, self-deception, and cunning flattery. Yellow symbolizes the center and the conscious act of the arrow. You must not take any lies or self-deception across into the new life. You cannot defeat lies with either diplomacy or politics but only with truth and honesty. The line says lies can be tactical, revealing truth cannot. The time has come to an end when it was necessary to conceal the weapon of truth, often from yourself as well. You can now bravely unveil your own "foxes."

3. A person who carries a load travels in a coach and attracts robbers. If he continues, he will be shamed.

This is accompanied by the threat of self-deception. The arrogance of the small man who has gained wealth and power attracts bad karma. This is not simply about the fact that his arrogance makes him unappealing in the eyes of others but also that it will get him into trouble sooner or later. *A person who exalts himself will be humiliated.* Don't overcommit yourself. And preserve your pure humanity. Other successes will not solve inner problems.

4. Free yourself of your thumb (mu) and you will find a true companion.

Do not insist on the past and what you have now outgrown. Shed what is unworthy so that you can grasp the worthy. (The *mu* sign means the thumb with which a person can grip strongly.) Forgiveness also means release. It means to release what has gone over. The weight of memories and habits pulls you down—not because they are heavy but because you are clinging on to them. Let them go to make space for the new.

5. A person is of a "Higher Order" who "solves" with his persistent strength. This is how the true self advances and the common retreats.

Our true self is the one who solves our problems. It is the director of our fate. The secret of victory is not to first do battle against the negative

but to see a positive goal out in front of us. If the sun of our spirit rises,   .
the darkness disperses. God cannot be defeated.

6. The prince shoots a hawk on a high wall. He strikes it. Everything is advantageous.

The hawk symbolizes arrogance and the selfish ego. It represents the dangerous person who gains power and brings trouble to the community. The hawk is invincible, obstinate, and tough. It is the prince's task to aim well and precisely and to shoot at the right time. The solution here is in one ultimate movement—it is just like cutting though the Gordian knot, like a healing operation.

41  *Sun*

Reduction

損

Character: A hand holding something and a sacrificial vessel.

When opposites unite, it becomes apparent that all growth is preceded by reduction. Before leaping forward, you have to take a step back. The low tide comes before the high tide. If a large boat comes, the water on the banks of the river starts to drop, it seems to get sucked away somewhere and the mud and stony soil appear. In order to accept something, you have to become empty first.

This is what this Oracle Sign is about. **You have to make room for something important and the way to do this is to empty out.** Sun, the 41st Oracle Sign, is the essence of the ancient tradition: let there be space within you so that you can receive. This is how the meek will inherit the earth and the weak of spirit will be granted the Kingdom of Heaven and he who humbles himself will be exalted. The Taoist sage always stays consciously behind and below in order to hold the whole world in his power.

We think differently now. We fatten ourselves and cling on, and we don't notice that this leads to bloating and a consequent fall. We hold Napoleonic fates in the framework of our envy while they continue to inflate and glow with improbable incandescence—the bursting and falling into darkness happens outside the frame; it is as if it didn't belong to that same life. Who would think of Hitler not at his roaring, triumphant peak but when he shoots his woman in the head in an underground bunker and then lifts the barrel to his own terrified and emaciated face? Today, shadow does not belong to light.

The I Ching sees unity. This means that there are not two threads but only one, and the whole web of life is woven from that one thread; Yin and Yang are the shiny and dull sides of the same thread. Because the goal of a happy life is harmony, it is the overall web that is important and that the threads should harmonize with one another.

There is now too much Yang. There is too much "I want" and "I need." There is too much toughness and obstinacy and not giving and "give it to me" and "that's mine." These need to be **reduced**. Have you realized that you always get things when you no longer seem to need them? What isn't really needed is relatively easy to achieve.

This is just as true if it happens to be an enormous task for others but is nowhere near as great for the person that reaches it. *The reason it became his is because it isn't natural for him.* (It is well-known in the business world that if someone handles a matter that they "really need," it won't succeed.) What is "really needed" is out of reach. The "really need" has to be sacrificed here. You don't need it. God will give it to you if he sees fit.

I can manage with less—if you think this deep down in your spirit, you understand the "tactic of sacrifice" when a person gives up all the desires, thirst for success, and egoism to make room inside for something more. Sun is not about bearing the low tide but about consciously creating a low tide within myself. I look around the world where there are millions of starving people and I say that—even with my daily problems—I am indescribably rich. I create superfluousness within myself. I do not tense myself to the point that "it isn't enough" but I relax to the point that "even this is a lot." I am happy with what I have—in the physical, mental, and spiritual sense of the word—and I do not keep myself in an ecstatic, thirsty, and dissatisfied state for what I do not (yet?) have.

The message of Sun: **Honest reduction means exalted blessings. Faultless. The road stands open. How should you do all of this? Two little plates are sufficient for the sacrifice.** The sacrifice is only beneficial if you know what it is that you sacrifice. It would appear that there were also hypocritical sacrifices in ancient China—the ritual needed nine little plates—but here we are told that we only need two if our intentions are honest. You sacrifice the power of your ego and the thirst for ownership in them. The more you reduce the weight of your ego, the higher you will rise and you will become more complete and more harmonious. "The True Man," says the sage, "restrains his desires and does not give himself over to his temper."

Our selfish self does not like the period of Reduction. It sees it as loss. It doesn't know that it is actual gain. Take a look back: the merit that you find in yourself and what has made you more, stronger, wiser, purer, and brighter you did not collect when you had a good run of cards but when you were able to make the sacrifice of dedication, renouncement, and patience.

All loss is a blow for the person who left the path—great, great promise and possibility for the person who stepped onto the path.

THOUGHTS

We modern people panic at low tide. Our egos take fright at the "it won't work," "it's no good" experience; we feel defenseless and think that our situation is hopeless. The weak are overcome by panic if they get into trouble. They start to thrash about helplessly with an anxious heart and with no hope. They thrash about not only because their external desires are not being fulfilled but also because this is the moment when our ego has to stand to one side and pass the sword to our Higher Self. And the ego is more frightened by this than any kind of external failure.

The answer to your question is, *you are in a period of low tide. Don't work against it, work with it. Move even further back, accept help, and sacrifice all of the fear and temper of your selfish self to give space to the Strong and the Helpful.* "Lack of strength" can be fantastically strong.

A perfect example of this from martial arts is provided by a student's account of his struggle with Ueshiba, the eighty-year-old aikido master. He attacked the old man who used the Sun tactic. The student could feel that the master was not attacking back but was absorbing the attack like a black hole and was literally sucking everything into a great emptiness and destroying it. The student felt as if he was fighting against the power of the whole universe rather than a frail, old man. This everyday miracle reads rather like a children's story but actually forms the basis of all religion and esotericism.

As one of the Parkinson laws says, "A real movement dies when it gets a headquarters." True spiritual masters remain poor until the end of their days even if they come from a royal family, like Buddha himself. If you search for real merit in the human world, it is always down below and far away from wealth and power—and if a valuable person rises to the surface, they take care to constantly examine themself to ensure that they remain down-to-earth. This is not modesty but the preservation of strength; the deep has amazing upward strength. Jesus and Lao Tse lived in "famous anonymity." Beyond the fact that they fundamentally transformed the history of humanity, we hardly know any genuine historic facts about them.

So, this is about strength—and not a small amount of it. This Oracle Sign teaches how to take advantage of the low tide (lack of success and apparent loss) to achieve genuine and long-lasting achievements. If you are poor, do not think that "I won't have anything to eat" but rather "I have still got a little more than enough." This is the strategy of Sun. If you use this way of thinking, you will not only make yourself more harmonious but you will create the preconditions to ensure that you have much more in the future. A consciously experienced low tide gives birth to the strength of the high tide. (This is known by stock market gurus as well as saints—it is a law that appears in all planes of being.)

LINES

1. Complete the matter (action) and quickly continue. No mistake. Consider (discuss) the Reduction.

This is about the correct degree of reduction. You should neither overplay nor accept a sacrifice that is too exaggerated. For example, mothers are often capable of exaggerating their love for their children. That is one problem. The other is when a growing child does not rebel in time against this overbearing love. You can transfer the same model to work, friendship, or any kind of social situation. For example, a good leader knows how much they can demand. A practitioner of martial arts sees the limit of an action here and does not go forward with full steam or back off. They stop, take a breath, and pull themself together. In music, this is referred to as the "auftakt." A person who does not do this makes a mistake.

2. Beneficent Oracle Sign, be steadfast. Strictness taken to extremes brings trouble. You can make others grow without reducing yourself.

Preserve your center point—the level is correct there. You feel this in yourself in the same way that you feel dignity and self-esteem. If you lose this, you are no longer humble but submissive, and you do not give out of your superfluous strength but out of your weakness and fear. It is one thing to wash the feet of others as Christ washed the feet of his disciples and another thing to polish the boots of your master out of servility. Know that you are rich and that is why you give.

3. If three roam together, their number will be reduced by one. The one who goes on his own will find his companion.

Before we speak about the everyday meaning of this sign, we need to understand its deep message. According to the I ("I" as in I Ching), the mystery is Two and not Three. It is not that "thesis," "antithesis," and "synthesis" form a wonderful family and the three of them go on to live happily ever after but that "synthesis" is nothing more than the sprout of a new "thesis" and the eternal dream continues.

Jesus said, "You will enter the kingdom when two become one." The mystery is man and woman. It is the love between the two of them. The child is the third—either woman or man—and its role is not to fit in between the parents but to find its own partner. In a family, if a child comes, it puts a stop to the dance of love between man and woman because it stands between them and draws the mother's love and the husband is pushed out. This is the cause of many ruined marriages. The couple needs to know that this is a dance until death. A child needs to break out of this and grow up and find the one with whom it can enjoy its honeymoon dance.*

This line suggests that you should reduce from three to two and if you are one, then grow to two and, in this way, you can live your own fate. Often the reason that we do not find a partner is because we get stuck where we are no longer needed. And sometimes we confuse solitude with being alone. Everyone has a companion. The "solitary saint" talks to someone and is alone least of all!

4. If you reduce your mistakes, others (shi) come hurrying to great joy. No mistake.

If you have dispersed the prejudice, hate, condescension, fear, rejection, and alienation within yourself, then you immediately magically transform your surroundings. The *shi* sign means "message," "messenger"; your inner transformation sends secret messages to the outside world and this is received by those it is meant for.

5. Ten pairs of tortoise divinations can only make things grow! Nothing can obstruct or say no. Great blessings!

Nothing can obstruct the blessings of the sky. Your fortune and your happiness are destined. Your plan is also helped by invisible powers.

---

*As a playwright, I have often experienced that all good scenes are dialogues. Great things always happen between two people. If there are three or four or a lot of them, the tension slackens but the crowd polarizes sooner or later with some moving closer to one and some moving closer to the other and the Two Parties are formed again.

6. You can expand without reduction. Faultless. Steadfastness is beneficent and your path has a goal. You have servants but you have no home.

Everything that you do for the common good and for the good of others is beneficent and can be fulfilled. You can receive a lot of help for this. This is timely now—not the narrow circle of your personal life. You serve community karma and you offer help to solve the fates of others. Your colleagues are now also your "life companions." This is not the time for turning inward but for active service.

42  I

Expansion

Character: A vessel overflows with material and spiritual reward.

This is a time of growth, emergence, development, fertility, and enrichment. The previous sign was Reduction—this is the period of Expansion. Low tide is followed by high tide. The message of the 42nd Oracle Sign is, **Expansion. Beneficent if you have a goal that you follow. It is beneficent to cross the Great Water now.**

The harmony of helping one another and growing strengths lies behind this Oracle Sign. You experience this like the period of realization. You waited for it for a long time and now it is here. What begins now, gains fair winds and travels far. This is the joint work of the Arousing (Thunder). Problems can be solved in this sign and relationships and plans begin to blossom. Make use of the fair wind. Have a clear plan, a planned destination, and put all your strength into your undertakings. You may be surprised at the amount of strength that you have. (It is the sign of healing and gaining strength and the enrichment of outer and inner life energies.) Your personality also becomes richer.

A person knows themself much better in successful periods than in unsuccessful ones because the good and bad characteristics that have remained hidden up to this point come to the surface now. A person who has hidden a desire for power now goes crazy with power and the egotist who enjoys a good run of luck has a tendency to claim every success as their own. The ultimate knowledge of this Oracle Sign is what Jesus says: "Man can take nothing that is not given to him from heaven." All people are unveiled in success and in the best case they are also revealed to themselves. It is a cliché to say that power makes everyone crazy.

It is the same with other temptations. Good fortune causes the ego to inflate and it tends to attribute all of its success to its own magical power. This is why the sage says, "At the time of expansion, the True Man, if he sees something good, follows it and if it has a fault, he abandons it." You can tell a good life plan from a bad life plan because the good one is also good for others and the bad one only brings profit for you.

"Crossing the Great Water" means that, even though you do not know what awaits you on the other side and how dangerous the road may be, you should **do it with confidence**. The Master knows what waits on the other side but does not say what it is. You need the bravery and spontaneous daring that you can only attain by leaping into the unknown. You only have one support for the time being and that is your faith. Believe in yourself and believe in your Master.

In the everyday sense, the Oracle Sign encourages you to act. Get stuck in and follow through to the end.

THOUGHTS

The I Oracle Sign is a fertilized and blessed state. It holds promise of a rich future. The invisible world will help. You will receive this help if you live your fate and fulfill your life plan. This is the good "wind direction." You will lose help if you diverge from the direction and if your blind ego takes control in your earthly life. Remain in tune, open, and sensitive to good. More people have failed in success than in failure. Be careful. A band of thieves falls apart when they start to share out the bounty.

In martial arts, *li* is the moment when the possibility of triumph appears after a long and oppressive period. This should be used bravely and consciously but you shouldn't sink into it. It is one thing to conquer and another to claim triumph. A person deserves victory but sooner or later will be crippled by triumph.

LINES

1. It is an advantage to dedicate yourself to the exhilarating, great deed. Great blessings. No mistake.
The time for passivity has come to an end. It is possible that you feel too weak or that you think the task is too great, but set about it with confidence, with enthusiasm and faith. You can depend on the help of good forces.

2. Someone probably expands! Do not reject a tortoise that is worth ten "peng" shells. Loyalty and persistence bring great fortune. The king presents his sacrifice to the Lord of Heaven. Great Blessings.
This is about a blessing that is not the result of our own efforts. It comes from the "outside" and, in the ancient sense, it comes from man, spirits, and God. "Persistence" means that you should remain on the Earth in good fortune; be humble if fate smiles upon you. (You could become dizzy and this is not good.)

3. Even unsuccessful and unlucky matters expand! There is no mistake if you are true and if you advance with the Center and you show this with the stamp of the prince.
The period of Expansion is so forceful that even unavoidable (karmic) problems turn to your advantage. They make you spiritually and humanly stronger, and this "inner expansion" will manifest itself in your external fate sooner or later.

4. Stay with the Center. Inform the prince of the situation and let him follow you. It is beneficent to make yourself useful when the city is relocated.
The ancient meaning of the sign speaks about the role of the medium whose inspiration saves their country from trouble. In ancient times,

a whole nation would move to another place to avoid an approaching war or natural disaster. Your role is to be an intermediary who is listened to down below and up above. You are neither leader nor led—you stand between the two. You have to understand both and this requires openness. It especially requires tact because you carry the truth that is in everyone's interest. The period is terribly significant; it will determine your future for a very long time. At times like this, it is vital that you preserve your center. New is being born. Take part in it, you need it.

5. You are true (yu fu) and your heart is unselfish and good. Don't ask: the road is open before you. (Great fortune.) Your true and unselfish heart carries your future reward.
Yu fu means that you are in connection with good spirits. "Unselfish heart" means that you involve yourself with others and that you are compassionate. This is the basis of your expansion and this is also valued by the visible world and the invisible world. You are good when you don't know that you are good; this is when your goodness is involuntary and natural. Then you are also compassionate because you don't judge, you don't classify, and you don't look to see if someone deserves it or not; you give because it comes flooding out of you.

6. You do not expand at all; perhaps you will also be punished (chi)! Your unfaithful, wavering heart is the reason. Trouble!
You are in a situation when you should give, but you don't give. You need faith and you are crippled with doubt. Your selfishness isolates you from the world and you bring out antagonism in others. If you carry on like this you, could get your knuckles rapped. This is expressed by the *chi* character (punishment).

43  *Kuai*

Removal

Character: A hand cleverly separates something. Today, this ancient sign is no longer used. There was a time when it symbolized digging a trench that cleverly diverted and put a stop to the dangerous power of the river in flood.

The good and gleaming is on the ascendant and only one dark force stands in its path. The final battle is always the bitterest. It is the same for a siege, a drama, or an external–internal war. The Oracle Sign protects you from a bitter victory. That is why the emphasis of words like *dedication, devotion, revolution,* and *breakthrough* is a mistake here. The Chinese know that we will not be dedicated if we attack what is bad with our teeth gripped tight. For them, **dedication means the lack of uncertainty.** It is when a person recognizes what is bad to its roots; it is as obvious as when a person has a splinter in their finger and knows that it will hurt until they pull it out. Our doubts cease. There are no two ways about it; this is what is causing the problem. This must be defeated.

If it is to work anywhere, then it will work in this Oracle Sign. The tactic used in martial arts is not to stand in opposition to evil—that will only strengthen it. It is better to divide its strength, tire it out, and leave it to be consumed by its own temper. Do not reach for a weapon. Retreat back to your neutral center point.

See the dark force clearly, whether it is inside you, inside someone else, or in your unclear life situation. Know your goal and know that only you can win—trust the rest to the help of the invisible world and know that you are its tool. Strength. Dedication. Openness. This battle is no longer hidden and takes place in the open with no compromise. Solve this problem with a determined spirit free of doubt and fear, with the kind of certainty and lack of emotion with which a surgeon operates or a dentist removes a rotten tooth.

The Oracle Sign—with no changing lines—primarily means a critical moment of self-development. It means the liberation from your own "bad." We can only be defeated through our faults.

THOUGHTS

Here, you need to express what your problem is. You no longer need psychology, analysis, or experience: you know already. Say it to yourself, say it to God, and ask for help. Don't ask for strength because you have it: ask for patience, the calm of not acting (that is the basis of all victorious acts), and the unshakeable faith in victory.

A rat is at its most dangerous when backed into a corner. Our ego is the most anxious when it is in ultimate danger; it is capable of doing anything when it panics. (The same is true for the egos of others.) The dancelike movements of Tai Chi lead to easier victory than thrashing at your enemy with a sword. It is not even certain that you need to strike. A person digs a trench and has already quelled the destructive force of the flood; this is what this Oracle Sign speaks about.

As an example, many people spend years trying to give up smoking and they don't succeed. A day comes along—the day of the Kuai—and we never light another cigarette again. Nothing special happens but a person suddenly realizes that they don't need it. It stops there and they turn away from their addiction. *This does not happen in a way that you would stab the smoker in yourself in the heart, but rather just pass it by.*

You distracted the smoker's thoughts. You no longer give yourself over to meanness. We are often the ones who keep our internal and external enemies alive. We nourish them with strength.

Kuai is the encouraging sign of spring and yet it still isn't easy. It wasn't like this a long time ago—this is apparent from the drama of the lines. It is difficult to struggle against the self-defense of the ego and the bitter and cunning way in which negative forces fight. The sages say that the very last moment before enlightenment is the darkest and the most hopeless.

Eugen Herrigel, who studied the art of archery in Japan, said that after years and years of failure, he eventually managed to fire an arrow well when he was ready to give the whole thing up because it simply wasn't working. This is about genuine selflessness and reaching "let thy will be done." This can often mean a change of fate.

LINES

1. Power in feet stepping forward. If he goes over, he makes a mistake. He is incapable of solving the situation.
Early step. He wants too much, too soon. He needs to stop. The situation is still unripe and an early challenge can only make things worse. I should only ever go into battle if I am more prepared than my opponent. But if the situation is reversed?—Stop!

2. Alarm and exclamation. Armed all night. Don't be afraid!
A person who is vigilant cannot be touched by trouble. Here, vigilance means that we see from the center point with the eyes of our Higher Self. That is why we can come to no harm. Only the ego within us can be afraid and nervous; this is never true of the Higher Self. Nothing can happen to it either now or in the future for which it would not know the instant and fear-free solution. Measure the situation with clear eyes: what could happen to you? You see that what your ego sees as bad is also good.

3. *Aggressive urge in the cheekbones. Trouble. One of Higher Rank prefers to avoid. He carries on alone and walks into rain. He is sprayed and accused—but he doesn't make a mistake.*

Neither an inner aggressive urge nor an outer exception can force you to act. The struggle will begin when the time comes. It is better to be accused and remain yourself—but wait for your time. It is not now. Avoid, be tactical, or leave the scene of the struggle and do not listen to the voice of accusation, or that of self-accusation.

4. *His thigh is wounded and yet he still pushes forward. If he allows himself to be led like a lamb, his trouble and sorrow will end. He listens to the advice but he doesn't trust it.*

Strength, blind faith, bitterness, or cramped will cannot lead to good now. The blindness and panic of the ego is the cause of obstinacy. A person who only believes in themself loses a battle because they cannot hear the voice of the master, the true Self, or their inspiration. You can hear but you don't believe. You think that not acting is the losing path when the exact opposite is true.

5. *Marsh weeds on a high plateau. Remove! Remove! Stay in the center! You will not make a mistake.*

The bad, the common, and the negative are in a high position. Struggle against them with dedication. But do not struggle out of temper, revenge, or fear but from the pure center of your being, free of all selfish emotion. This is the psychological moment in martial arts. It contains no doubt and no anxiety. Now or never!

6. *No warning. This can lead to trouble.*

It appears easy to put an end to the bad. There is trouble if a person is careless and does not work to the roots. It is pointless having a successful operation if conditions are not sufficiently sterile. We do not have one single negative quality that we could completely defeat. The sage lives on a sword's edge—he is eternally cautious. "Only God is good," said Jesus when he was described as good. The lack of vigilance is the problem. It is nothing more than forgetting the self. A careless person takes the shoot of trouble with them into their new life. Pay attention. Be forward-looking. There is trouble if someone doesn't hear when they are being spoken to: the seed of bad can sprout again.

44 ䷫ *Kou*

Contact (Temptation)

Character: Sexual union.

In this Oracle Sign, "contact" means meeting and coupling. Sexuality has had a double message since ancient times. One is that it is the root and basis of the life of nature. The second is that it presents the greatest temptation because a person remains prisoner to the material world. The ancient law of Eros binds people to the body.

The ancient force of Yin steps in under five Yang lines and the image says, **Contact. The woman is strong and fills him with life. But it is not advantageous to take and keep (chu) her.** Of course, the message of the Oracle Sign is symbolic and varied. One answer to your question is, *welcome the unexpected into your life as well as that which is fate-like or suddenly strikes that which gives strength and enthuses.* This relationship comes and goes and yet still, like a fertilizing embrace, has a universal cause and goal. These embraces could be events that provide joy, meetings, or intimate and fertile moments. They could also be intense events that—speaking symbolically—do not give blessings but only sexual pleasure.

Kou means "good." It means good for man. At the same time, all of the lines warn you not to become bogged down. You should not try to keep it. In fact, you should search behind its apparently harmless mask for the Great Tempter. "Temptation" could be an individual, a promise, an emotional contact, a negative thought that appears and tries to enter into your life—you don't even notice that it *strives for power* and if you give yourself to it permanently, then it will tie you to the earth sooner or later and you will lose your wings.

One part of the tradition advises you to welcome the fact that you can become part of the Creative Force of the Universe. What happens is fate. The other part says that you should stop the apparently harmless desires in your heart before they take control of your whole life.

The superficial meaning of the Oracle Sign is the danger of "female aggression" that appears harmless. It symbolizes the tempting and flattering approach that covers a hidden desire for power. (A hyena is appealing when it is still a puppy.) Nip all negative thoughts, transient fears, and gloomy signs in the bud. The Oracle Sign warns you to handle tempting and apparently promising situations with great care. Chinese soothsayers see unexpected and passing events in this sign.

THOUGHTS

We are spiritual and earthly beings. We are both mortal and immortal, and it will remain this way until we return to God. This is why blessings and sexual pleasure, earthly joy and spiritual happiness cannot be truly separated. I think that the message of this sign is that you should be happy about the good but do not become its slave. You should enjoy life but do not become attached to it. You should know that what you receive is not permanent.

This is all that you need to know and nothing more: accept God's transient gift and do not try to make it permanent because all you will achieve is to make yourself transient. The temptation is unnoticeable. What is bad in that? The answer is nothing. You can enjoy food, drink, love, success, fortune, and everything that is sensual and does not last forever—*just do not become its prisoner.*

The Chinese character *chu* depicts an ear and a hand. This means that a person is not satisfied with what is heard and what passes through their spirit but wants to hold it and close it in their hand—they want to own goodness and shout, "You are mine!" Such a person becomes a prisoner in that exact moment. They lose control of their own fate and become a slave to money, success, desire, fame, love, hope, and power. If you receive something, thank God with joy then place it on the altar and carry on. A person who tries to put any gift into their pocket will be unhappy.

An example of Kou: a woman received this Oracle Sign who was in love with a man twenty years younger than herself. They gave each other a great deal; the woman received passionate love and the young man received wisdom; the opportunity of a higher world opened up before them. As far as I know, they parted amicably with heavy hearts but both had been enriched by the relationship. Their meeting was short but fateful.

LINES

1. Braking with an iron brake! The road lies open. But going after a selfish goal is trouble! A skinny pig kicks with its trotters.
Stop, don't continue. When something steps into our lives—a feeling, a thought, a desire, or a person—the effect is still weak. The temptation has to be overcome in the very first moment—it will be very troublesome later or perhaps not even possible. You find something important in the silence and the motionlessness: what is it? Do not leave your true path. Put a brake on yourself. Contrary to many books, in Chinese tradition, the "pig" not only symbolizes well-being and wealth, but also unworthiness. Many languages attribute more than one meaning to the word *pig*.

2. Fish in the sack. The situation does not conceal trouble. Do not welcome guests.
A simile: the mother's womb is expectant with plenty. This cannot be divided because it too needs "nourishment." This is the positive

interpretation of this line because the fish is the symbol of plenty—as they swim in pairs—of love and of fertility. There are some, however, who are wary of the situation: all earthly desires and thoughts need to be closed in a "sack" before they betray our lives. You have to achieve all of this in secret. No one else should know about this ("do not welcome guests").

3. There is no skin on his thigh; he can walk but with difficulty. Trouble. If he finds the Great within himself (he doesn't allow himself to be led on a leash), he will avoid the problem.
A desire that—luckily—cannot be satisfied. You suffer for it but it would not be good if it were to be fulfilled. It is better to look into yourself and to look upward. Sometimes our limits are beneficial and our suffering is useful. You will, in time, realize that this is true and you will say, "Thank goodness it didn't happen because I would have suffered so much because of it." You can realize this now if you "find the Great" within you.

4. There is no fish in the sack. Trouble.
This is the sign of the "infertile womb." The Chinese *pao* means "cocoon," "patience," "to take responsibility," "to become engaged to someone." The character shows a baby in a mother's womb. A person who is closed inside themselves is without supporters. At times like this, they say of a politician that they have "lost touch with the people." The cause of the problem is that you aren't able to accept others. You have to change this.

On a psychological level, the Oracle Sign advises you to accept yourself along with your good, bad, and "low level" characteristics. You are all that you are. This includes the world of your instincts, the world of your desires, and your suppressed longing: you are all of these things. A person who doesn't take notice of their own entirety dries out.

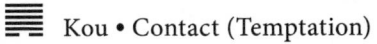

5. Willow branches cover the melon. They hide (protect) its beauty (chang). And it falls into your lap like a gift from Heaven.
Go about your business quietly. Do not be aggressive to yourself or to those around you; let everything develop on its own. Your devoted meekness brings blessings. The greatest things are not created by man but left to ripen. Your question determines whether this is a work, something creative, or a beautiful phase of your life. Great times are approaching. The meaning of *chang* is "beauty," "shining," "well-composed whole," "glorious creation." The magical process of creation takes place in hiding because there is nothing more perishable than a glorious creation. It ruins self-will. What does "gift from Heaven" mean to you?

6. Contact with words. Shame and commotion—but no mistake.
It can happen that we "hurt" the low ranking within ourselves or in others. It is common to be arrogant with those who interfere. This is not wise conduct—but neither is it a mistake. Since you are doing what you have to do, it isn't important what others have to say about it. The sage is sometimes rude. Jesus kicked over the stalls of the money changers in the temple. The message of the Oracle Sign is **explosive temper is not advisable but if it does happen, then it isn't a mistake.**

45 ䷬ *Ts'ui*

The Gathering (Collection)

Character: Thick bunches of grass collected by a servant.

What needs to gather are strength, energy, knowledge, and faith. In order for us to carry out a more significant act and especially not alone but together with others, we need to collect strength, faith, and certainty. In order for you to gain companions, you have to become appropriate to the task. People only join another person who is complete within. A person who is not complete within and who gives off uncertainty makes others uncertain. You are only complete within when you can transform your principles and thoughts into deeds.

Gathering is ripening—ripening for true communion, ripening for the leading of a true communion. The foundation of a genuine community is a strong leader who is trusted and who is followed with devotion and joy, in the same way that soldiers march to a campaign and forget about their fear. Gather strength, faith, vigilance, and self-confidence.

The message of the 45th Oracle Sign is, **The king approaches his temple. It is desirable to see the Great Man. And it brings success. Persistence. Great sacrifice brings blessings. Directed departure is desirable.**

The Great Man lives in us all—if we awaken to it. (If not, we should listen to the advice of those in whom it has already awoken.)

The ancient meaning of "temple" and "sacrifice" is that a shared community cannot form without a shared foundation of faith, shared goals, and without the sanctity from the spirit world above. So that you see the endless outlook of this sign, the "Great sacrifice" is when the "king" sacrifices himself. This is what Jesus did who gave his life for the life of his friends. The willingness to make sacrifice is great for a great affair.

The Oracle Sign signals foresight of the leader of the Gathering. It indicates vigilance that is prepared for all unexpected events. The basis of "together with others" is "togetherness." I first have to gather myself before I can hold the hand of another. The Oracle Sign is encouraging but only if the shared undertaking is directed by the Great Man. If we listen to it, there will be no division, betrayal, lack of faith, or resignation.

THOUGHTS

Like all other Oracle Signs, Ts'ui has many analogies. It depends what you ask. In the bodily sense, it is time for *gathering* energy. In the spiritual sense, it teaches you how to *pull yourself together*. In terms of community, it teaches *how to live together with others*. It could also be all three at once.

The point—on whatever level—is three things. A central will is needed around which to gather. A central goal is needed for which they gather. And there is a need to make sacrifice in the interest of the goal and unity, otherwise nothing will come together at all.

We do not think like this now, and this is why a good community is a rare thing; it is just a jumble of people who have been lumped together accidentally and who are not held together by anything at all, only the rules. If you were to translate the three points above to the operation of a football team, then the message of the sign would be obvious: the central *will* is the coach who decides on the central tactics. Beyond this, every team has a *leader figure* who directs the others. The central goal is clear—to win. The player who does not realize that this requires *sacrifice* will never make a good football player and such types are pushed out of all good teams. If all this is present, then we speak about good **team spirit**. (Savor this phrase because it contains the spiritual secret of this whole Oracle Sign. Unfortunately, we are only familiar with it in sports now.)

This is how all good "gatherings" operate. That is to say that they do not operate democratically. The crowd does not seek a center point but the center point attracts the crowd around itself. The apostles didn't choose Jesus, it was Jesus who chose his apostles. Pontius Pilot held a democratic referendum and the people chose Barabas and condemned Jesus to death. This is a good example of what happens if a lot of ignorant people decide the fate of one single individual.

The center is the important thing within yourself, your true self. And if you socialize with people—for whatever reason—then your center will be the point of reference. *Know who you are, know what you want, and make sacrifices for it.* There is no place for arrogance in the center—only humility.

And something else: the sign warns caution. It talks about invisible obstacles that stand in the path of those gathering. **The True Man renews his weapons (*chu jung*) to prepare for the unknown.** The Chinese advice (chu jung) can be interpreted in one of two ways: *Renew your weapons*, so that you are prepared for the unknown. Or, *do not think about using weapons* and be vigilant instead (forward-looking) so that you are prepared for the unexpected. One is the tactic of Confucius and the other is attributed to Lao Tse. Practitioners of martial arts use both.

The important thing is vigilance. A person who is vigilant is never afraid. It is impossible to frighten them because their spirit is so flexible that they quickly adapt to the most unexpected of events. Things that would frighten others are completely natural to them. We would say that "their heart is in the right place." The point is that a good leader knows that a good community can pass through numerous storms but the leader must know how to ride the waves and keep a firm hand on the wheel.

LINES

1. If you are genuine but not completely genuine, there will sometimes be chaos and sometimes a gathering. If you call your helping spirits, they come. When you hear them your indecision turns into cheerful laughter. Regret nothing! To go on is flawless.
Doubt is only useful until Unity appears. From then on it is just useless hesitation. Your surroundings only reflect your own confusion and doubts. As you commit yourself to devotion—because your reservations have stopped—you find companions. The situation is uncertain because you are still uncertain yourself. If you can already see what is good, do it, and don't hesitate, and the hesitation will stop. A person who sets off is already expected.

2. If he allows himself to be pulled: beneficent. No mistake. If you are true, then a small sacrifice will bring blessings.
Like spirits attract one another. This is what creates togetherness. A deeper analysis of the line shows a person who allows themself to be led and doesn't follow their own head. They listen to their inspiration. If the spirit is open, there is no need for great sacrifice. The character for "being pulled" (Yin) depicts a new tensing bow. A gathering needs harmony—"I" and "mine" are replaced by "us" and "ours." The matter is more important than your own interest. Your true and priceless joy is hidden in the matter.

3. Gathering, sighing. Nothing is at all desirable. It is no mistake to carry on, only a little shame.
You are sometimes not accepted. This can have two reasons. One is that you are too selfish and not a team player. In this case, you need to learn humility like a Zen pupil who—before being accepted by the

community—is sent into the kitchen to serve. The other cause is that perhaps you don't belong here. There are problems with togetherness and that is why you sigh. Do not force the solution—trust in time.

4. Great blessings. No mistake!
The road is open. You sometimes have to go alone but if you are faithful to your inner Leader, you will still reach your goal and your efforts will be crowned with success. If you are faithful to God, then the opinions of people are secondary. They will change them in time. It is only worthwhile living upward. Don't listen to all the different opinions but follow your goal because you know that it will be good for everybody. A lot of people together only make a community if they share a guiding star. (This is also true of friendship and marriage.) That is what you have to follow.

5. You have rank in the gathering. This is not a mistake. But you are not yet true! Work on yourself constantly and the regret will stop.
If you are religious, I would say the following: whatever community you are responsible for, ask God every day whether you are doing it well or not. You were "someone" first and you have to become suited for it after the fact. Selfish intentions. Ulterior thoughts. Purify yourself and then you will hear the higher voice. You still can't hear. You know, don't you?

6. You pay with tears, sighs, and moans. No mistake.
You are not accepted. You are not valued. You are misunderstood. You suffer because of this but it is not your fault. Do not be upset by something that you are not able to change. That is all the ancient text has to say on the matter. There is one soothsayer who advises to wait because they are changing. There is another one who tells you to carry on. It is possible that there are those who still don't truly value you; their eyes will open with time. It is also possible that you are knocking on the wrong door.

46  *Shêng*
Upward Ambition

升

Character: Measure of fermented drink, one shêng
(approximately one liter).

This is a time of growth, the realization of plans and ideas. *Shêng* today also means "upliftment," "promotion." Shêng is when someone emerges from the mists of obscurity and becomes known. The meaning of the ancient character is deeper. It shows that the essence slowly fills the measure: it distils drop by drop. Only a few liters of brandy from a hundred kilos of fruit.

Everyone's life has an essence. We don't just live—we live *for something*. We have to do something and draw something out of ourselves. It is difficult to determine what it is—the most important thing. It is a goal that is both internal and external at the same time. It is a life plan that I can only fulfill if I grow up to it, if I become the person I need to become. This is what happens in the sign of Shêng.

The lines show how a tiny tree appears from the innards of the earth and starts to grow tall. In answer to your question, the Oracle Sign says, **Success depends on your efforts.** You have to work conscientiously from day to day, from hour to hour, from cell to cell. The "tree"—say the sages—needs effort in order to force its roots into the dense soil and to grow tall. The message of the 46th Oracle Sign is,

Upward ambition, great result. See the Great Man. Do not worry (do not doubt). Southern campaign is beneficent.

The superficial meaning of the Oracle Sign speaks about a slow and unobstructed rise. It speaks about recognition: "you grow slowly out from under the earth," and they eventually see who you are and what you hide. All dreams—for which a person works hard—come true. This process is underway now or you are standing just before it. Here, hard work does not mean aggression but the exact opposite; you always have to find the direction of least resistance like the thin veins of the wood or the windblown branch. You have to avoid, adapt, gently penetrate, grow, and slowly enrich and gather strength.

The deeper meaning of the Oracle Sign conceals the secret of Taoist yoga: the path as you discover your own essence and spiritual identity. For this, the help of the "Great Man" is advised who knows this road well because he has already trodden it. Follow your star—you grow closer to it by the day. Your efforts will be rewarded. "Don't be afraid" means "believe in yourself." The result of steady work is that you get to know yourself more and more and you realize that you are strong. You have the power to create fate.

When you set off, you are worried because you have no faith, but as life reassures you for the first time, your worry is replaced by confidence. This is the period when you can bring the best out of yourself. What is hidden in you can come true now. It isn't ready—you can make it ready now. The Oracle Sign says "don't worry" because the process is a slow one.

THOUGHTS

The reason for worry is lack of faith. A person lacks faith who forgets that they are the child of the Omnipotent One and have inherited his Magical Power. And when this power lays dormant in someone for a very long time and when their dreams are not realized, they become frightened and say, "Oh, nothing ever goes well." Life slips out from their control, they become weak, a victim, and increasingly dismayed at being unable to realize their life's great plan.

The slumbering Magician awakens in this Oracle Sign. This might be due to an internal or an external cause, I don't know. This works differently in nature: we call the "faith" of cells "instinct." This is invincible magical power with which trees, flowers, and animals multiply from within themselves; they realize everything that was in the dreams of the seeds—but instinct is not enough for the human being. They need conscious faith, faith in their own magic, in their "omnipotence" to realize their life plan.

Something has started at last but the goal is still a long way off. There is a voice inside you that says, "I'll never make it!" And another that says, "Oh, but you will!" Choose your faith. **All wonders can be yours and you can build your most daring dreams—but slowly, one brick at a time.** It takes patience to place each brick, persistent hard work, and especially faith—so that this may one day becomes a house. You need to be able to see the house as you place each brick. That is faith—as the disciple said, "The reality of things that cannot be seen."

LINES

1. Genuine upward ambition brings great blessings.
Your inner effort agrees with the will of your fate. Your faith says the same thing. You are in tune with those on whom the realization of your will depends. They trust you because you trust yourself—and they help. The situation marks the good beginning of a movement that is helped by the spirit world.

2. As your inner self is in harmony (fu) with your outer world, your small sacrifice brings results. Faultless.
"Small sacrifice" does not mean that you are miserly but that you are not yet able to do magic with powers. *Fu* means "harmony." Harmony with

yourself, with the outside world, and the invisible spirit world. The wind direction is good and you are moving in the right direction. Joy.

3. Your upward ambition takes you to an empty city.
Your progress is unobstructed; it is suspiciously unobstructed. It is like when someone bangs on a door and it swings open. Don't ponder on this, carry on. Take advantage of the fact that you have built up momentum. Realization always has a phase when we run into something unknown. We take fright at times like this. We become uncertain. We imagined something else. We wanted something else. We counted on something else. Reality is an empty city. I had this very same experience with my first stage success. I felt totally *empty*. I thought that it would make me happy and instead it made me feel disappointed. Reality was rather two-dimensional compared to my dreams. It was confused, disturbed, and not at all pleasing. Is that it? Is this what it feels like?

4. The king makes a sacrifice on the Chi Mountain. Blessings. The road is open before you. No mistake.
Whatever you achieve in life, place it on the altar and give thanks to God. Do this even if you think that it comes as the result of your own efforts. For one thing, you didn't see and you cannot see the forces beyond you that have helped—the other thing is that the energy inside you is God's.

5. The road is open before you. Move up the steps.
Do not leave out even a single step. We have a tendency to go rushing forward when a process gets underway and starts to make spectacular progress. We are thirsty for swift success.

6. Upward ambition in darkness. It is favorable that your solid faith should not be shaken. (Wealth and plenty are lost.)
The lines can be interpreted in a number of ways. This is the one that I think is correct. The basis of "upward ambition" is faith—I see what

I have to become. Here, faith wavers, man goes blind and stumbles around in the dark. He didn't believe and he is led by his ego, his greed, his emotions, and his vanity; he sees only what he projects from within himself. This is not reality but a selfish nightmare. Do not continue in darkness. Stop! There is no way forward. Today, everyone rushes blindly on. No one is able to stop in time. This is why "plenty is lost." Regain your faith. Do not want more than God gives.

47  *K'un*

Oppression (Exhaustion)

Character: A tree cannot grow because it is surrounded by walls.

The sages say, "There is no Water in the Lake: this is the image of exhaustion. The True Man follows his goal and fulfills his Fate." The situation appears hopeless. It is as if nothing works. Everything appears to be standing still. Life is tough, mean, unsuccessful, oppressive, and hopeless—at least that is how you feel. Today, we call this depression. When it descends on us, we instantly ask, "Is there any reason for this?" Traditionally, this is not the question to ask. Confucius says, "Oppression (K'un) is a situation in which a person should not be oppressed."

The Oracle Sign does not clearly say whether or not you are living in a genuinely difficult and unsuccessful period or whether that is just how you interpret matters. This question is unanswerable because this is your fate: what you find difficult might be easy for someone else. You are definitely finding things hard at the moment, but don't forget one thing: the True Man is never depressed. For him, nothing can be so oppressive that he would abandon his goal and not fulfill his fate. In fact, he sees difficult problems as a challenge. He sees each one as an excellent opportunity to strengthen his character. The True Man may be bitter, sad, and vengeful, but enough to give up?

No one in real trouble is depressed. People fight with all their might in a war or a mass flood and find powers that they never knew that they possessed. They battle without food or water but don't give in and keep on slaving away and manage to carry loads that would be unbearable in peace time.

K'un warns you that the material world has taken control of your spirit. Perhaps you have become tired out and exhausted. All your energy has sapped away. You have lost your faith. Things haven't turned out the way that you wanted. You live with the oppressive experience of failure.

Today, a person with depression is told to rest while being analyzed and treated with drugs. They are surrounded by caring attention. It used to be exactly the opposite: people were exposed to tough tests and, rather like shock therapy, they were put in dangerous situations so that they could marvel at their own strength.

Life energy (chi) and faith have a reciprocal relationship: people with a strong faith have masses of energy. Exhaustion rarely has a physical cause (even athletes know this)—it is much more common for the spirit to be tired and it abandons its distant goal and sinks into the hopelessness of everyday life. Lack of energy always stems from a **lack of Faith**. Regaining Faith requires *death-defying bravery* rather than pampering.

The message of the Oracle Sign is, **Oppression. Success. Persistence. The influence of the True Man is beneficent. It is not your mistake! Whatever you say, no one listens.** Your words have no authenticity. No one will listen to you. Is there no strength in your words? Or is it an age of deaf ears?

Whatever the question, the answer is that you should stay quiet. Do not try to convince anyone—except yourself. The answer is not in the organization of external—apparently lost—matters but in the merciless bravery with which you stand up against your own weakness and ill health. Wake up to the fact that the spirit of God is alive within you. This means that you are stronger than your faith! A mortal and immortal self lives in all of us. The K'un Oracle Sign warns,

"Do not let the mortal win!" Do not let it talk you out of the fight, the triumph, and the happiness. Do not allow it to convince you that "nothing ever works for me; I'm a loser, and I always will be." The True Man is tensed by a difficult period just like a bow—the more tense it is, the farther it shoots.

THOUGHTS

The light Yang line is stuck between two dark lines in the lower Water Kua and this symbolizes the **spirit trapped in the prison of the material**. This is the general situation in the modern world: that is why we live in an age of depression. It is not only a widespread complaint but a sense with which we all live. It often becomes physical illness rather than mental illness, or simply a difficult sense of oppression and helplessness. It can only be ended with the use of "untimely" tools. We have to wake the divine, the spiritual, the immortal within ourselves, and we should not identify with the general mood of the age that drives man into the ground and sentences him to death as a material being.

We often throw this sign when we are well on the way to suffering a psychosomatic illness as the consequence of our mental state. K'un is the unavoidable state of the spiritual path. We did not find our way here by accident but because of fate. The light that lives within us has to collide with darkness sooner or later. The reason that the battle is so difficult now is because you do not get any support from the community in which you live. The community is also depressed and unable to help itself. This means that all you have is your own light that you are currently stifling. Your external circumstances may be unfavorable at the minute but do not expect the answer to come from there.

The Creative Magician who has been playing dead inside you needs to be resurrected from his coffin of negative thought and dark emotions. "You are gods," says Jesus, quoting the holy tradition. Wake to yourself because your true Being is the only thing able to transform your life. *If it succeeds on the inside, it is sure to succeed on the outside.*

LINES

1. Your waist is pressed by dry branches. You come to a sad valley. You don't see anyone for three years.

Depression—if you give yourself over to it—feeds on itself. You see the situation as hopeless and it paralyzes you, you do nothing or you play to lose and then everything really does become hopeless. Lift yourself out of this vicious circle—by your own hair if you have to.

2. Oppression next to food and drink. High-ranking, red-belted people approach from all angles. Sacrifice is beneficial. To aim upward would bring trouble. No mistake.

We often "live well" and yet still we are depressed. This may be due to a lack of recognition or unfulfilled desires and hopes. What appears here represents high rank and means respect from the community. But sacrifice has to be made for it. If you do not ask it for yourself, you will receive it. This is the peculiarity of the situation. The "red belt" that represents high rank is really within. This line can also mean spiritual help.

3. Stone presses down, you cling to thorns and thistles. You enter into your house but you do not see your wife. Trouble!

The worst possible thing that we can do in a tight situation is to thrash around and bash our head against the wall. We reach for tools that not only injure us but make the situation even worse than it was before. A reckless and hysterical person even topples his own house: he poisons his private life with his failure. An apparent or insignificant problem can soon turn into a Great Problem. Stop!

4. He arrives but very slowly and dejected in a golden carriage. He is shamed but he eventually reaches his goal.

You can only control an oppressive situation if you do it with sufficient energy. Something has begun here but everything is very leisurely and very slow. The "golden carriage" is temptation, the reward of the weak and the "small good fortune" that can be bought by those who wanted to escape trouble. Do not settle for this and this alone. Your goal is more than this and higher than this. The sign can also mean that we hurry too quickly to someone's aid.

5. His nose and legs are cut off. The one with the crimson belt also holds him down. Joy still approaches slowly. Make a sacrifice!
The situation is difficult and oppressive. When we battle with depression, we reach a state of complete hopelessness—and this is the moment when everything turns. We find the hand of God when we have lost everything. This is the turning point when we wake to ourselves. The line warns you to see difficulties and blessings. The deepest point is the turning point.

6. Vines wrap around him. He isn't certain in his movements and he says, "If I move, I'll regret it." But if he does set off: blessings!
Throw away your crutches and walk. You have grown used to them and it will be difficult without them, but realize that you no longer need them. Realize that you are now stronger than your surroundings. Put an end to anxiety, uncertainty, and self-pity—shed these things like outgrown, dirty clothes—and fight!

48  *Ching*

Well

Character: An estate divided into eight parts that has a ninth part in the middle. In ancient times, this area had to be cultivated together: this is where the well stood.

A pure spring lies deep in the well; this is the "water of life," the eternal value and knowledge that make a man a man and a community a community. The sign says find your way back to your humanity hidden deep down in your being. Rediscover yourself and God—do not forget this and do not allow the "well" to fall in or become dirtied as a result of any outer or inner madness. A person who drinks the water of life will have eternal life—a person whose spring dies out has reached the end.

The Oracle Sign says wake up to yourself and look for the essence deep down in your question. Do not be satisfied with any kind of self-delusion or deceit. The essence is simple and eternal: love ... immortality ... happiness ... that you are a spirit from the spirit of God, this is the essence. This is deep down in the well.

The water of life not only provides Knowledge but also inexhaustible *energy*: a person who drinks from this is rejuvenated. Their depleted strengths are restored and renewed. The water of life is shared. It is in you and in others. Deep down in our souls, we are all one and that is why, without exception, the long-term happiness of every community depends on whether or not the "well" works and whether people drink its water or not. If not, the community will decay and disintegrate, whether that is a marriage, friendship, business venture, nation, society, or a human spirit.

The Well sign message is, **A person can transform his city but he cannot change the Well. Things come and go but the Well remains the Well. If the bottom becomes muddy, if the rope is too short, if the bucket breaks: trouble.**

Here is the opportunity not only for you to find yourself, to discover your true values and opportunities with deeper self-awareness and to eventually discover your accepted fate in the world—but also to find the hands of others with whom you truly share fate. We not only see ourselves more clearly in this Oracle Sign but also others. You will develop spiritual insight and you will be able to catch a glimpse of what is of value in others as you do the same within yourself. This is what connects you with them.

The heart of all communities is the Well: it is the center of all cultures, religions, and societies. Despite the wildest differences, people gather around the well and feel united because this is where the water bubbles to the surface—the water of life—that is in us all.

The Ching Oracle Sign is not only exquisite but also threatening: the well needs to be saved, otherwise everything will end. *You commonly receive this sign if the Well is in danger*—if you give yourself over to the fashions and fads of the time, if you feel and think superficially, if your inner voice of inspiration falls silent and chaos and doubt take control . . . if you let go of the hand God.

This sign speaks at the deepest point of your spirit: if "your rope reaches that far" and "your bucket doesn't break." It is time for true self-awareness, knowledge, spiritual development, physical healing, gaining strength, and meeting with those who "drink with you" as much as it is a time to discover and put an end to the curse that meant none of this was able to happen so far. Free yourself of all things unworthy.

THOUGHTS

Prejudices differ—the essence is one. There are many religions and wisdoms—what is true within us is one. A person whose well does not work looks for what divides. A person whose well does work looks for what unites. If you have drunk from the pure water of the well, you will realize that all men are your brothers.

Jesus refers to himself as "living water" and in one of the beautiful scenes from the gospels, he meets a Samarian woman by the well—who is the only one to whom he reveals his identity as the Messiah—and he tells her that whoever drinks from him will never grow thirsty.

Wells are in a disgraceful state today in the dark age. This is why we find no better word to describe the age in which we live than *inhuman*. Humanity has shared philosophy, shared law, shared tasks, and shared origins above all ideas of nation, race, and religion. It is timeless. Heraclitus, Buddha, Krishna, Lao Tse, and Jesus do not "go out of fashion" and are becoming increasing contemporary.

You draw from the well when you ask advice from the I Ching. It advises you to look into the well and deep into yourself. You cannot receive advice or help because the solution and the strength are within you. If your rope reaches the water and if your vessel doesn't break, you will be surprised to discover quite *how much you know* and the invincibility of the strength deep down in your spirit. You wouldn't have thought it!

This unexpected discovery of your own strengths and merits also leads you to realize that *the same is true of others as well*. And you no longer see what repels in other people but what attracts—and this may form the basis of a new cooperation. You do, however, have to reach this encouraging finale. The drama is in the lines.

LINES

1. Muddy well, no one drinks from it. Birds don't even come to a ruined, old well.

The Oracle Sign warns of two things. First, what has gone too long and has passed needs to be left there. You have to move past your problems, sorrow, and bad experience. Second, life and value are one. If a person loses their values, they will stop living and simply vegetate. They drink from a swamp and not "living water" and are all alone. A culture dies out if its well dries up. When a true value is no longer a value, life deteriorates, and a person is left alone. We know this state well. We call it a crisis of values and loneliness. Look for the pure source!

2. A person catches a fish (fu) at the mouth of the well. His jug breaks and the contents flow out.

Your heart is where your treasure is. Here, you abandon your genuine values for the valueless. You sell your spirit in exchange for money, success, well-being, profit, and fleeting pleasure. A person who runs after their own values loses themself and people around them. The genuine content also evaporates from your relationships with others, if there was any in the first place. The symbol depicts a "lucky fisherman" who is fishing for bleak fish in Life's Eternal Waters. (The *fu* is a freshwater fish that swims with its mate and makes love—rather like a bleak.)

3. The well is pure but no one drinks from it. It pains me because it would be possible to drink from it. If the mind of the ruler was light, we could enjoy the blessing of the well water together.

Your values go unrecognized although they are genuine. The mind of the ruler is also dark in a dark age; he does not recognize the difference between a blessing and a curse. At times like this, talent, good intentions, wisdom, and genuine love are all abandoned. Those in power do not consider these to be values. "In light ages," says Hamvas, "the talent of man is a blessing for the nation. In a dark age, it is its own tragedy." Rubbish times need rubbish and no one has a requirement for pure water. That which is beautiful, noble, immortal, and divine is not timely. All the line says is that this pains you. It does not give advice about what to do.

One thing may reassure you: stupid "rulers" come and go but the Well remains. Pure water is an eternal asset. If your love for someone is not reciprocated, carry on loving. If your goodness toward someone is not reciprocated, carry on being good. If you are talented and it is not recognized, carry on creating. (This is exemplified by the life of Jesus. He was the "light that shone in the darkness but the darkness did not accept him.")

The inner, psychological message of the line is somewhat different: there is a bad and foolish king ruling in your spirit. You are not able to live according to your inner values. You know what is good and yet you still do bad. You believe, but you don't live according to your beliefs. It really is atrocious if someone knows what true value is and yet they still lead a wretched life. *Look for your real, light king.* Only then will the fu be yours along with the blessings of the sky and the spiritual Force.

4. The well is being repaired. Faultless.

This is now about you. Do not involve yourself with the world but with yourself. You have an encouraging future ahead of you but this needs you to "sort yourself out." This is a time of inner development. Don't feel pained because of the delay. Put a sign outside saying, "Closed for alterations!"

5. There is pure, cool, and drinkable water in the well.

Give thanks to God for everything that you have received and what you have managed to become. It is another matter as to where your values are appreciated, your blessings are shared, and your light gives light to others. The darkness has a reason. Take joy in your light. You are suitable to use it so that others may follow you. Whether or not your "followers" are suitable is their problem.

6. The well has no head. The water at its edge is everybody's. Exalted blessings. Great fulfillment.

Everything is good. The source of life is open and belongs to everyone. This line says, *"As we have confronted our own faults, we have become understanding of others.* That is why they approach us with greater confidence: we condemn no one." We are brothers for better or for worse. They come to the well. The time of healing, understanding, fulfillment, reciprocated feelings, and significant realizations is approaching. It promises fulfillment.

49  *Ko*

Renewal (Revolution)

Character: Picture of a shed (removed) skin.

Renewal. Your day will come and you will achieve inner and outer oneness. Fundamental success. Sorrow stops. The snake sheds its skin. The situation is untenable. Only fundamental change and renewal helps. You have to overcome an outlived inner and outer situation. Something that has protected and preserved you until now has become a thing of the past—you have to renew yourself. Shedding does not mean that that an animal pulls something from itself but that it has new skin underneath that throws off the old. Before the sun rises to its zenith, your outer fate will harmonize with your inner state. Regret and problems will stop (hui wang).

Ko is made up of two trigrams, Fire under the Lake. These are two incompatible elements together symbolizing a state of *boiling*. The Oracle Sign says that you stand before a revolution. The True Man pays increasing attention to timeliness in such periods of fundamental change and renewal. He does not act too early and he doesn't act too late. He watches the signs of the time. Clear, seeing eyes—is the positive quality of Fire; Joy—this is the strength of the Lake.

The Oracle Sign has faith in your success.

THOUGHTS

It is hard to come away from the old. The things that you have become used to have grown on you like skin and protected you for a long time and then slowly turned into a restricting prison. It is painful to give them up. The new is already ripening underneath. All new things are first born *within*—you stand before a new life cycle.

Two things are needed for renewal: decisive moves and careful waiting. It is a problem if you are late but more of a problem if you move too early. Yu fu, this means that the change on the inside harmonizes with the outside. It also means that the spirit world helps with the renewal process. In the same way that a child is not abandoned when born and a hen keeps an egg warm and watches over it while it hatches, the invisible world looks after us—especially when we are "reborn."

The lines of the Oracle Sign offer tactics for this *revolution* which is not to be confused with rebellion. Although each may have a genuine cause, the difference lies in the fact that a revolution wins and a rebellion loses. It loses because it initiates its acts blindly and does not fully appreciate the true nature of forces, and it especially doesn't see that you do not have to step on the outside but you have to renew on the inside.

The point of a revolution is not that the situation on the outside is untenable but that something new is ready and waiting to be born. "I have had enough" is insufficient for a revolution. I also have to see what I would create to replace it. A genuine revolution does not recognize impatience or aggression. It only knows patience and strength. A genuine revolution is preceded by *careful inner and outer work*. Consideration, calm, faith—and especially infallible judgment.

King Wen considers revolution to be a natural state. Everything is continually reborn. It first enriches, expands, grows, and stretches in terms of quantity and then snaps over into a different *quality* condition. We are rarely able to carry out this natural process and either act too early or when it has become too late. We can become stuck in what has gone on too long, become overripe and started to rot or—if we don't see clearly—pull the old skin off too soon, and the new isn't there to replace it.

What you leave behind is your past: your habits, feelings, desires, and a way of thinking that has petrified into characteristics. You feel that they support you even if they are bad. You cling to the old out of instinct. People have also grown used to you as you are. What will your spouse say if you "renew yourself" when they have grown used to the old you?

Renewal is not a solitary act but always a communal activity. The *rebel* only reaches the point of disruption—wanting to flee from their overburdening fate and not considering where others are in their lives. The rebel spirit has given birth to a lot of divorce, escape, and emigration and it often transpires that the rebel brings all of their yet-to-surface problems with them. The revolutionary feels a sense of responsibility for the human community in which they live. As one senses timeliness, *their act will be successful.* The most important thing is to *begin the renewal on oneself.*

Only a new man is able to create a new world. This is what was missed by the revolutions of modern history. *You first have to change yourself and then the system.* The same is true of our situation in life. "Renewal" does not mean moving the furniture around in your apartment. You should never start with what surrounds you. Renewal is always an inner step. It is a step closer to God. It is a step toward fulfillment. This is the way of development in the spiritual sense. We have to renew ourselves many times in our life. Pressure from within is able to initiate just as much as the pressure of outside events. But you should know that the outside world is a mirror image; there is no point in smashing it if you don't like the look of your face.

The Oracle Sign recommends **radical transformation**—but in the Chinese way. This means that it should be done with wisdom, consideration, inspiration, and joy.

LINES

1. He is wrapped in yellow cowhide.
You are ripening and so is the situation—like a baby in the womb. The urge is strong, but do not do a thing. Do not interfere in anything. The only thing you have to do is to ripen.

2. You become renewed on your own day! It is beneficent to go to war. No mistake.
The revolution can begin. You can see this from the signs of the time. Your vigilant glance is not that of the rebel but of the sober revolutionary.

3. Going to war brings trouble. Persistence is dangerous. If rebirth has been mentioned three times, you can dedicate yourself and you will receive confidence.
Do not set off yet. This can lead to clinging on too tightly and uncertain, immature, and weak deeds. Genuine dedication is neither too careful nor too daring. You need to see more clearly. Consider things three times before you take a step, then you will be ripe to act. And others will also see that you are now ready. Your deeds can only be effective when you see clearly what you are doing and what the consequences are. Be careful because what you see as clear vision is not. You still have many false beliefs from self-deception to disperse.

4. Regret ends. Oneness with the world and the spirit world. Renewal is fate. The road is open.
Doubt disperses. You can act. This is the moment of great deeds.

5. The Great Man renews like the tiger. The higher world supports him before he asks for a divination.
This is when the True Man makes a move, the "Chief's Son," who knows what to do without a divination. What he does is universally

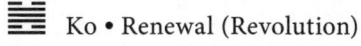

true. He can feel that the Whole is with him. And just as a tiger's new stripes appear after molting—so the visible results of the renewal appear.

6. The True Man renews like a leopard. The small man who has not yet fully grown only changes his face. To continue is trouble. Stay in your place; in this way the road stands open.

The state that follows a revolution: things never quite work out how we had dreamed they would. We ourselves don't change a great deal and our environment has not exchanged spirits, just adapted to the new circumstances. The True Man accepts compromises. To continue would be great fanaticism and would lead to trouble. All creators are disappointed in their work—that isn't how they expected it to be. We have to accept human weaknesses. We also have to accept our own weaknesses. All results are partial results—and the new already conceals the sprouts of the next renewal. Stopping is a greater art than starting. You should do this now and not involve yourself with disappointment.

50  *Ting*

Sacrificial Vessel

Character: Image of a holy sacrificial vessel.

"Exalted blessings. Success," says the commentary. The hexagram of the 50th Oracle Sign shows that Wood burns in Fire. All blessings are born out of sacrifice. Blessings are the sky's response to sacrifice. This is the most ancient thought: the world was born from sacrifice. It was born from divine sacrifice. You can only be reborn from sacrifice. What do you have to sacrifice? You have to sacrifice anxiety, fear, selfishness, old habits, false beliefs, and the fixed idea that what happens with you is against you and not for you.

Ting is the symbol of high Chinese culture. It is an ancient artifact belonging to all great families and dynasties. It was used for the alchemy that made the earthly heavenly, the material spiritual, the barbarian cultured, and humankind divine. Our roots are not in the earth but in the sky. Our real experience of being is not mortality but immortality. Few people understand this now because few people carry the burning fire of sacrifice inside themselves. Few people know that they themselves are spirits and their home is "not of this world," and the primary goal of their existence is not the mad struggle to survive and not the satisfaction of desires—but the realization of spiritual values. The pyramids will last longer than New York—because those who built them lived in the knowledge of immortality whereas New York was born in a time of panic and insane ambition of obsession stuck in the material.

You go through inner maturation in the Ting sign. You are past the revolution and *now the new needs to be founded*. You must free yourself of all the infectious memories of the old. You now need to become giving and that is why you need to take care: what is the principle, who is the person, and what is the future to whom and to which you will give yourself? Throw everything onto the sacrificial fire that you have outgrown, that only holds you back, and that until now you considered as a value when it wasn't. Throw your selfishness onto the fire.

You now know that it is only worth fighting for that upon which there are blessings. There are only blessings on your Fate and not on just your life. A difficult fate may be blessed and happy—an easy life may be unhappy, worthless, and full of anxiety. You can now recognize and solidify your fate.

THOUGHTS

The sign conceals the secret element of Chinese yoga, the practice of which was similar to mind control. The magic of imagination pushes the unworthy away while imagining a worthy and pure future at the same time. The power of symbols and archetypes is enormous. The worthy and new will appear if there is sufficient unworthiness in Ting. A person who uses this for selfish goals attracts weighty karma. The **magic of renewal** is beneficent if it works in the direction of the accepted fate. This is the basis of all true religion, culture, and art. Real culture makes a person spiritual and it keeps the memory of heavenly origin awake in them—subculture does not know about one's divine origins or it denies it. *Subculture is not only godless but also inhuman.* It is satanic mind control that serves death and transient belief.

A qualitative change takes place in the sign of Ting. You can transform your thoughts here along with your feelings and human relationships. After this, you will more easily accept your fate, even if it is difficult—and you will see your life as being more valuable, the blessing of which you have already experienced. Even raw ingredients cooked in the sacrificial vessel become refined nourishment. The message is to live upward. The invisible world will help.

LINES

1. Sacrificial vessel with turned up feet. It is advantageous to remove the remains. Marry your mistress if she gives birth to a son. Faultless.
Free yourself of all bad memories, negative feelings, and thoughts. Do not classify either yourself or others. Starting with a clean sheet means that something can succeed that has never before succeeded. Do not carry the burden of old reflexes, habits, and fears with yourself. What has been a source of problems up until now may now bring blessings. What you have seen as unworthy until now concealed the gift of your fate. It is the dawn of a new age—do not take your oppressive dreams with you.

2. The sacrificial vessel is full of values. My companions are tortured by hostile thoughts—but this does not reach me. Blessings.
The small hate the large because this involuntarily reminds them of their smallness. Beneficent deeds bring out hostile feelings in the world: envy, ill will, and rejection. People want to drag down those who begin to live upward. Do not allow the poison arrows to touch you. Socrates said, "They can kill me but they cannot harm me." A person with a full vessel needs to protect themself not only from the outside world but also from their own inner voices. Protect yourself from lack of faith, fear, and negative thoughts. You should know that darkness does not wish to accept light. Also know that darkness cannot triumph over light.

3. The handle of the sacrificial vessel has deformed. The deed is obstructed. Regret. Eventually blessings.
The new is now complete but there is no vessel for it. It takes a new time for the recognition of new values. It needs to ripen. Do not be

worried that you will be left alone with your treasures. Your time is ripening. Sacrifice holds the reward in itself. "I do not take glory from people," Jesus said. Rich-spirited people are alone in the world and the spirit world is their companion. Everyone is only able to receive recognition from deep within their spirit or, the same thing, from God. In everyday terms, this line encourages you not to be worried by initial problems. The blessed rain is late—but it is coming.

4. The foot of the sacrificial vessel is broken off. The prince's food spills. It sullies everyone. Trouble.
Do not follow this path! An ambitious person causes serious damage to themself and those around them. False sacrifice means that you have over-fattened your ego and this will lead to failure. Life becomes more beautiful and noble around modest people who are full of faith. The careerist lies about their "faith" to themself and sullies life. Hold careful self-examination.

5. The sacrificial vessel has golden handles. It is beneficent to act with solid faith.
You can now act from within, from your heart and the center of your spirit. Be persistent. You now make your fate, and those who help in this will find you.

6. The handles of the sacrificial vessel are made of jade. Great blessings. Everything is pushing forward.
The birth of a new world. New values begin to work. You can now experience the happiness of the sage and his tamed power; you do not depend on external circumstances. Good luck, bad luck, joy and sorrow, success and failure, above and below: they come and go. The happiness of the sage depends on no one. He wanders through the difficulties of life with a triumphant smile.

51  Chên

Arousing (Shocking)

Character: Rain pouring from the sky and the image of a woman hiding her blessed state. Today, this character means "time"— in ancient times it meant "shock."

The herald of all rebirth is shock. From coldness, new life waking from the dead causes alarm at first. The celebration of spring begins with thunder and lightning. The divine—if it enters fate—initially causes fright. Saul fainted and fell off his horse when he first met Jesus and he only woke up later when he was a new man, Paul. All rebirth has two phases: a shocking, alarming, and frightening phase—when the joints of the old suddenly split open and become nothing—and the joyous, uplifting phase when the new takes the stage.

All artists know that it is only possible to access true values through shock. And all people with faith know that contact with the divine is preceded by fear of God—something too bright and too enormous steps into our life that initially frightens us. People who have returned from death say that, at one point on their journey, they were frightened by the sudden blinding light of love that appeared. Our eyes have become accustomed to shade. We are afraid of freedom.

The message of this Oracle Sign is, **Do not be afraid of the thunder, the crisis, and the alarming news—this is all the herald of new life.**

Our modern age lies totally in the sign of Chên. There are a great deal of crises, earthquakes, and alarming news—this not only symbolizes the end of something but also the start of a new life cycle.

KEYWORDS

Thunder

Tremor

Shock Effect

Fertile Inspiration

Spring used to be celebrated with elaborate ceremonies. The priest held a brimming sacrificial vessel up to the heavens with such calm that neither earthquake nor storm could have unnerved him—*he did not spill one single drop.* This is **presence of mind**; this calm and inner certainty is the key of this Oracle Sign. Create peace with your heart. Look calmly at the storm. Do not adopt the resonance of others and do not be afraid—time is working for you. A beneficial deed can only be born out of calm. The urge is very strong now: you must act. Act with your inner self. Calmly take aim. Do not rush the shot.

Know from the quiet center point of your spirit that you are going through two states on the outside: one that is shocking and distressing—and one that is bright and joyous. These are the emotional companions of a new phase in your life. There is trouble if you get stuck in the first phase. A person who is not afraid can walk on water.

THOUGHTS

When something begins it is shocking and disturbing. The new is born howling. It is the beginning of something new that creates fear. This could be a new plan, new undertaking, new phase of your life, or a new approach. The alarming thing in the Oracle Sign is that it is terribly dynamic. And it is apparently unexpected, rather like an explosion. Really great things can't simply slip into our lives unnoticed. Energies are released. Things take on a momentum. In this sign, you experience that your Fate *shouts*. This is the shock effect of great experiences.

LINES

1. A shock is on its way: uh, oh! This is followed by laughter: ha, ha! Blessings.
The thing that you fear now turns to your advantage. A person only knows afterward what is really good for them. It is what shocks them—and brings good luck. Perhaps it is the shock itself—that you eventually see yourself clearly.

2. Danger accompanies shock (li). You lose your wealth. Climb up the ninth hill and don't run after it. You will get it in seven days.
The "danger" (li) means the haunting spirit from your past. Karmic debt, unsolved fears, complexes, disturbing experiences that return to you in dreams and terrorize your present. The "shock" will now wash all of these things away—and a lot of other things besides that you will interpret as a great loss. The "ninth hill" is a place from where you can eventually have an overview of yourself and your fate—and you realize that a new cycle is being born inside you and around you. Something that you initially considered to be a problem now brings blessings.

3. The shock leads to rebirth. Let this knowledge lead.
"If we have not made an inner situation conscious, it appears on the outside as Fate," says Jung. This now becomes conscious in you. And this opens new horizons before you.

4. The shock stirs up the swamp.
You don't see clearly. A lot of things come to the surface but the time is not yet right for understanding or acting. While you still can't see clearly and while you are ruled by fears, anxieties, and negative thoughts, do not take a single step! Beneficial deeds need calm. Aim for this. Do not become the prisoner of minor feelings.

5. Shock and trouble come and go. Do what the center wants.

Build your house even if lightning is striking all around you. Pay attention to your heart and not the difficulties, and you will not experience loss. Do not be the plaything of those around you. Follow your inner self. An aikido master, speaking about the tactic of this line, describes one who cannot be defeated if he is attacked from eighty-eight directions. He says, "If my concentration is in the Center, I do not live in time. My inner calm halts constant and multidirectional trouble around me and I answer everyone in turn and in time." Events speed up in panic and slow down in calm. A juggler who is calm can keep sixteen plates in the air but will drop one if they panic. Be calm and do what you want. Do not focus on your fears but on the task at hand.

6. Shocks come one after the other. The spectacle causes panic. If he steps now, it brings trouble. The trouble has not reached his body yet but only that of his neighbors. No mistake. His companions reprimand him.

Everyone experiences shock differently. There is no unity at times like this, not because of selfishness but because no two people have the same image of the future. Do not adopt the panic of others and do not try to convince anyone. If you are woken by Arousing, new norms apply to you than the ones that you have lived by up until now—this is why the others speak. You have become "alien." A new life often also means a new community. This is socializing with new people and you are only joined by like-minded people from the old circle. A person who learns from the fate of others is able to solve their own crisis more easily. This line offers advice to people living in the modern world: do not adopt the doctrines of others, their fears, or their negative thoughts! Do not adopt the feelings of all those who have become stuck in the present. **Modern society is sick, do not adapt to it as it will make you sick too.** Do not concern yourself with slander, rejection, lack of appreciation, or whether you are seen as a genius—follow your own path. At the same time, you should remain aware that you do not see clearly either—you are not better, just different. Do not act out of fear or uncertainty. Wait for the light.

52  *Kên*
Calm (Mountain)

艮

*Character: Someone's eye looks back to see what has led
to the present situation.*

You have reached the **boundary** of something. A cycle has ended; it lasted until now—another cycle starts from here. This is the time of reckoning. It will now become clear what has become realized of your dreams, desires, and efforts. All things invisible will become visible and solidify. What you now face is **reality**.

There is need for reckoning because our life is made up of movements, and if we do not become conscious of the fact that one movement has ended and another is being born and *what lessons were to be learned from the closing movement*, we will take all its faults across with us into the new movement and repeat them ad infinitum. Repetition is our fundamental weakness and it causes the most trouble. A good example of this kind of repeated separation is when someone does not learn from a relationship that has gone wrong and remarries and gets divorced again in the same way for the same reasons—because they carry a faulty "virus."

Reckoning requires a state of calm. At times like this, the True Man inspects his heart and does not leave his place. The person "who has not yet fully grown" runs mindlessly on. The sage warns that the Kên

Oracle Sign only carries the quiet and motionless calm of the Mountain on the outside while it is very dynamic and tense on the inside, and that is why neither the events of your life nor the subconscious strength of your spirit will be able to create calm. You need to make that yourself.

Calm that we create ourselves is called **meditation.** I am not thinking about the retreating into a dream world that is so fashionable now but that heightened state of self-awareness when you look down on your life and on yourself as if you were looking with the eyes of God. You look at your being and your actions like a bystander. You need to do this now: stop and look back with clear eyes—at the boundary between the end of something and something new that is just beginning. Meditation expresses the essence of judgment.

The message of the 52nd Oracle Sign is, **He keeps his back calm. He does not become attached to his personal self. He retreats into his inner court; he doesn't see his people. No mistake.** The general answer to your question is, *stop and calm your heart! Retreat into your inner court; your responsibility now is yourself—no one else. Do not allow your fear, anxiety, desire, hope, or will to hound you any longer.*

In *Fiddler on the Roof* when the matchmaker bursts in and starts to announce the good news, the sage stops her and says to her, "Let's first sit down." This is the advice of this Oracle Sign.

THOUGHTS

Do not explore the past or the future. Be here and now. Do not be disappointed or hopeful. What will be, isn't. What was, isn't. Everything just Is. Eternity not only means a long, long time but also that there is no time—just continuous Present.

If you hold a glass of wine in your hand, there is just a glass of wine and just your hand. Frozen image. At other times this image flies by—now it stops and you look at it in detail. It is as if you are seeing it for the first time. It is as if you are seeing it for the last time. Take a look at yourself in the mirror—the very same way. Take a look around in your life—in just the same way. Take a look at your question—in just the same way.

There is no greater miracle in the world than reality. From this sober, solid, and desire-free state, you are able to decide what to do. If everything appears to have stood still for the moment, see it as a blessing. If it moves, stop it. If you can't stop it on the outside, try on the inside; inner calm is achievable "on the way" but it is extremely difficult. ("The best place to meditate is the market square!" said a Zen master.) You now need to *stabilize* your affairs. Your situation is a *solitary task* and not shared. It depends on you. This is why it is important to give it your full consideration.

In martial arts, you need to create a situation in which you are able to pull yourself together. In boxing this would be holding, as this provides the opportunity for a rest. Tai Chi Chuan recommends a similar tactic that would put the opponent in a blocked position ("take the tiger back to the mountain").

Gathering strength and resting may be the general goal of the Kên sign.

LINES

1. Calm in your feet. No mistake. Continuously advantageous.

Once something has been put in motion, it brings a long chain of consequences along with it. It has not yet been put in motion. The heart and the head are pure. You can see what would happen if you were to set off. But only begin if you see it as good. All events start within us even if we are responding to an external challenge.

This line teaches us that true beginning is not the first step but the step *before* that, when our spirit has still not set off and is able to decide what to do. Should I be temperamental? Should I get angry? Should I allow myself to be fertilized with various plans, emotional and intellectual sprouts? A considered person always takes the best step within the parameters of a given situation—just as in *Hamlet*, Horatio "is not to stir without great argument." Afterward all you can do is to stifle the fire and bitterly abort matters that have gone wrong, Here, you are still free. You can clearly see what you are getting involved in. Have faith in the fact that you see well.

2. His legs are calm. He is not able to save his followers. His heart is not joyous.

Doubt, fear, and lack of faith force a sudden standstill. They appear after things have gained momentum—they stayed silent when you set off. At times like this, a person runs to the ego in order to stubbornly and aggressively take their fate "in hand." This does not lead to good. Follow your path with devotion; this is one piece of advice. The other is that it is really painful if others will not allow us to help them. You need to take account of the fact that people are only matured by their own experience—and that is rare.

3. Forced calm in the hips. Danger. This strangles the heart (sun).

On the first line, you decided whether to light a fire or not. It is burning with large flames here and you try to put it out. No form of extinction is correct. The "strangle" (*sun*) word also means "smoke"; the smoke of unsatisfied desires and unfulfilled hopes stifles. Take a look and examine what is causing you to "suffocate." And if you see it, don't hide it away in yourself again, don't sweep it under the carpet but free yourself of it. Meditation, rather like harmony, should not be wanted but allowed to happen. You may have dark thoughts about yourself or about others: let them rise to the surface, look at them, and let them leave, and do not focus on them.

4. The calm of the body (personality). No mistake.

Here, the heart quietens; unsatisfied desires, ambitions, and fears do not torment you too much. The ego has still not given up entirely but it no longer interferes in the game. You finally see what is yours, what you will reach, and what is not is not worth torturing yourself over. If

I become calm, it is as if I were another person and I can see another world around me—people become suddenly "different" too. It is like removing a pair of misty spectacles. You will not regret anything you do with this approach.

5. The calm of the jawbone. Your words have order and so you will have no cause for regret.

We often regret something that we say. It is then that we realize that we are not considerate. What does consideration mean? It means to speak from a state of calm and not inner disruption, doubt, or role-play. We not only express something with our words but we also create. "A good phrase," writes Béla Hamvas, "is like an oath: it cannot be altered." Speech is magic and a person is responsible for every word that leaves their lips. Watch what you say and who is speaking from within you.

6. Magnanimous calm. Blessings.

There is only one true calm: when a person is at peace with their fate. They don't rebel but realize that they are living a blessed life; everything is a gift. Emotional stability and calm of the mind spreads and attracts goodness. Such a person no longer wants anything and that is why they get it.

53 ䷴ *Chien*

Gradual Development

Character: Water and cutting. This is the symbol of the Chian River: its source, in the Chou Kingdom in the mountains of Central China, cuts through vast regions, growing fuller and wider before pouring into the sea.

The answer to your question is, *things are moving quickly but slower than you would like.* Two comparisons from nature will help you to understand this situation. The first describes a thin stream that sets off, twists and turns, and fills out, taking in water from other sources before spreading out and becoming a vast, surging river. The second one looks at the two Kua: a Tree grows on top of a Mountain. How long does it take? Also, an external eye can only see its leaves and not its roots. But the roots are what make a tree truly great and strong as they grow deeper and deeper into the dense, dark layers of the earth. What you can see grows from within and from below. Inner solidity helps the growing process. It is the certainty that says, "It will be as I dreamed it would." Things can only grow tall on unshakable foundations.

The other essential point is external ability to adapt. What does this mean? It means always following the path of least resistance. It means pushing in everywhere, finding a handhold, and flexibly and toughly and continually adapting to external opportunities. Growth is struggle—but its aim is not to defeat the outside world but to achieve

fulfillment. Growth is obstructed by impatience. The roots will smash rocks in time and send their soft threads into hard stone but, if **you rush this slow process, it will all come to nothing.** This is about cellular growth—step by step, gradually. There are days when nothing happens at all. There are days when it looks as if the whole thing is actually regressing; the situation often appears to be totally hopeless.

In the Oracle Sign, you learn that your fate does not move in a straight line but in a zigzag where every zig and every zag are not cul-de-sacs but unavoidable stepping stones on the path to maturity. At times like this, you lose your faith. You would like to run on ahead. As Nietzsche says, "to will is to want." A voice inside you shouts, "The whole thing will come to nothing. Let's go, we don't want to get stuck here!" And afterward, it transpires that what you thought was a side-track was actually a pivotal station on the road to your development.

The deeper meaning of the Chien sign sees the development of your being and the being of others here: the True Man solidly defends his moral and spiritual strength in order to develop the common man. Whatever you ask, the answer not only contains the opportunity of distant fulfillment but also that **you have to grow up to the task.** You are still too immature to receive it immediately.

THOUGHTS

Patience. Don't worry about tomorrow. Lasting values take time to come together. Do not attempt to aggressively take control of your own fate because you will disrupt the maturation process. Early and sudden success can crush a person because they have not grown up to it inside. There is no greater challenge—and misery—for the spirit than when it is faced with sudden wealth, success, or great power.

All an external eye sees is that the sudden burden distorts character and a person becomes ugly—or as they say, "goes mad." If you look inside a person who has been puffed up by a sudden excess of pressure, you will see that, deep down in their spirit, they do not believe that *all this is theirs.* It is as if they had stolen it, or there is a hidden feeling that it could be taken away at any time. This is because the person shoved it in their own pocket.

We feel that agitated greed in every moment of our modern life. We rush but not to get anywhere in particular—because the goal is no longer in front of us. Iron Age man did not know what "happy fulfillment" is and that is why we rush around, because we know that our whole civilization is terribly unstable and will not last much longer. The psychological cause of our "speeded up life" is a *guilty conscience.* We rob one another and the world—and we know that we have to hurry because the world will only last for a couple of days and we will have to return everything!

Genuine fulfillment needs **lasting foundations**. The Oracle Sign symbolizes fulfillment with a girl who is to be married. The various lines of the Oracle Sign describe the various stages that a wild goose has to pass through before it can find its mate. It flaps its wings in flight to express the slow process of maturing and increasing readiness. Here, "wild goose" would once have meant the snow-white bird of the spirit whose goal is to be increasingly perfect and spiritual. It was thought that a wild goose only had one true mate. If it loses its mate, it never mates again.

This means that there is a real wish for fulfillment behind your question rather than a fleeting desire. It is the kind of thing that you have to grow inside yourself because it is your fate. Work patiently on yourself so that you will deserve what you are waiting for. And don't hurry others either.

LINES

1. The wild goose swims toward the shore. The young boy encounters difficulty. It is just gossip. No mistake.
The "spirit bird" has set off but it is still a long way away from its destination. Advance but with patience. Do not let the opinions of others disturb you or the fact that you are on your own. Time is working for you. Overcome your negative thoughts.

2. The wild goose moves slowly toward the rocks. It eats and drinks and celebrates! Blessings.

The "spirit bird" reaches its first passing success and this fills it with joy. Learn to take joy in the little things. Do not look at how far you still have to go but at what you have managed to achieve. That's just as beautiful. At the same time, you should know that you still have a long way to go. If you are raising yourself, you need to know that the best balance is between self-congratulation and self-condemnation and between satisfaction and dissatisfaction. You cannot develop without joy but neither should you lose yourself in joy. Carry on with joy in your heart.

3. The wild goose moves slowly toward the plateau. The man leaves his path and does not return. The woman is pregnant but she does not give birth. Trouble! It is desirable to defend yourself against robbers.

We often reach an arid plateau during the course of our development. We didn't want to end up here. But do not be mistaken because this is not the end of the road. It is merely a stopping-off point. The first thing to do in an unsuccessful situation is to examine the direction that you are taking. The second thing to do is not to continue if the direction is false. The third thing to do is to protect yourself against all weakening and paralyzing thoughts. Don't let anyone rob you of your strength. Failure and challenge only strengthen true faith. The line presents you with the difference between an exalted goal and ambition. In the same sense, it also warns that you will manage to achieve your ambitions but this will cause real suffering for your true being. The I Ching sees an empty "career" as trouble. This is when the ego sells the immortal Spirit for thirty pieces of silver.

4. The wild goose slowly moves to the trees. May find an empty branch. Not an error.

Resting on the Great Road. Best to think about this and accept the situation with contented gratitude, whatever it is. Be happy with what you have. Even if it's just an empty branch.

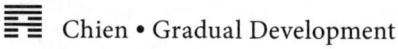

5. The wild goose slowly lands on a hill. The woman does not fall pregnant for three years. But eventually nothing is able to beat her! Success!
This is the final challenge before fulfillment. The last phase of development is the most encouraging—and yet it is still difficult having to wait for it. "Three years" means a long time. This is especially true for someone who is impatient. The challenge—just like those in a fairy tale—may also be an external obstacle; it essentially means that we receive all genuine things *when we become right for them.*

6. The wild goose flies into the sky. Its falling feathers are used for holy rituals. Blessings!
Fulfillment. The achievement of a high ideal. The "feather" and "ritual" refer to ancient shamanic ceremonies. *I* means "ritual" but it also means "origin," "ancient energy," and fundamental "good." This is not simply about reaching a goal but about the fulfillment of fate. Goals are not earthly or heavenly; all our goals are heavenly goals. Development starts down below but ends on high. So, this is not about worldly success but about spiritual glory. It is possible that the modern world doesn't see things like this. Only God sees that you have fulfilled what you undertook. If your question came from your heart—however insignificant it may appear to be—then the answer is praise. Blessings!

54  *Kuei Mei*

The Bride-to-Be

Character: Girl and wedding procession to which the girl arrives as the mistress, as the "second wife."

You are in an inferior and subordinate position. **Undertakings bring trouble, there is nothing that can be moved forward,** is the message of the Oracle. In this situation, your desires, ambition, and illusions have swept you along and you have not measured the inner intentions of others or the command of your own worthiness. All illusions are followed by disillusionment and the fulfillment of every desire brings disappointment. Your actions are directed by your wild imagination rather than clear, inner vision. Now you have to somehow cope with the situation.

The Chinese tradition depicted this subordinate and often really humiliating situation with the image of the "mistress." She is not the main wife—she is simply a lover. She has no dignity or respect and she is just used. In fact, she is taken advantage of. What can be done? Put up with it? Run away? Fight back and demand our rights? It is not beneficial to passively put up with a humiliating situation. It isn't possible to duck out of it because this situation has been created by your desire and longing. It is too late to attack and demand—it should have been done before your thoughts became fate. This is how those around you pity you with no dignity and you are valued just as much as you value yourself. No one listens to you.

The only thing that you can do is to preserve your dignity in an undignified situation. *Kuei* also means "conversion" and "return." It means to return to ourselves. This first requires you to recognize the creative powers of your own desires in this "I don't like it" situation. No one else is at fault, only you. It didn't work because of you and the fact that you badly measured your inner and outer situation and that of the others. Again, you have to return to your own dignity. The great lesson that the sign teaches is that I only have to follow the voice of my real Self. The siren voices lead me astray.

THOUGHTS

No one listens to you. Events take place without you and not in a direction you'd like. What was beautiful in your imagination turns out to be bleak. It's shocking. It is hard to accept that you dreamt all of this—but that is the truth of the matter. You are now learning the difference between *imagination* and *illusion*. Both of these have magical power; something that you imagine or see in "illusion" comes true sooner or later. But while *imagination* sees both the light and dark side of things beforehand, the good and the bad that goes with it, *illusion* only sees the best side of things, the sweet flesh and not the bitter pip.

That is why disappointment is so hard. Your desires create your world—this is the power of imagination and illusion. From now on, if you desire something, use imagination rather than illusion and imagine both the light and dark sides of the fulfillment. If you long for a baby, don't only picture a small child but lifelong responsibility, and not just parental joy but also the burden of fate. And if you imagine a shared plan with others, do not force your own ideas onto them—it is better to pay attention to where they are and what it is that they want for themselves.

Everything has a price. But our dignity is priceless. And humility is not the same as humiliation. The fate of Jesus is a perfect example of how a person preserves his dignity in the most undignified of situations. Kuei Mei speaks about the tactics of recovering dignity. It also deals with something else.

Chinese sages are realists; it is said that millions of beings in the world are born in this sign. In other words, they are born from illusion. We are all "love children." Our parents imagined us to be more beautiful than we became, and yet still we are here. Realization is always accompanied by disappointment.

As with all the other Oracle Signs, it is just as important here to identify whether your question refers to a future step, or are you already inside the energy field of the sign? If *you have not yet taken that step*, it warns that you are not being directed by your clear vision. If *you have taken that step*, it offers tactics to enable you to modestly cope with the situation and regain your harmony.

LINES

1. The bride-to-be as an extra wife. She limps but she can walk. Disciplined action is beneficial.
The situation is not ideal—but you took it on. You knew beforehand and yet you still chose it. If you modestly accept the role of second fiddle, you are safe. In fact, with sufficient self-discipline and standards, your action may also even succeed. This is the line of great bit-part actors who more or less come to terms with the fact that this is their real role and that other people play the leads. Compromise may also be beneficial if it is conscious and it takes place in the interest of fate.

2. A one-eyed man who sees. It is beneficent to stay in the shadows.
Illusions and wild imaginings of the world of desire have blinded you in one eye. But the other one does see clearly and authentically. It can see that there is nothing you can do now other than to retreat into your own center point. If you have been fighting up until now, you should

step back and remove yourself from all actions. You are in need of purifying solitude.

3. *The bride-to-be is still waiting. If she doesn't do this, she will only become a second wife.*
Sometimes it isn't only our desires that sweep us into undignified situations but also our impatience. Why are you hurrying? And is what you want to do in harmony with your self-respect? Take a good look at your heart, your plan, and your circumstances, and especially your feeling that "the time has come." And if you feel that you will never get the real thing—do you really need it at all? Do you really need a fraction of the real thing or a counterfeit? The head man says, "No!" The heart man says, "Yes!" The sage stays silent and trusts you to make the decision, but his silence suggests that you should wait.

4. *The bride-to-be postpones the date of matrimony. Even if it is late, she will wait for the right time.*
All good and beneficent things have their own time. You need to wait for them to mature. While it is maturing, so are you, as well as events. Your clear vision will come and others show their true face more honestly. This is when a good coach asks for time out. You can work out a lot of things in this time. One example is "to know a tree by the fruit it bears." But this will only work if the fruit is ripe. At times like this, you either say, "But that is what I was waiting for," or it falls straight into your lap because the time is right. What you had imagined happening happens because it has a genuine foundation. What you saw in your illusions does not happen because it doesn't have a genuine foundation. But there is nothing wrong with this.

5. *Emperor Ji gives his daughter's hand in marriage. The princess's clothes aren't as ornate as her serving girl's! A nearly full moon brings blessings.*
This line promises a blessed future. In historic terms, the above text describes the beginning of a new dynasty. Here, the king gives his

daughter's hand to one of his subordinates who instantly accepts the situation with modesty and dignity. This relationship is not illusion but common sense, and it shows the respect of inner values before anything else. The "nearly full moon" is the triumph of accepting Yin—the full moon would already be starting to wane. Whatever happens to us, it isn't important whether we end up in a superior or inferior position but that we preserve the center of our being. The thousand-year-long Chu Dynasty—China's golden age—was born from this conduct. The eye cannot see true ornament because it is inside; it is spiritual. Two strengths dominate this line: modest humility and wise foresight. Fulfillment is still a long way away.

6. The woman's basket is empty. The man sacrifices a sheep but no blood flows. Nothing is beneficial.
The whole thing is an empty performance. It isn't important what you do but with what heart you do it. A formal relationship is infertile. It doesn't live and this is symbolized by the bloodless sacrifice. The difference is the same between reality and appearance as it is between imagination and illusion. Do not build on appearances!

55 ䷶ *Fêng*

Abundance

Character: Cornucopia. Vessel brimming with sprouting seeds that is fed from below by fire.

Fulfillment and the state of culmination. Your sun is at its highest point and what has ripened now blossoms. "Do not be sad," says the sage. "Find your sun in the center of your spirit." We excitedly await the blossoming of our desires but when they are eventually fulfilled, we still feel sadness. There are several reasons for this. Firstly, we know that after reaching the top of the hill, the road starts to lead downward. We also see that reality is not exactly what we dreamt. It was *more* in the dream, more beautiful and more joyful. Now it is here but it isn't enough.

This sign means the joy of realization as well as the associated sadness. Fêng consists of the Fire and Thunder Kua. Life shines brightly in a sudden flash of lightning; it's here and it disappears just as quickly. All success is accompanied by a feeling of transience and that it was all in vain. The sage gives the following advice: "Do not keep for yourself what you have achieved. From now on, do not aim upward but spread your achievements and share them with others."

You should know that development works in a spiral and one loop has just come to an end. In order to step into a higher loop of the spiral, you have to come to terms with the mistakes and results of the loop that you have just completed. You have to deal with the good in order to strengthen your faith. And you have to deal with the bad so as not to take it with you. Look around and take in everything that you haven't seen before because it was hidden, and then carry on your way. But not upward. Make all revolutions of the spiral wider and more spiritual. Do not continue what you have been doing so far. Only a hamster stays in its own wheel. Your hope has just come true or is happening this very moment and a karma shoot is ripe for harvest—a new age is beginning. Step up! Dream more. New plans, new companions, higher ideals.

It is only possible to close the old if you look out with clear eyes from your center and you soberly examine your achievements to date. Then look further. Look higher. The sage knows that the symphony of our life is made up of many movements and that is why he does not fret when one movement reaches its end. In fact, if he played it beautifully, then he even enjoys this moment.

In modern terms, this is also where the mental problems of retirement belong. People are generally incapable of starting a new life and a new karmic cycle. This is not a question of age but one of vigilance. Only the path of the body is finite. The path of the spirit is infinite. (This is known by all those who age wisely.)

THOUGHTS

You can only judge things if they become real. This is Fêng. What you believed, hoped, and wanted is here now. The photograph, with multiple exposures, has emerged from the developer and now you can see what things look like.

One says to oneself, "Is that it?" For the sage, this is *the moment of sober judgment.* We make all judgments primarily about ourselves and when something is fulfilled in our fate, we not only see what we consciously wanted but also everything that we subconsciously nurtured in the process. We take the completed image and project onto it our weakness, clumsiness, and cowardice, as well as the sense that we rushed things, ruined things, and we were stupid.

The completed image also shows the world in which we lived. The life plans of a lot of people need to coincide in order for something to happen. The *judgment* is also about what I can do and what others can do. The key question of self-knowledge is how much is the fault of the world and how much is my fault? You can tell everything by the fruit that it produces.

Looking in the mirror is always a risky business. A person keeps another image of themself in their mind than the one that can be seen on the outside. Our face is just like a developed picture; everything is recorded on it. It shows the things that we deny to ourselves as well as what life has inscribed on it. A person's life work is written on their face.

The fate-creating Magician that lives inside us is being assessed in the sign of Fêng.

LINES

1. He meets with his like-minded master. Faultless throughout a whole life cycle. If he goes there, he is appreciated.
Someone helps and teaches. A "life cycle" can be a short or a long period of time while things mature. You open up to something or others open up to you. Often, "appreciation" is not recognition from this world but praise from the spirit world. This "well done!" is an experience like no other.

2. A curtain covers the sun. You are only led by the Pole Star. Continuing leads to doubt and hatred. Let your faith lead you and the spirit world help you. Beneficent.
Despite the fact that things are not turning out the way that you wanted them to, do not lose your faith. Fulfillment does have phases of darkness and the forces of resistance can sometimes be so great that our faith is shaken even though it is faith that creates. The same is true of help from the invisible world. Great ambitions cloud your clear vision. The fruits of "I want" are bitter. The fruits of faith are sweet.

3. Darkness at noon—solar eclipse. The eyes are deceived. His right arm breaks. No fault.
This is not the moment to act. You have to wait for the time to come. This is also described as a productive state of shock. A lot of things happen at once and you still can't put things in place. Whatever the case, you still don't see clearly. Wait.

4. A curtain hides the sun. Seeing the stars in the dark. He meets with his (hidden) like-minded master. It is beneficent to act.
You still don't see clearly but the darkness passes. You can begin slowly—you receive inside and outside help. You receive an answer to the question, "Where to from here?" "Darkness," in the sign of Plenty, symbolizes unnecessary disappointment just as much as intoxication caused by the results achieved. It may also show that you have grown tired of the struggle. The "like-minded master" can mean a companion or wise adviser, as well as our unmistakable voice from within. "Hidden" means that, when it appears in our life, we do not suspect what it is. It appears insignificant and yet it still gives a lot.

5. Glorious light comes. Blessings. Appreciation. Success.
A new and beautiful phase of your life is beginning. When the light of recognition is born within us, our being harmonizes with the creative will. This also attracts others and leads to coincidence—such acts are blessed. There are no personal blessings, only shared ones.

6. Plenty in the house. He covers his house. He peeps out of the door but doesn't see anyone. A solitary period. Trouble!
It is trouble if a person lives for themself. It is trouble if they think anything is their own. It is trouble if they are not able to share their achievements—it is trouble if they close their spirit away from others and even greater trouble if they look to the sky and forget about their spiritual origins. The material approach is spiritual imprisonment.

56  *Lü*

The Wanderer

Character: People gather around a flag.

Your temporary situation is similar to that of a traveler or a guest. You are not at home but in a strange place a long way from home. You can only count on success in minor and insignificant things—nothing is yours here and nothing will be yours permanently.

Jesus said, "Be passersby." He meant it in relation to this whole earthly existence: live as you are here but do not think that you have been condemned to this place. Everything passes here. This is not your "kingdom." The Chinese character indicates that people come and go to "the flag" but not to you, and you need to stay loyal to your spiritual roots. If you accept that you are just a wanderer, your situation may even become pleasant. But you should always know that this is not your world and that people are strangers. You share no deeper fate with them.

The situation does not usually last for long. A fleeting adventure may also be lasting—but if you are not cautious, you may lose your dignity. The image is of running Fire on the Mountain. Meeting and separation: this is your life here. Do not consider what is temporary to be permanent. Remember that you are among strangers, so be careful and tactful with people. Choose where and with whom you spend your time. **Plan for the short term.**

THOUGHTS

Strangely enough, I always threw this sign when I was traveling. This is not important but just typical of my "foreign" experiences. The important thing is whether or not God comes with me.

A person wants to immediately adapt in an alien environment; we look for a home for ourselves, settle, and try to put down roots—and while this happens, we forget about our own home, we forget about the spirit world. A spiritual person can never have a home in the earthly world. "Foxes have their caves; the birds of the sky have their nests—but the son of man has nowhere to rest his head!" You can only live acceptably and relatively comfortably in an alien environment if you know *where you belong.*

There is only one genuine form of homesickness, and that is the longing to be reunited with God. All other desire is illusion and the self-delusion of the wanderer. Neither country nor nation nor family nor lover are permanent on the Road. You can only experience a deeper relationship with those who *arouse a familiar feeling of like-mindedness within you.* These feelings bring the mysterious messages of your true home.

You are in foreign climes. You may have work and even enjoy being here—but it is not permanent and wanting to make it permanent would be a great mistake. Ambassadors experience this; they represent their country in a foreign land. They are careful. They are good judges of human nature. They carefully select the time and place for everything. Their relationships are friendly but not deep and not permanent. They clearly see their situation but they do not encourage conflicts. In the deeper sense of the word, they are companionless.

It is in this sign that a person learns the trust in oneself and one's own being that gives warmth everywhere. If our self-light goes out, we take fright and become dependent on others and a plaything of the circumstances.

The topics of the Lü Oracle Sign include adventure, discovery of the new, sense of belonging, and the limits of adaptation. It is the preservation of the permanent in transience. It is being a gust. It is quickly recognizing the situation. It is the common character of the *wanderer* in folktales whose fate takes place in a foreign land with foreign customs, laws, and especially foreign people. They are not from around here and do not know the fate and spiritual life of those who live here. That is why their judgments can only be fleeting. They don't know what it is really like to live here.

The Chinese Wanderer is more cheerful than a Hungarian émigré and does not see their homelessness as a tragedy. They know where they belong—to their own heart—and that is why they live their whole earthly life largely with the spirit of the Wanderer (Lü). The key is not to become attached to anything—only to the "flag!"

LINES

1. He loses his security, becomes involved in a common situation, and attracts bad luck.
There is nothing worse than when a person forgets about himself and imagines that he depends on his surroundings and not on God. We often cause ourselves external trouble—subconsciously—to help us rediscover God.

2. The wanderer finds a calm lodge. His belongings are safe. He finds a young servant.
God gives temporary accommodation to good guests. This means security and the preservation of values. A good guest is one who does not forget that what they share a part in is a gift.

3. The traveler's lodge burns down. He loses his young servant. Trouble!
A person who, in arrogance, thinks that what was received as a gift is actually his own, hurts himself and others, and becomes unworthy of the situation. To demand your rights instead of expressing gratitude is a serious mistake.

4. The traveler stays at the lodge. He guards his ax. His heart is not happy.
Anxiety can have two courses. The smaller one is that a person is not clear about their surroundings, sensing danger whether justified or not. The more significant reason is that the relationship with God loosens and one's security is lost. Such a person is not loyal to the "flag." It isn't a problem if someone is careful, but it is a problem if they're afraid. Anxiety is nothing other than the psychological symptom of lack of faith.

5. Shooting a pheasant with a single arrow shot. This eventually brings him good fortune.
Your plan will succeed. Sometimes you find a home in a foreign country—where you can fulfill your destiny. Some comments here speak of high spiritual supporters. In the earthly sense, a person's destiny is always where they can realize their life plan and become who they ultimately need to become.

6. The bird burns its nest. The traveler laughs at first, then he cries and complains. He loses his cow because of his thoughtlessness. Trouble.
Do not give up eternity for passing pleasures. We sometimes say, "I forgot myself." Such forgetfulness is not without its dangers because our acts have consequences. The cow is the symbol of humility and the nest is the house of the spirit. If you lose your vigilance, you will pay a large price for momentary pleasures. Don't forget about the "flag."

I is used instead of *thoughtlessness* in the Chinese text. It means the same as it does in I Ching, where it means eternal change. This sign warns that everything can change, but *loyalty* cannot. People who practice yoga would perhaps substitute "disorganization" of the mind and the karmic repercussions of lack of concentration for *thoughtlessness*.

57  *Sun*

Influence (Wind)

*Character: Things stand on a foundation or basis
that subtly influences them from below.*

The message of the 57th Oracle Sign is, **Influence. Success in little things. Desirable to know your goal. Desirable to see the Great Man.** This Oracle Sign describes two kinds of influence. It talks about how you influence the world and how the world influences you. We are not generally aware of the fact that we "influence" others as we are not aware that others "influence" us. This influence is the finest and most undetectable force in life—we only recognize it once it has materialized.

We need to influence like the wind. According to Nietzsche, "If you shake a tree with both hands, it doesn't even move. But the wind, the invisible wind, can pull it up, roots and all." This is the kind of invisible influence that is being described. It is about the radiance of our feelings, our thoughts, and our spiritual energy. *If these influence in one direction for a concerted period of time, a person is able to unnoticeably influence those around them and bring about fulfillment.*

Fulfillment does not take place in this sign. Here, all you do is blow like the wind, delicately and penetratingly. You disperse the resistance and noticeably shape and alter what appear to be fixed circumstances.

The wind is only strong if it blows in one direction for a long time and if its energy is concentrated. This is how you should approach your goals.

You are still too weak for great deeds—do not take things to the point of deciding. Do not collide but rather influence change and delicately guide processes. Do this with empathy from below and behind—invisibly. Follow the path of least resistance. Do not fight, do not bash yourself into a brick wall. Meek strength is effective because it does not lead to resistance; it is virtually undetected and yet still it finds its way into everything. It gets in among the cells and also manages to change our subconscious world with its fine suggestions.

This is the strength of sages. This is the strength of gentleness that gives birth to long-lasting results. But this all happens very slowly, very slowly and gradually.

THOUGHTS

This Oracle Sign encompasses all forms of suggestion, hypnotism, and propaganda, and that is why you need to ask yourself, what kind of influence am I under? This can be the influence of the pure sages or the Powers of darkness. Don't let yourself be influenced. You have to separate the influences of light and darkness in this Oracle Sign.

Its key is the following: *The influence of light makes you free. The influence of darkness makes you its slave. The influence of light makes you a creation of God; it makes you strong, brave, and dignified. The influence of darkness makes you helpless, weak, dependent, no one.* It is no excuse, even according to the earthly justice system, if someone acts under "strong influence." Do not allow yourself to be *influenced* even by yourself! Jesus—quoting King David—said to his people, "You are gods." This is what good advice recommends.

The answer to your question is, *assimilate. Gently, determinedly, patiently, with faith, with feeling. Every tiny detail is important. The process cleans and purifies.* Gentleness means conduct that is selfless, is free of aggression, devoted, adaptable, and that goes with the flow of fate. Look at every direction of the "wind." Let a good wind make you fly—far, far away!

LINES

1. Advance, retreat. The persistence of a warrior is beneficent.
You are unsure. Forward or backward? Doubt can easily lead to desperation. The fault indicated by the whole Oracle Sign can manifest itself in this one line and that is weakness. People are unsure at times like this. The problem is not with the direction but with your resolve. Just do it!

2. Influence under the bed. You need a lot of shamans and those who remember old things. The chaos disperses. Blessings.
The situation needs to be clarified. The bad influence is partly from the past and partly from negative spiritual influences. You need to disperse these. You need to look "under the bed" and in the hidden depths of the subconscious. Secret or subconscious harmful motifs are at work inside you or others. You need to expose them to the light of day and their power will disperse.

3. Repeated influence. Humiliation.
Obstinacy is gratitude for the deed. It is sufficient to consider something twice. If you don't act after that, then it's simply stupidity. The line also says that you tend to act aggressively in your confusion and this only makes things worse. Both explanations point to a weakness of will. It is better that you gather strength and do not make a mistake.

4. The sorrow passes away. He kills three kinds of game in the field.
The road is open before you. Your doubts disperse. You can be successful on a spiritual, mental, and physical level.

5. Persistence is beneficent. Sorrow ends. There is nothing that isn't desirable. What doesn't start well may finish well! Before it is ready: three days. After it is ready: three days.
Everything improves. However it started out—the end can be good. Be considerate in this temporary situation. Don't hurry and don't hurry others.

6. Influence under the bed. He loses his holy weapon. Persistence: trouble. Do not carry on. You no longer have sufficient strength. Too much gentleness is weakness. Don't search any further, the time is not right. Do not dig any further for the hidden causes. It doesn't lead anywhere.

58  *Tui*

Joy Shared with Others

Character: A person's open mouth. It is talking and singing.
Feet below and hands above as if they were dancing.

I want to give you a real sense of the kind of joy that a person from ancient China imagined. The root of the character means "speech." It means exchange, openness, give and take, transfer of inspiring thoughts; it means being together with friends and also the joy of the marketplace where people happily go about the business of buying and selling. We can be happy with our eyes closed and alone, but we like to share joy. And if that works, people move mountains and, as the text says, "do not even fear death."

The theme of this Oracle Sign is joy, happiness, and openness shared with others. Give of yourself and welcome people in! Step out of the armor of your solitude that you fashioned on yourself out of self-interest. Open your heart and do not be afraid that others can see you. Make yourself welcoming so that people don't shy away from you but actually like you and dare to open up in front of you.

All people are social animals. They only retreat into solitude. Now you have to step out, go over, speak out and listen, and enjoy being "together." Genuine joy is rare these days and so is good companionship. When our ego dictates how we live, our heart is not joyous, we fear others and we can't share our fears. We live in a state of permanent self-defense: we either attack others or defend ourselves. The ego does not see another person as a companion but as an enemy. You can finally step out of this vicious circle. Give yourself over to the dance! Do not be afraid.

The reason that the Oracle Sign advises this is because it sees you as being *strong inside*. True joy can only be based on inner strength and self-confidence. Only a strong person who fears no one can be happy. Strength makes us freer and more secure so we can eventually allow ourselves the luxury of being soft and welcoming on the outside. This is the **joy of strong people**. They have nothing to be afraid of. In fact, the knowledge of strength also makes one happy.

This also applies to people who are physically strong. They smile the most and I know from personal experience that they make really good friends and enjoy companionship. I have had a strong sense of this with friends of mine who are involved in wrestling and boxing. Friendships through sport—if they are not later ruined by career clashes—last a lifetime. "Old boys" enjoy eating and drinking together, often until the end of their days.

The Oracle Sign says, "The True Man discusses things over and over again with his friends." What does this mean? It means that he shares his joy with them. It means not only exchanging "information" but also joy. They chatter and chirp like happy little birds. Joy needs to be practiced just as much as dance. This is joy yoga.

The deepest point of our spirit resonates in joy. It comes from a much deeper source than cognitive thought. God also sensed this when he created the world. According to the Bible, he exclaimed, "Tov!" Jewish people still say "mazel tov" today. *Tov* means the joy of the heart. It means be happy—joyful and happy. It means that life is good. A person who is spiritually strong is capable of influencing and inspiring a whole community with their joy. This is the secret of actors who are so adored by audiences. They exude joy and happiness.

The Oracle Sign gives you the task of finally **opening up to joy.** Allow yourself to feel happiness. But at the same time, you should be vigilant and differentiate the joy of the heart from false joys. This is what the individual lines teach. The I Ching knows that joy is ultimately a sentiment and a mental state: it can easily come from not only divine but also dark sources of temptation. Just like the fairy tale, it can be the joy of freedom or the deceptive joy when you cast your eyes on the gingerbread house.

In answer to your question, the Oracle Sign says that *even the impossible can succeed with joy*!

THOUGHTS

The Oracle Sign encourages you to open up to other people; it also warns you not to become dependent on them. This apparent contradiction holds a great deal of wisdom. The greatest joy is to *give* joy. But if your joy depends on whether or not others give it to you, you are in a lot of trouble. Regardless of the fact that you are a social animal, the source of joy is within you. This is why you cannot pursue true joy on the outside via entertainment, superficial enjoyment, drink, and unworthy company—because this is not genuine joy. Genuine joy always holds the scent of freedom. It says that there is no death. That is why we call Jesus's message "joyous news." This is despite the fact that his human story is tragic, only his divine story is joyous.

Tui is the sign of the arts. Art is born out of joy and gives joy. Any art that behaves differently is not art. Milán Füst demonstrates that when a writer sings about the death of his mother, his heart is filled with joy, otherwise he wouldn't be able to sing. Art is born when death, mourning, and catastrophe turn into joy. If that doesn't happen, all a writer can do is complain and say, "It hurts and it won't work!"

Take joy in life, with abandon and joy. Be the source and inspiration of joy to others. Everything can work with joy.

LINES

1. Peaceful joy. Good luck.
As they say, "You are good with yourself." This is joy of satisfaction. It is not disturbed by either doubt or uncertainty. It is as if you are in God's hand. Pure, childish joy has a magical effect even when external events give no cause for joy—they will. Even this isn't important at such times; a person who is on good terms with themself on the inside sees external events as being secondary.

2. The joy of openness (fu). Blessings! The end to problems and sorrow.
This is the joy of fu. It means honesty and a state when a person reaches harmony with the visible and the invisible world. This joy is based on the sense of one's own joy. Only the strong dare to open up, as they have nothing to fear. Richard Wilhelm also sees that people differentiate between levels of joy. "The end to problems" has come because the source of joy is not in the transient.

3. Joy coming from the outside. Trouble!
True joy comes from the inside. If you look for it on the outside, it means that you cannot find yourself. It is a familiar state: I want to feel good and that is why I wander from place to place, chatting and having a good time in order to free myself of my inner restlessness—but that doesn't happen. We try to "shed" our bad mood onto others like passing on a cold, and we try to suppress and forget but all to no avail. The joy is within and this is where you have to go.

4. Calculated joy does not bring calm. Free yourself of your protective shell and you will be happy.
The protective shell is the cramp of self-defense. The ego is constantly calculating, anxious, keeping an eye on profit, and seeing everything as trouble and everyone as an enemy and traitor. This is where our "negative" thoughts belong. The ego also has its own "joys" but these are

miserable joys. There are fleeting triumphs, worthless compliments, and "emotions" bought for money. True joy is the joy of abandon; here is the chance to forget yourself! The sage sees minor disharmony (illness) in this that can be solved, and that is followed by good luck.

5. Openness—to the point of total nudity (pao). Danger.
There are two types of advice linked to this line. I don't know which one is correct; the difference depends on the interpretation of the word *pao*. The first says that you should not be open to those who are dark, flattering, or common as they will exploit it. In joy, a person forgets self-defense. Our joy is shared—but not with everyone. So, this is about that **disruptive danger that threatens values.** The other advice suggests fundamental change. It says that such change is difficult and dangerous but necessary. You have to finally free yourself of the outlived and oppressive memories of your past—these still stand in your path to joy. Tear off from yourself what is unworthy of you!

6. Tempting joy.
This is the joy of the "common man." Béla Hamvas said, "You can turn whole nations into idiots with entertainment." There is a joy that replaces genuine joy, in the same way that intoxication replaces true abandon. "Tempting joy" can also mean a person temporary gratifies themself with their vanity, ambition, or hunger for success. The I Ching does not comment on this because it has no specific problem with such "joy"—only if a person becomes its prisoner and becomes attached to it. If I don't identify with it, it can even make me happy.

59  *Huan*

Dissolving (Reunification)

Character: Water and breaking and dispersing ice.

The ice melts, the mist disperses, overbuilt structures collapse, and dividing walls eventually come tumbling down. This is where all inhibitions, prejudices, false beliefs, complexes, anxieties, and habits dissolve. It is also where all blocked life energies and flows, divisive emotions, frozen situations, alienations, and misunderstandings dissolve.

This is ultimately about the armor of the ego that not only separates but also protects, and that is why disintegration happens both "upward" and "downward"—upward toward boundless spirit and downward toward chaotic instincts. You need to dissolve upward, toward Love, Unity, and the entirety of God. This needs to happen toward a higher ideal that is shared. If the armor of the ego falls apart and the consciousness does not expand upward but downward, it is just like intoxication. A person who has lost their boundaries does not fly upward but sits down on the ground and becomes directed by the forces of the tumultuous world of instinct.

That is why the message is, **Dissolving. Success. The king approaches the temple. It is desirable to cross the Great Water. Advantageous Oracle Sign.** The symbolic explanation goes as follows:

"Wind blows over the water. Dissolving. At such times, the ancient kings raised churches and made sacrifices to God."

The moment eventually arrives: what has inhibited and divided now stops—because you were able to stop it. An ancient commentator says, "The time has come for opportunity, undertaking, and the achievement of distant goals." At times like this, the hardness of the heart dissolves along with repeated negative thoughts that had frozen into a system and you suddenly realize that nothing is impossible for God.

Your boundaries widen. For this to happen, emotional knots need to be untangled and the storm needs to blow away your negative thoughts ("It won't work," "I'm a loser," "No one loves me," etc.). Let them go and don't run after them. Look for what links you to others rather than separates you. Look for what is far off and not only what is close by. *Nothing is impossible!*

THOUGHTS

Something dissolves. In you? Around you? We'll see. Give it a helping hand. Arrogance, fear, inhibitions, prejudice, the anxiety of past experiences—which have become almost instinct—false beliefs, selfishness, bad moods, loneliness, failure, lack of faith: these are just a few chunks of ice that could do with melting and being washed away. This is especially true of egotism.

The "ice" symbolizes a lack of love. "Ice" is the false belief that I am alone, I have no companion, I have no God, and neither do I have magical powers. What is it that has frozen inside you and that now needs to melt? What forms the veil of mist that needs to be dispersed? *Say it out loud and overcome it.* You cannot apply tough tactics; be soft like water and gentle like the wind. And, of course, you can melt as well as the world around you. Your horizons may broaden. When an icicle melts, the distant sea also becomes its own . . . because it flows into it. All unification is preceded by melting. Do not be afraid of freedom.

LINES

1. Race to the rescue on horseback. Strength and enthusiasm bring results.
Hurry to solve the problem before the subject of your question "freezes" and before the knot becomes even tighter. You still have the chance. The deed is timely. But this can only be a deed that is selfless, free of aggression, and full of love.

2. Dissolving. His bench (support) is swept away by the water. Problems and sorrow pass.
Old habits don't help; in fact they now obstruct. Let go of the old, let the "floods" from the thaw wash them away—look forward toward your future. This is a future of "together" and not apart. Your hope is maturing. When a person throws away their crutches and begins to walk, they start to love life again, maybe even start to like people again.

3. He dissolves himself. He doesn't regret it.
The goal is more distant and also higher than the tiny desires of your ego. Throw aside your selfishness and anxieties and serve greater things. Serve the divine. Do not look at your interests—be "abandoned!" This line of the Oracle Sign suggests that you have a goal that you can only achieve if you dissolve your cramp. It is well worth it.

4. He unties himself from his team (his flock). Exalted blessings! He becomes untied above and below. Meeting on the mountain peak. The desired place cannot be hidden. (It glows!)
There are several interpretations of this line. I think the sense is that all communities that are not based on love are transient; they pass away. Interests, fleeting friendships, and party alliances disintegrate. A nation, a race, or a society only remain if they are *communities of love*. If it isn't, untie yourself from it.

The "mountain" (chiu) is where sacrifices were made. In other words, this high point is, in fact, the genuine center of the community.

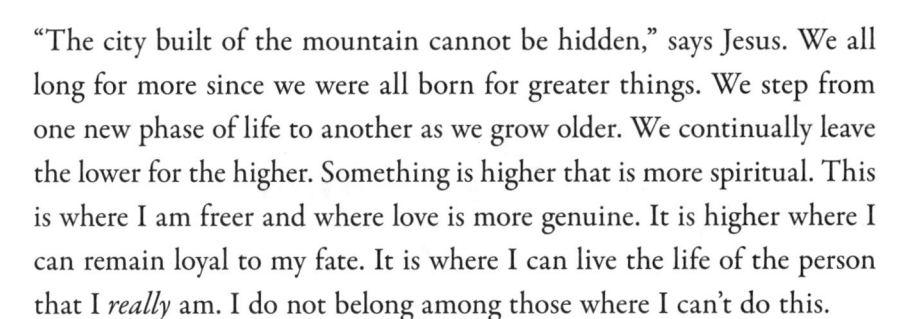

"The city built of the mountain cannot be hidden," says Jesus. We all long for more since we were all born for greater things. We step from one new phase of life to another as we grow older. We continually leave the lower for the higher. Something is higher that is more spiritual. This is where I am freer and where love is more genuine. It is higher where I can remain loyal to my fate. It is where I can live the life of the person that I *really* am. I do not belong among those where I can't do this.

5. Drenched in sweat, he gives a great command. Everything disintegrates (the floods come) and only the king's throne is solid. No mistake.
Healing sweat comes out of the body at the peak of the crisis. The line says that the *permanent center* lies hidden in all disintegration that will create new unity (health). The old is passing and the new is emerging and this transition can only be carried out with solidity and vigilance. You are the king. When your life is in transition, you need a solid center point from where melting and setting takes place.

6. He spills his blood (chue). He leaves and drives away harm. No mistake.
Dissolving everything that may cause trouble, pain, or injury and that may lead to "bad blood." As with the other lines, this doesn't only apply to us—we also have to protect those with whom our fate is shared. The tactic may be dissolving and driving out anxiety but it may also mean that a person leaves the scene and doesn't enter into a battle unnecessarily. *Chue* can mean "blood," "life force," "money," or "property." Master Li reads it as *chu*, which means "sorrow." In this case, the line may mean that sorrow disperses and sadness passes. It means dissolving, forgiving, and forgetting wounds even in thought. This is what makes a person free. The best cure for sorrow or an aching wound is *not to think about it.*

60 ䷻ *Chieh*

Restriction (Moderation)

Character: The stiff rings on a stem of bamboo.

The Chinese character says that the strength and height of a thin bamboo pole is thanks to its "restricting" rings. You have to confront the "limitless" stirring emotions, desires, mysterious dreams, and fears or guilt within you. Dreaming is limitless; imagination is precise and defined. That is why dreaming will lead to nothing—but our imagination has the power to make things happen (such as mind control and various therapies). Our fears are limitless. But if we **express with words what it is that we fear, fear loses its power.** Many things move around and around in our mind with no restrictions. This Oracle Sign encourages you to express these fears in words and to say them out loud. The second that you name a demon, it loses its power.

If you precisely express your goal, you will achieve it. This Oracle Sign advises you to divert the river into a channel and dam it. Great civilizations have emerged on the banks of regulated rivers, but turbulent waters that go unrestricted may flood. Scheduling, daily chores, economizing, the creation of real limits, advancing from one day to the next, sensible moderation, self-discipline, and frugality all belong here.

The Oracle Sign warns that something may *wash you away.* Some kind of instinctual turbulence needs to be diverted into a sensible channel—something that is immoderate needs to be moderated. The message is, **Restriction: success. Bitter (overdone) restriction is harmful**. This is seen as the wise, middle way: proportioning is good, miserliness is harmful; self-discipline is good, self-torture is harmful; precisely expressing my problems is good, gossiping about them is harmful; working "precisely and nicely like a star in the sky" is good; working like a robot is harmful.

The Oracle Sign provides the key to realization: **be realistic**. The only plan that will be realized is one that you make happen with correct moderation, a lot of sacrifice, self-discipline, and devoted effort. Anything that is not prepared in this way remains nothing more than an unrealistic dream. God also builds cell by cell and molecule by molecule and he is omnipotent. Only expect of yourself and of others what can be realized. Do not be *too*. Don't be too direct, too reticent, too extravagant, too tightfisted; build useful dams; otherwise you face the threat of flood.

In one instance, this Oracle Sign pointed to my irrational fears. They dispersed within three days—because I dispersed them. I expressed what really frightened me and I used common sense to build a dam for my fear. This was a wonderful feeling: something turned from being a flood inside me into a fertile river.

THOUGHTS

You should know what concerns you and what doesn't. What belongs to you—solve; to what doesn't—say a definite, "It's got nothing to do with me!" The Chieh sign says that our spirit is indescribably large and its subconscious part works chaotically; it sucks all external influences in with no selection, like the sea and poisonous oil. It also has unformed desires, ambitions, anxieties, bitterness, and fears swimming around in it and there is no way of telling when a specific feeling will rise to the surface.

We long for the mountain peak that has ten paths leading to it but we don't follow any of them. We would like to do a lot of things all at once but none of them so much that we would put all the effort that we have into just one. "The Eagle," says the sage, "selects one single lamb from the flock." In other words, it restricts its unlimited greed—but it is sure to get the one that it wants. We want all of them but not one will be ours.

"Self-awareness" essentially means that we recognize our limitations. We know what we can expect of ourselves and what we are capable of doing—and we do exactly that, despite whatever sacrifice we may have to make. Overestimating or underestimating myself means that I am never going to do anything that is worthwhile. It is an even greater mistake to *wrongly estimate our fellows* (friends, colleagues, spouses, business partners, and even our enemies). We either underestimate them or expect far too much of them.

This Oracle Sign is about things **coming true**. Everything came into being in the sign of Restriction: the seasons, days, hours. But we were born with our own character, body, and fate—every single person is infinity *living within restrictions*. Only mist has no limit: it falls to earth as a round raindrop or a hard ball of ice. The Kabbalah says, "God restricted himself into worlds."

In response to your question, the Oracle Sign advises that Restriction is the antidote to all internal and external chaos. It requires **self-discipline, life order, moderation**. And you need to live by this for better or for worse. The spirit needs to be cultivated just like the earth—it can't be left to its own devices. All religious asceticism, self-improvement, training, and yoga belong here. This means that you set limits for yourself and don't allow yourself everything (and do the same for others).

Restriction is the rule of the spirit over material and instinct. You should know where the limits of responsibility lie. *Do everything you can up to this point and do nothing beyond it.* Find the right level. And especially the things that hurt. *Express where the focus of your spreading problem lies.* The more precise the diagnosis, the more effective the cure.

The great spiritual figures of humanity were always their own sternest critics. But they even set limits for self-criticism; they set levels.

It is generally true in life that if we don't place restrictions on ourself, life will do it for us. It is the order of creation to set limits to chaos. If it doesn't happen on the inside, then it'll happen on the outside.

LINES

1. If you do not leave your inner room through the door, no mistake.
The situation is immature. The external obstacles are larger—it is still too early to act. We need to prepare "within" and do it in secret. "Secret" means that you shouldn't allow the gathering energy to escape but ripen inside yourself.

2. If you do not walk in your court and beyond your door, trouble!
Now is the time to act. Not sooner and not later but *Now*! The time has come. It won't come again. This is the moment when you can realize the results of your inner restriction. The message of this line, as it could also mean the beginning of something new, is that your actions are no longer directed by old habits. You used to be inhibited in certain situations but this is no longer the case. In martial arts they say, "In the moment of great action, the warrior is completely free." The restrictions only lead up to the act and the act is totally free.

3. If you know no restrictions, you will have cause for complaint.
What we do not resolve on the inside will fall on us on the outside. This is how we live today: we don't know how to treat ourselves. We are prisoners to our desires, our feelings, our anxieties, and our bitter thoughts. We are incapable of gathering our mental energies, organizing our lives, and raising ourselves. We have let our fate slip from our hands. That is why we are afraid, anxious, and unwell. In Chinese the question is *Shui chiu*? "Whose fault is that?" It is a very

good question. In fact, *chiu* means a person who is not what he should be. He is not living as himself. He does not direct himself and he is "at fault."

4. Peaceful (calm) restriction. Success.
You know moderation. You only want what you can have and you only do what your circumstances allow, and that is why you are not tense or unsatisfied. The sage takes reality into account and that is why he is able to achieve great things.

5. Sweet restrictions bring blessings and appreciation.
A person who is triumphant within themselves is invisible. "Sweet" or happy restriction is what happens out of love of God, love of other people, and love of oneself. Sweet restriction is when a mother dedicates her every waking hour to her child. It is when work—however difficult and tiring—brings enjoyment. A true yogi enjoys yoga. A true priest enjoys serving God. A true scientist or artist enjoys dedication to their work throughout their whole life. Of course, this is a special kind of "enjoyment." This is the secret delight of the Magician who knows that, **to change others and the world, he first needs to change himself.** And he does this—however difficult—with joy in his heart. Such people are respected even in this age of depravity. Even though they may be far from the bright lights of fame, exemplary figures still do exist.

Not only do I greatly respect them, but a person has a great influence on me who does not want to aggressively change me but who works on themselves and involuntarily pulls me into the energy field of their modest personality, which has been created with so much effort. A good cobbler is respected by his apprentice. There is a lot of work, sacrifice, and "restriction" behind the quality of his work. He influences and teaches with this as he himself was taught by a master. In fact, he is still constantly learning his craft. This line says that the work we do on ourselves will bring joyous results both inside and out.

6. Bitter restriction. If it continues, trouble. Sorrow passes away.

"Restriction" (life order, discipline) that takes place in the name of freedom. If we do something because we are forced to, it will lead to trouble. Trouble will ensue if we force ourselves or others to do something. True discipline makes a person greater and stronger while aggressive force causes misery and leads to rebellion. Buddha achieved enlightenment when he abandoned his overly strict asceticism. The Oracle Sign advises you to relax. Good coaches know that their athletes need relaxation and enjoyment the day before a competition—not tough exercise. Do not be too strict with yourself or with others.

61  *Chung Fu*

Truth of the Center Point

*Character: The familiar sign of Chung—the Motionless Center.
And Fu: the foot of a bird above its young.*

Whatever you asked, you know what the answer will be. Not with your mind and not with your instinct but with your heart. Whatever you asked, you know the truth deep in your soul. *Chung* here means "heart." Love radiates from the **heart**. This is not emotive and selfish but understanding and adequate love. This love has magical power. You understand others, you understand yourself, and you discover what Fate has planned for you all. Whatever you do from your center point is blessed. This is true even if your ego doesn't see it as such.

"Me! For me! Mine!" You have been living in the false belief that the center of your being is the selfish "I." This isn't the case; the ego just usurps the position of your True Self. It has used blind selfishness and incomparable cunning to draw the spotlight onto itself and pushed the main character to one side—while your True Self quietly watched and waited. Where? In the motionless center of your being. It now says, "If I direct your life, everything will be just fine. They listen to me and not to you. They trust me and not you. They fear you but they don't fear me. I can clearly see your faults, not just those of others. They sense that I do not want to conquer them but that I seek the Truth that is mine and also theirs. My secret is that I love them just as much as I love you!"

When are you in your center point? When you are calm. There is peace at the heart of the hurricane. This is the peace of the heart. This peace has a subduing strength, especially in today's distorted world. A single person is capable of preventing a massive fight. Sages define this conduct with a dolphin; the advice here is, **The Truth of the Center Point. Dolphin, beneficent! It is desirable to cross the Great Water. Beneficent divination.** The dolphin is the symbol of Universal Love and Harmony, while in ancient Chinese tradition it signifies Great Good Fortune.

You can now see everything from within with no arrogance, vanity, or selfishness. You see into things. You understand people even if "they know not what they do." (Often, you don't know either!) The spark of your vigilance has just flashed. Don't let it go out—nourish it. You can now attain harmony with yourself and with others. You are finally able to organize your affairs with sight rather than blindly as before. Blindness means prejudice and this can now fall away from you. This clear vision (fu) is just emerging; like a new being in an egg, it lies hidden inside you. The six lines describe the various stages of "hatching."

In Chung Fu, you are now able to achieve harmony with others and also with the spirit world and you are going to feel this—a person sometimes shudders if they sense that they received praise from "above!"

THOUGHTS

Chung (center) is the basis of all metaphysics. It is the first character in the word *China*. Everyone has experienced this for a minute or two but it takes a lot of practice to be able to remain in it. This is meditation. It is the foundation of the ancient East and real human life. One who sees from here, according to Béla Hamvas, is "vigilant." What does this mean? Imagine that your life is a stage play in which you play the lead. You live the whole drama based on your own self, your own interests, passions, and obsessions. You see everyone through your own spectacles.

Then, through some miracle, you step out of yourself and you suddenly see the whole thing through the eyes of the author. This is the author who wrote history and who lives in us all, including you, and who thoroughly understands and loves all the characters.

You would suddenly see the entire reality. It would be like waking from a dream, as if you had been crazy and suddenly come to your senses. It would be as if you were not looking out of your own head but watching the play though God's eyes. Just imagine the story that you would write if you transformed your whole life with this clear vision. That is chung!

It is a person who sees the world from the heart and not only gets to know and understand other people—but the first thing they notice in their life is *what effect they have on others*. We never sense this. We may say that our spouse's behavior is impossible and it never occurs to us that this might be a result of the effect that we have on them. You can see yourself in chung and you discover the magical key to the formation of your fate: **you must transform yourself if you want to alter your fate**. If you change on the inside, the outside will change too.

The other word, *fu*, not only means "truth" but also "honesty." Honesty means that you say what you think and you do what you say. We live in the opposite direction; we do not say what we think and we do not do what we say. In fact, we lie to ourselves with such skill that we don't even notice that we are lying: *without as much as a blush, we say and think that we are Christians without having the tiniest drop of love in our souls*. And if someone kindly reminds us of this fact, that this is not Christianity, we mentally—and, sadly, sometimes actually— cut their throat. (All in the name of love!)

You can achieve harmony with yourself in the sign of Chung Fu. You can also achieve harmony with others and the world around you. This is often possible without you having to do anything special, as the radiance of your spirit travels great distances and it transforms your outside world. But you have to start on yourself. If you long for outer harmony, you first have to create it inside yourself; if you long for love, you have to love; if you long for a companion, you have to make yourself suitable for companionship. Your *inner magnet* attracts everything and if you long for something else, you need to stop your "magnet." If a person's inner magnet starts to work, they do not want to suppress or manipulate anyone else but they attract people in a way that allows everyone to enjoy their own freedom. People sense this. This irresistible strength of attraction is called *love*.

Chung Fu is an "untimely" Oracle Sign. We live in lies and we do not know real love. We all know what this is accompanied by: anxiety, meanness, confusion, loneliness, and the constant fear that the whole thing will soon collapse around us. Chung Fu advises the exact opposite.

The Oracle Sign advises you to **get going as you will be accompanied by good luck**. See with your "heart," like the fox in *The Little Prince*, and your judgment will be immaculate.

LINES

1. Caution is beneficent. If you get involved with others, you will not have peace.
You should work on yourself first and not on others. You need to change yourself and not others. You need to find your own center point and you should not do this on the outside. A person who constantly blames the world has surely not found themself. This person lives in the false belief that they depend on others.

2. The crane calls from the shadows and its son responds. I've got a cup of fine wine, let's drink together.
A person who has found their center point radiates a great distance! Their call sign travels around the world and the person who it speaks to hears it and responds. Do not fear that you will remain companionless. Your heart is transmitting and you will find your soul mate. Everything depends on the strength and clarity of your transmission.

3. He runs into the opposite. He sometimes beats a war drum and sometimes stops. Sometimes he cries and sometimes he sings.

Your situation is not good because you do not depend on yourself. Whether you are battling or loving, always be your own master. Never place your fate in someone else's hands. If your center point is on the outside and not on the inside, your joy and sorrow depend on others. The same is true whether this person is a friend or an enemy. You will lose in both love and war if you are directed by others.

4. The moon is nearly full. The horse gallops out of the enclosure. No mistake!

If you follow your star, your life will also change. Old habits, views, and companions are left behind. Others come to replace them. This is natural. As we grow out of our childhood and puberty and we leave feelings and friends behind, our purifying spirit is attracted to the wider world and it creates another community around us. This is accompanied by sacrifice, but this is how it has to be.

5. The Truth (honesty) ties together. Faultless!

This is the heart of the whole Oracle Sign. It is true unity with yourself and with others. This cannot be infected by lies and self-deceit. What you do is fate and others will recognize this in time. This is the moment of action in martial arts.

6. The crowing reaches the sky. Continuing like this is trouble!

It is self-deceit to believe that you are what you say. There is no point in you knowing about truth if you are not True: your words are empty. Your time is better spent working on yourself and not preaching. Beware of vanity and ambition. True values need no propaganda. Whatever you asked, look into yourself. Do your words cover the truth or not? The wrapping is pretty but what's inside? Do you think that others don't see this?

62  *Hsiao Kuo*

Advantage of the Small (Moderation)

Character: Little, few—and passing footprints.

The forces are increasing but the time for great action has not yet arrived. The sign is dynamic (Thunder) and, at the same time, restricted (Mountain)—in other words, *you feel a strong urge but you must not follow it.* The urge may be a castle in the air, illusion, ambition, sudden temper, or the attraction of a distant plan that is still not established. There is a lot of inhibition and disharmony—you are still not as strong as you think you are. If you were to move now, you would not do it with the consideration, vision, and action of the Center but with empty ambition, temper, and vain hope. This would only lead to bad.

The Oracle Sign's message is moderation. This will bring good luck. **The advantage of the small. Maturing. Persistence is desirable. You should do little things and not take on large things. The flying bird that has forgotten about itself says, "It isn't good high up! It's good down below!" Great good luck!** Everything is in this. The image of the ambitious bird accompanies this Oracle Sign throughout. You have to do small things. These are tiny and apparently insignificant, everyday things. "There are no negligible moments for a person who has set off on the Road," says Béla Hamvas. The situation is temporary.

Success is hidden in the small things. All small steps prepare for the large one. You need to take things one step at a time and one degree at a time. Do not stare into the sun; pay attention to what is in front of you and what you are living at that exact moment in time. Keep your feet on the ground. Appreciate what there is. Build your house one brick at a time.

You live your life like a sower of seeds: you don't know what future will sprout out of the tiny seeds.

THOUGHTS

This sign is the exact opposite of the previous one (Truth of the Center Point). The center point is missing here. Even the "Spiritual Man" is unable to find it and he is left with no other option than to choose the lesser of the "evils": small rather than grand, over tactful rather than insulting, and tightfisted rather than extravagant. He is overcautious rather than reckless. Master Huang says, "You are better to drive within the allowed speed limit than over it because this will only mean that you lose time and you risk nothing more."

You now need to work on the foundations. You need to work on the small details. Keep your everyday problems as holy tasks. In martial arts, this is the *preparation period* for the great action. At times such as this, the warrior *gets ready and prepares* his opponent for the moment of Action. This requires sober and patient work and often a large degree of caution to ensure that the action doesn't explode too soon.

Moderation, reserve, and careful groundwork will be worth their weight in gold in time.

LINES

1. If the bird flies up, it will fly into trouble.
You understand, don't you? Don't listen to your urge.

2. He doesn't meet with his ancient father and his ancient mother. He doesn't meet his Ruler, just his servant. No mistake.
A person who accepts their situation as a fate task with humility will receive help. "Motherly help" comes either from the spirit world or from the earthly plane and never satisfies our ambitions but only our needs. It knows well enough what we need.

3. Do not continue, be cautious as you are walking into danger! Trouble!
Blindness can bring a great deal of trouble. Do not act because you think you are right or because you have simply had enough. You can't see yourself or your situation and especially what takes place behind your back. Stop and take a look around. Things can still improve if you don't continue.

4. No mistake. He meets it and doesn't pass by. But it is dangerous to continue. Be careful. Don't act! Remain steadfast!
Take joy in small achievements. Do not want more—the time isn't right. The apple that has fallen from the tree is yours—do not want the apple tree! The voice that says, "Now! This is it. I have to act now. I've had enough!" will only lead to trouble. It is better that you learn from the mistakes of your past.

5. Thick cloud in the west but the rains don't arrive. The prince shoots and hits inside the cave.
"Rain" is the symbol of fulfillment but this is still to arrive. You feel that you are alone but as you are loyal and patient, you discover a special companion in these barren and difficult times. The companion may come in the form of a friend, strength, or spiritual help that fate joins you with. The "cave" is the mist of not knowing. It is a place of inner depth and not radiance—as Hamvas described it, "Famous anonymity." This is where the great and true are born. Here, a person sees the "little" not as a compromise but as an achievement and even glory.

6. He passes it without meeting it. The flying bird leaves! Trouble! Bad luck and damage!

The message of the Hsiao Kuo Oracle Sign is to be satisfied with small things. This isn't happening here. Arrogance and ambition launch you high in the sky and there is a point of no return. The bird burns in the sun or ends up in a hunter's net. Great deeds need great times and these are not great times. You aren't ready either. You need to realize this; otherwise you will end up in trouble.

63  *Chi Chi*

After Fulfillment (Crossing)

Character: Crossing a river with the sign for "completion" next to it—someone just about to finish a meal.

Something that we set in motion in the past has just arrived. What we have been striving for has happened . . . or is being **fulfilled** right now. Everything runs its own path of struggle and arrives somewhere; this is what became of it. It has emerged from the mold and, like it or not, this is how it has turned out. The cycle appears to have closed. It is being fulfilled.

At times like this, our creative powers achieve a balance. Fire and Water don't fight against one another but help one another. Something that we spent a long time creating now becomes visible, it comes into being. This could be a relationship, a love affair, a revolution, a social transformation, a piece of work, or a house that we started to create some time in the past and that we formed and shaped until it was complete.

It is now that troubles come! A pure revolution is followed by a corrupt world and a happy marriage sets out on the road of boredom and ruin; chaos and disharmony move into our new house. *There is nothing more fragile than the split second of fulfillment.* No sooner has it been formed than it starts to decay; it becomes surrounded by disintegration and entropy.

The Chinese say that nothing can be completed because life is endless. You can run a lap but it doesn't ever end because **it is a spiral** and not a circle and no sooner has one lap finished than the other begins. The endless spiraling chain just keeps on going.

What can we do if we have badly run a karma cycle? Chi Chi gives us some advice: **After completion (crossing), Success is in the small things. Beneficent Oracle Sign. Beginning (new step) is advantageous! Completion is chaotic.** The sage adds that, "The True Man thinks of problems, prepares for them, and protects himself from them."

What does this mean? Firstly, it means that he makes minor repairs to the situation. He can't do large things as the deed has emerged from the mold. He can correct little imperfections here and there, but nothing more than that. The deterioration process can be delayed but not stopped. It is more important to start something new. This grows organically out of the previous one and yet it is still new.

I will give an example. Let us say that you desire someone in the physical sense. That person will be yours. The peak of embrace is the Chi Chi state: Fulfillment. If you no longer need the other one after this, the unity that you felt at orgasm falls back into the two separate solitary states of being. If, following this gratification, a deeper spiritual attraction begins, the relationship will continue to last. A new age will begin and lead to love and possibly marriage. Marriage is a new Chi Chi state: Fulfillment. If a new age doesn't begin after this and love doesn't lead to a new fate communion, and the two people involved don't adopt their new roles of "father" and "mother," the marriage runs into difficulty and disintegrates. The fate communion (love) is a new Chi Chi state: Fulfillment. But when the children grow up and the old couple is left behind, the task is the same again. Will something new begin in the form of a relationship that goes from strength to strength or will the two of them fall back into solitude and turn into two bitter, old people who spend all their time attacking and criticizing each other?

The end of every cycle is the beginning of a new cycle. Nature works in exactly the same way. A plant is barely formed and it already carries the seed of new life deep inside itself. This is a great secret. Preserve to renew and renew to preserve. Nothing is intimately "completed" in this process. If you take the above example to its conclusion, behind the joy of old age lie the age rings of all the experiences fulfilled as happy parents, husband and wife, and lovers.

Refine and "perfect" . . . and what will the new be?

THOUGHTS

The dynamic of the Chi Chi sign is a fundamental, cosmic law: everything that has been created begins to decay and decomposes to create something new. The ego thinks in freeze-frame and that it why it says, "Finished at last." The best-known analogy for the Oracle Sign is a political one. The long awaited "change of regime" in Hungary appears to be "complete" but in reality is never fully complete. The most fragile moment in life is when something is created. This is when you need to have your wits about you. And you have to know that being is in fact constant renewal.

Every hour of every day is renewal. The True Man lives in the endless process and that is why he stays forever young. This—and I will say it again—does not mean that he rejects the old but that he continually transforms himself and is reborn. He is where things are *created* and not where they are *completed*. The True Man is a "Resource Man."

Jesus said to the Samaritan women at the well, "Whoever drinks of this water will thirst again, but whoever drinks of the water that I shall give him will never thirst. But the water that I shall give him will become in him a fountain of water springing up into everlasting life."

A person "who has not yet fully grown" thinks that if he has achieved something, then that is that. He holds it in his hand and there it can rot. This is true of all his "regimes," religions, institutions, cultures, periods of history, and also of his love affairs, friendships, moralism, and knowledge. No sooner has he attained something than it starts to decay in his hand. His temples are filled with the smell of rigidity and death.

The True Man knows that things are not finite but infinite. He does not freeze the frame of the film of his life that is running in his head because he knows that the moment he does, it will start to smell and decay and burst into flames. He turns his attention to rebirth. "How can I be reborn from this situation?" "How can I magically renew my situation irrespective of it being the result of a great deal of my hard work?" The home of a wise housewife is never complete. She is always renovating, inventing, and changing something. And her foolish husband, who doesn't understand the secret of Chi Chi asks, "Why don't you like the old that was so comfortable and expensive?"

LINES

1. He brakes his wheels. The fox's tail touches the water when it crosses. No mistake.

Stop! Do not start out too early. Do not listen to your inner instincts or external temptations although they may appear encouraging. Do not be greedy.

2. The wife loses her hair ornament. She doesn't look for it—she receives it seven days later.

You will receive what is yours when the time is right. Do not struggle for it. The masters of your fate know that it is yours. Do not act on the example set by practical, bustling, ambitious people. Your goal is higher and your value is greater.

3. The Great Ancestor disciplines spirits everywhere. He brings them under his control in three years. Do not employ common people!

The goal is great and the work that stands before you is long and tiring. Be strong, persistent, and preserve your faith and prepare to defeat the small, weak, cowardly, and faithless within yourself as part of your struggle. Prepare to defeat your own shadow. The Oracle Sign says that the goal is magnificent but you cannot achieve it with unsuitable companions. It is the last phase of fulfillment when something has been achieved that you wanted and now it has to be solidified, or is it the

start of something new? I don't know. One thing is certain: your work requires strength, persistence, and faith. It mainly requires discipline in the face of your own low strengths and those of others that could undermine the whole venture. Do not allow self-interest, faithlessness, comfort, and cowardice to interfere.

4. Beautiful clothes also turn to rags and you can use them to plug the holes in your boat. Be careful all day long.
The Oracle Sign warns of the dangers of the "crossing" (venture) in a moment when things appear to be going well. It is such a shame that the captain of the *Titanic* was not familiar with this sign as it would have helped him to avoid trouble. The trouble was not the iceberg but the fact that he forgot about it; glorious clothes are only rags and the passion for the highlife can drag a person down to the depths. Be careful. That is all you need to remember and there won't be any trouble.

5. The eastern neighbor sacrifices a whole ox but this doesn't carry the same blessing as the modest sacrifice of the western neighbor.
A person is blessed who is genuine and honest. This is a person who is true to themself and lives their fate. There is no blessing on power, glory, or money if it is spiritless. It is a sure sign of ruin if something becomes formal. Birth is simple and poor even for a king: a naked body appears from the mother's womb and cries. The funeral is spectacular and magnificent even for a simple person: an elegant corpse lies in a gold-plated coffin surrounded by a forest of flowers. The difference being that birth is organized by God while a funeral is organized by vain and foolish people who only believe in material things. Be pure, modest, and devoted and you will receive great rewards.

6. His head touches the water. Trouble, danger.
Do not get stuck in the old. You have to start something new. Whatever you have achieved and whatever point you have reached, do not identify with it. You have to carry on. The road is infinite.

64 ䷿ *Wei Chi*
Before Completion (Crossing)

*Character: Chi depicts fast water running through a ford and Wei shows
something that has not happened yet or has not been fulfilled.*

You stand before something very important. This might be a decisive
turn of fate. The way forward also depends on you. You require two
things for a beneficial deed: strength and precise recognition of the
situation. You have to precisely analyze your inner and outer circumstances before you take that vital step. You also have to gather strength.
Your undertaking may prove successful if you are not careless.

The sage speaks about a daring fox cub that runs across the treacherous ford but does not reach the far bank because "its tail hangs in the
water." This is the Chinese image for thoughtlessness: the little fox cub
not only failed to consider the depth of the water and thought that the
far bank was much closer, but it never thought that its own tail would
cause trouble. A fox does not normally approach water—the problem is
that this is not your "natural environment."

Here, the task is nothing less than stepping from chaos into order.
You have a tendency to rush things because harmony attracts you and
also because you consider your present situation to be untenable. Do
not listen to the urge of "I want" or "I have had enough." Only listen
to your wise, calm heart and the sober and seeing center of your soul.

The last sign of the I Ching is encouraging despite the fact that Water and Fire are in the most disharmonious tension (Water extinguishes Fire and Fire turns Water into steam). However, the promise of harmony still hides in this virtually untenable situation. The situation is difficult and contradictory but also promising.

THOUGHTS

Wei Chi shows a **situation that is about to change in terms of its quality**. The moment of quality change arrives after a large number of quantity changes. We live through the quantity period as if nothing was happening. Things just build and build. More and more of the same. I can increase the temperature of water to 60, 70, or 80 degrees and it remains water. It only starts to boil at 100°C and then it becomes steam.

As we know, everything will flip over into its own opposite sooner or later. The desire for order is never as great as when the disorder becomes virtually unbearable. There is a point when we have just had enough of the unfortunate situation. We stop sinning, we stop making mistakes, we give up drinking, smoking, or any other bad habits when we have had enough. A person who drinks himself into the grave has not had enough. He would rather die than to say, "Enough!"

We can be terribly agitated before a great change, eventually losing patience after what appears to be a series of fruitless experiences. We think that this is how it will continue and now an opportunity finally appears, we make a *reckless attempt to break out*. We shouldn't do it. *We shouldn't do it right now!* It is now that we need calm and strength. Instead of instinctively jumping, we should take a step back and gather strength. We should coolly examine the distance to the opposite bank.

Do not rush things. You are not strong enough to carry the weight of the task. You need to gain strength. The masters of the sword call this moment the Great Action. Little action is when you attack and stab or cut. The Great Action is when you prepare yourself for the attack.

Do not attack until you are ready inside. You are ready inside when you find the quiet center point in the heart of your being mixed in among the fear, passion, will to win, and fear of loss. This is where all beneficial deeds begin.

LINES

1. His tail is in the water. Shame and confusion.
You are not ready to act. You cannot see through your situation. Do not listen to your urges. You should know that you still don't know.

2. He brakes his wheels. Beneficent to persist.
Wait although the cart is full. Take a look at your goal from the center of your being. Wait to receive a sign from inside—or outside—before setting off.

3. Aggression can only bring trouble before crossing. But it is advantageous to cross the Great Water!
The time to act has arrived though how you act is vital. If you act out of anger, temper, revenge, or fury, then you could end up in a great deal of trouble. And if you are weak, continue to gather strength or companions. You cannot create order with aggression, only with strength. Strength is calm, determined, and understanding. The good samurai is merciful. He is merciful toward himself as well as others. If your heart is calm, take a step and you will win. If your heart is still agitated, do not make a move because, if you do, you will lose.

4. Beneficent Oracle Sign. Persistence redeems and regret stops. The shaking force defeats the house of demons in three years. Gifts and celebrations in the city.
The moment to act has arrived. You can "cross the Great Water." The struggle was with yourself or with others about someone or something. You now have the strength, knowledge, and inspiration—as well as

faith in your victory. You can expect a long battle—negative thoughts, feelings, habits, and fears will not give up that easily. Persistence! You know that the sky is darkest before the dawn. Badness is most dangerous when it stands to lose. Persistence means to want for a long time and faith means to remain loyal. A person only declares a lightning war who has no faith in their victory.

5. Beneficent Oracle Sign. No regret. The light of the True Man shines. Blessings, success.
You are following the path of your fate. A person who follows the fate of their path, shines. This path may be easy or difficult—the main thing is that it is a beneficent path. This is the Christian fulfillment of the "will of God." "Shining" means that you become visible to others. This is the glorious crossing from chaos into harmony.

6. Beneficent Oracle Sign. No regret. It is right to celebrate with a drink (chiu). But wrong to become intoxicated.
You have reason to be happy and celebrate. This may be your victory or a pre-sense of it. You should experience this joy on your own, with your fellows as well as your spiritual supporters. *Chiu* means both "drink" and "spirit" in Chinese. When grape juice turns into wine, the good and the bad spirit separate in it; *self-abandon* is good and beneficent—*self-loss* is bad and harmful. Wine is holy in moderation but without moderation, it becomes a devilish drink. In the same way, the self-abandoned joy of a person following the Path is holy but if the joy blurs their vision and its meaning becomes distorted, it is harmful.

This line partly warns you to experience all minor successes because joy nourishes your soul—but do not confuse joy with Happiness. Joy is transient—Happiness is permanent. This experience is still before you.

And this promise closes the Holy Book of Changes.

Recommended Reading

Anthony, Carol K. *A Guide to the I Ching*. Stow, MA: Anthony Publishing, 1988.

Blofeld, John. *I Ching: The Book of Changes*. New York: E. P. Dutton, 1965.

Huang, Alfred. *The Complete I Ching*. Rochester, VT: Inner Traditions, 2010.

Javary, Cyrille. *Understanding the I Ching*. Boston: Shambhala Publications, 1997.

Jung, C. G. "Foreword." In *The I Ching, or Book of Changes*, by Richard Wilhelm. Translated by Cary F. Baynes. Bollingen Series 19. Princeton, NJ: Princeton University Press, 1967.

———. *Man and His Symbols*. New York: Bantam, 2023.

———. *Synchronicity: An Acausal Connecting Principle*. Princeton, NJ: Princeton University Press, 2010.

Karcher, Stephen. *How to Use the I Ching: A Guide to Working with the Oracle of Change*. Reading, MA: Element Books, 1997.

Legge, James. *I Ching*. New York: Bantam Books, 1969.

Lim, Kim Anh. *Practical Guide to the I Ching*. New York: New Age Books, 2002.

Liu, I-ming. *The Taoist I Ching*. Boston: Shambhala Publications, 2005.

Murphy, Joseph. *Secrets of the I Ching*. West Nyack, NY: Parker Publishing, 1970.

Ni, Hua-Ching. *The Book of Changes and the Unchanging Truth*. Los Angeles: Sevenstar, 1994.

Schönberger, Martin. *The I Ching and the Genetic Code*. Santa Fe, NM: Aurora Press, 1992.

Whincup, Gregory. *Rediscovering the I Ching*. Garden City, NY: Doubleday, 1986.

Wilhelm, Helmut. *Lectures on the I Ching: Constancy and Change*. Princeton, NJ: Princeton University Press, 2019.

Wing, R. L. *The I Ching Workbook*. New York: Dolphin/Doubleday, 1979.

BOOKS OF RELATED INTEREST

The Complete I Ching — 10th Anniversary Edition
The Definitive Translation by Taoist Master Alfred Huang
by Taoist Master Alfred Huang

As a native Chinese speaker, Master Huang has imbued this I Ching with
an accuracy and authenticity not achieved in other English translations.
He also returns to prominence the Ten Wings, the commentaries by Confucius
that are essential to the I Ching's insights.

The Numerology of the I Ching
A Sourcebook of Symbols, Structures, and Traditional Wisdom
by Taoist Master Alfred Huang

A must for serious I Ching students, this is the first book to bring the
complete Taoist teachings on form, structure, and symbol in the I Ching
to a Western audience.

The Occult I Ching
The Secret Language of Serpents
by Maja D'Aoust

In this illustrated guide, Maja D'Aoust provides a history of the I Ching oracle
and explains the mechanisms at work behind it. She provides a new analysis of the
64 hexagrams, exploring each hexagram's meaning in depth, and offers tools to
help you interpret the I Ching based on your own individual experience.